What We Can Never Know

Also available from Continuum:

What Philosophers Think, edited by Julian Baggini and
Jeremy Stangroom

Great Thinkers A-Z, edited by Julian Baggini and
Jeremy Stangroom

What Philosophy Is, edited by Havi Carel and
David Gamez

What We Can Never Know

Blindspots in Philosophy and Science

David Gamez

continuum

Continuum International Publishing Group
The Tower Building   80 Maiden Lane
11 York Road   Suite 704
London SE1 7NX   New York
                                                             NY 10038

British Library Cataloguing-in-Publication Data
A catalogue record for this book is available from the British Library.

ISBN: HB: 0–8264–9160–X
            9780826491602
            PB: 0–8264–9161–8
            9780826491619

Library of Congress Cataloguing-in-Publication Data

Gamez, David.
    What we can never know: blindspots in philosophy and science / David Gamez.
            p. cm.
    Includes bibliographical references.
    ISBN-13: 978-0-8264-9161-9
    ISBN-10: 0-8264-9161-8
    ISBN-13: 978-0-8264-9160-2
    ISBN-10: 0-8264-9160-X
    1. Theory (Philosophy)   2. Science–Philosophy. 3. Knowledge, Theory of. I. Title.

B842.G36 2007
001–dc22

2006024029

Typeset by Free Range Book Design & Production Ltd
Printed and bound in Great Britain by MPG Books Ltd, Bodmin, Cornwall

Ad maiorem dei, deorum et/vel nihili gloriam

This is the perfectly pure demonstration of the perfection of wisdom. No one has demonstrated it, no one has received it, no one has realized it. And since no one has realized it, no one has therein gone to final Nirvana. Nor has this demonstration of Dharma ever made anyone worthy of gifts.

The Large Sutra on Perfect Wisdom

I listen and the voice is of a world collapsing endlessly, a frozen world, under a faint untroubled sky, enough to see by, yes, and frozen too. And I hear it murmur that all wilts and yields, as if loaded down, but here there are no loads, and the ground too, unfit for loads, and the light too, down towards an end it seems can never come. For what possible end to these wastes where true light never was, nor any upright thing, nor any true foundation, but only those leaning things, forever lapsing and crumbling away, beneath a sky without memory of morning or hope of night. These things, what things, come from where, made of what? … Yes a world at an end, in spite of appearances, its end brought it forth, ending it began, is it clear enough? And I too am at an end when I am there, my eyes close, my sufferings cease and I end, I wither as the living can not. And if I went on listening to that far whisper, silent long since and which I still hear, I would learn still more about this.

Samuel Beckett, *Molloy*

Contents

Acknowledgements

Redemptive moments:
People who love me and people who care about my attempt to do
Philosophy
Have occasionally **cut through** the grey traffic days and silence.

Above all I would like to warmly acknowledge my father and mother who have supported me both financially and emotionally throughout my attempt to do philosophy. I can't thank them enough for everything they have done for me over the years. My thanks also to Simon Critchley for supervision during my time at Essex, to Lucia Pizarro and Havi Carel for comments and support whilst I was writing this, and to Carl Humphries for helpful and positive feedback about the final draft. Many thanks also to the staff at Continuum, especially Sarah Douglas, for their input into this project and their help bringing it to a wider audience.

Introduction

Insight into the multiple ambiguity of philosophizing acts as a deterrent … and ultimately betrays the entire fruitlessness of such activity. It would be a misunderstanding if we wished in the slightest to weaken this impression of the hopelessness of philosophizing, or to mediate it belatedly by indicating that in the end things are not so bad after all, that philosophy has achieved many things in the history of mankind, and so on. This is merely idle talk that talks in a direction leading away from philosophy. We must rather uphold and hold out in this terror.

(Martin Heidegger, *The Fundamental Concepts of Metaphysics*)[1]

I open my eyes and see a star. Open eyes absorb colours and thrust them out again; open eyes allow starlight moving at 299,792,458 metres per second to stream inside; open eyes open wide as the ice pick slides between them; open eyes can be cured by aconite's glistening similitude. As the distant star shifts through the sky at 0.0000727 rad/s I turn and offer words to my companion: I speak about the star in time using language. The star is external to me, heavenly, a divinity, a G2 star with a lifetime of 10 billion years.

Theories structure our world. Theories are our world. Theory is not just something practised in the academy by a collection of 'specialists'. We see our theories everywhere. We *are* our theories.

Some people study theory by taking a written sample and examining it extremely carefully. Perhaps the text contains internal contradictions or self-reflexive paradoxes that disintegrate it into nonsense or silence. Perhaps the text is structured by sets of oppositions – such as male-female, high-low, or speech-writing – and the relationship between these oppositions can be reversed. Perhaps the text can be reduced to the cultural patterns that prevailed when it was written.

A problem with detailed readings is that it is easy to think that the difficulties raised by them are local to the text that is being examined. Perhaps some minutiae of the text could be easily changed, and we could continue to interpret the world within its framework. Another problem with detailed readings is that they often ignore the everyday theories we use to interpret the world around us. They remain trapped within a 'criticism' that has little impact on our general worldview.

Theory can also be studied by building a *model*, which extracts common features from theories within a particular domain. Many theories have many features in common: they share a picture of the world and disagree over minor details. This picture acts as a framework for the disputes between theories. Without this picture, different theories would have nothing to talk about: they would not be arguing about the same thing.[2]

Scientists and philosophers create pictures of the world that are also absorbed by non-specialists. Although they might not master all of the mathematical details, the non-specialists do gain a rough understanding of the view of the world that is set forth. The (wo)man in the street today discourses on the big bang and DNA; (s)he sees the world in terms of these theories, even though (s)he does not fully understand how they work.

An abstract model of a theoretical domain enables us to understand it in a way that is free from many of its obfuscating details. One can see the metaphysics behind it and examine the self-reflexive problems that it presents. If a picture of the world is unable to account for the fact that it is spoken about in language, then this cannot be solved by looking at some of the details and perhaps changing an equation or two. This kind of question can be better addressed by creating a model of the theoretical domain and analyzing how it functions at a more general level.

A second reason for abstracting out a model is that most of the time we only deal with small parts of single theories and vagueness fills in the places where it is all supposed to cohere together. We perch upon the mountain tops of particular theories and never venture down into the valleys where they unify into a single range of thought.

On the surface my wife is a beautiful creature with smooth skin, full breasts, brown eyes and curly dark hair caressed between curving hips. But when I slit her open and slip inside, I discover a beating heart, bloody liver, squishy lungs and shit-stuffed guts. These gruesome organs are essential to her functioning, but softly tucked away beneath her supple skin.

The theories that I am dealing with in this book present themselves with flawless complexions when we touch upon them in our day-to-day doings. But they are as frightful as my wife inside. If the brain hypothesis is correct, our phenomenal experiences *have to be* patterns in firing neurons and there *cannot* be any stretching out of our minds into the world. This is perfectly coherent, and yet it is also an extremely counter-intuitive claim when its full consequences are worked out. The process of condensation and abstraction into a model can highlight how utterly absurd some theories are; how they are all-embracing monstrous metaphysical visions.

It could be argued that the monstrosity of the theories in this book comes from my treatment of them, and not because they are inherently implausible. You will have to make up your own mind about this as you read the detailed expositions in the later chapters. One claim of this book is that our current theories of perception, time, madness and knowledge become outright incredible when they are taken *seriously*.

The theory theory in this book operates in three interlinked stages:

1) A generalized model is abstracted from a theoretical domain.
2) The self-reflexive limitations and breakdowns of this model are described.
3) This abstraction and analysis make the metaphysics and monstrosity of the model more apparent.

This methodology is applied to philosophical and scientific theories of perception, time, madness and knowledge that are deeply embedded in our everyday way of interpreting phenomena.

The first chapter is an overview of the self-reflexive relationship between theorizers and their theories. When I create a theory about the world I am also creating a theory about myself because I am part of the world that I am describing. A self-reflexive circle is set up in which the description is part of what is being described. Within this self-reflexive circle a theory can support its status as a representation of the world, but it can also undermine the possibility of theory altogether when a theoretician writes a theory which, explicitly or implicitly, makes theory impossible. This analysis of stable and collapsing theories provides the background for the chapters that follow.

The second chapter examines perception. Neuroscience hypothesizes that the brain is a physical object whose main operational components are billions of interconnected neurons and the firing of these neurons or groups of neurons generates (or actually *is*) our experience of the world. However, when we perceive colours, scents and sounds it seems as if the brain is reaching through the senses and placing the end products of its processing into the real physical environment. Neuroscience can only explain this semi-miraculous observation by claiming that our bodies and environment are *both* represented within a single virtual reality model that is entirely contained within the brain. Although this interpretation of neuro-science is unavoidable, it suffers from the fatal problem that it is based on evidence taken from our experiences with real brains, and yet claims that we have never seen or touched a real brain.

The third chapter examines objective theories of time. This covers both our ordinary notion of time as some kind of flow or thing and the spacetime of relativity theory. Both of these are essentially cinematic and this chapter develops a model that pictures time as a projector of a sequence of static nows. Everything within the world is placed inside the static now and all changes are reduced to the replacement of the current now by a now in which everything is slightly different. This has the result that objects no longer move *within* time, but are moved *by* time through a succession of states. The problem with this model is that it eliminates the people who are describing it. If time is objective, people become helpless puppets in the hands of time: objects *into which* language is projected by time, and not subjects who use language to describe time. Furthermore, although a vague notion of objective time is something that we all believe in, it becomes an absurd metaphysical fantasy when it is concretely developed as a cinematic model.

The next chapter draws on antipsychiatric literature to model madness as a quantitative difference in the qualities manifested by people. All people share the same set of qualities, but some exaggerate the schizophrenic style of being, whilst others exaggerate different collections of qualities. This interpretation of madness is developed through labelling theory and by highlighting the schizophrenic dimension of childhood, art and knowledge. The outcome of this merging of madness and reason is a homogenous zone that incorporates the mad and the sane within a single space. This is a compelling interpretation of madness, but it suffers from self-reflexive difficulties connected with an excess of madness, an excess of sanity and the proliferation of 'mad' theories in the homogenous zone.

The final chapter is a study of knowledge and scepticism. It is an empirical fact that the thoughts, languages, ontologies and forms of life of people are synchronically and diachronically different. Positive scepticism is a theory that accounts for this fact by modelling the world as a labyrinth of overlapping aspects structured by different thoughts, languages, ontologies and forms of life. Although this theory describes itself as an aspect, this does not invalidate it (the relativist's problem) since there is not necessarily anything more real behind aspects that could invalidate them. However, positive scepticism is self-reflexively challenged because it does not place the aspect of positive scepticism above others. This forces the positive sceptic to endorse aspects that directly challenge it, and positive scepticism is led by its own arguments into an unstable sustaining/negating relationship with the labyrinth of theories around it.

Taken together, the theories in this book integrate into a single picture of reality that can almost be believed in, even though it cannot be coherently described, justified or even thought about. Within this picture, the models of perception and time in chapters 2 and 3 form the invisible metaphysics and chapters 4 and 5 analyze the thought that currently thinks this metaphysics. Although this vision is to some extent a caricature and simplification of our everyday theories, my claim is that it corresponds to them in their essential aspects – it is a caricature with all their metaphysics and self-reflexive contradictions intact. We are so immersed in this picture that we cannot escape from it and even if we could break free, it is far from clear where we would go. Any alternative would inevitably suffer from similar self-reflexive difficulties and absurd premises as the theories that we are currently inhabiting.

One can think of this methodology as dialectics. Not negative dialectics or an ascent towards Absolute Spirit, but an attempt to sense the self-reflexive *movement* of the theories that we are thrown into and find around us. As we think about these theories they collapse, shift into a different space, and then we find ourselves returning to embrace them again.

It is worth noting that few (if any) of the theories in this book are my own. What is important is the way in which they break down at their self-reflexive limits. In many ways what I am engaged in here is similar to deconstruction – but this is a deconstruction of philosophical and scientific worldviews, not Continental texts.

Mortals cast away from God, we are damned to a land of shifting theory in which self-reflexivity is our only possible support. However, this is almost impossible to talk about as it ceaselessly reawakens the limit points where speech disintegrates into nonsense or silence. Contrary to Lawson,[3] I do not believe that we can freeze the quicksands with yet another semi-stable theory. This book attempts to move through the unstable moments and perhaps chart a little of them as they evanescently shimmer and glimmer in the moonlight. When philosophy is pushed hard enough it dissolves through its own logic and any attempt to describe this dissolution dissolves as well. This total liquidation is the circling limit of philosophy.

> Philosophy sets limits to the much disputed sphere of natural science.
> It must set limits to what can be thought; and, in doing so, to what cannot be thought.
> It must set limits to what cannot be thought by working outwards through what can be thought.
> It will signify what cannot be said, by presenting clearly what can be said.
> (Ludwig Wittgenstein, *Tractatus Logico-Philosophicus*)[4]

1 Stable and Collapsing Theories

Beginning ...

> The very point of view, which originally is taken on its own evidence
> only, must in the course of the science be converted to a result – the
> ultimate result in which philosophy returns into itself and reaches the
> point where it began. In this manner philosophy exhibits the appearance
> of a circle which closes with itself, and has no beginning in the same way
> as the other sciences have. To speak of a beginning of philosophy has
> meaning only in relation to a person who proposes to commence the
> study, and not in relation to the science as science.
>
> (Georg Hegel, *Logic*)[1]

There is a whole load of stuff that exists. This is often called
'reality' or 'matter'. This stuff appears as trees, bees, computers,
rocks, chimney sweeps and chairs. I can touch this stuff, smell this
stuff, taste this stuff, listen to this stuff and see this stuff using my
body, which is also composed of stuff. I can speak about this stuff
using language.

Every man, woman and child stands before the world and
declares: 'This is so!' However, some people specialize in creating
theories. Theologians, scientists, sociologists and philosophers are
examples of such people. Generally their theories are proclaimed
out loud or written down in books or journals. People write books
because they wish to communicate their theories; they want to
persuade other people that their theories are correct. Libraries
contain books filled with many such theories.

I am David Gamez. I am a person composed of stuff and I can
speak about the stuff, as I am doing now. I am 33 and have lived

in Britain all my life. I am healthy and of sound mind. The year is 2006 (according to the most popular calendar system in my country). I speak English. I am male. The age that I had when I started this book may occasionally make it naive and idealistic. The problems that I am interested in have been determined by the times and places in which I have lived. I have been influenced by science and by analytic and Continental philosophy. Philosophy since Nietzsche has been morbidly preoccupied with the collapse of philosophy and this has influenced me too. I have also been influenced by science, mysticism and by the idea of alternative logics and languages. The structure of the thoughts and arguments that I am presenting in this book may have been entirely determined by capitalistic Western culture.

These are a few of the presuppositions with which I am starting to write this book; assumptions about the world and myself that seem extremely self-evident to me. However, someone from a later or earlier time might think that I have different presuppositions from the ones that I am explicitly articulating here – deeper underlying presuppositions that make my explicit thematizing of these presuppositions possible.

I have just set out what seems to be a fairly common-sense view about stuff, people and theories. This is what I have been brought up to believe. However, it could be argued that the unifying concept of stuff is pure metaphysics *in the bad sense*. This *simplistic* picture of people unproblematically describing the stuff could be said to assume *far too much*. Furthermore, every word that I wrote contains a rich depth of further presuppositions and meanings. To *really* set out my presuppositions I would have to append a footnote to every word that I wrote and add a footnote to every word in the footnotes.

I am meditating upon the beginning and upon my presuppositions. But these clanking carriages of thought did not spring from nowhere. I am discussing the beginning because I know what ends and presuppositions are; because I place a value on being transparent to my presuppositions; because I already assume things and make deductions from them. The notion that the beginning is important is itself a presupposition.

Genuine beginnings are *naive*; they do not know what beginnings or presuppositions are; they do not *need* to find a starting point because they are *already at* such a starting point. We can only thematize the beginning long after we have gone beyond it.

To really begin, to genuinely start from a few simple assumptions, is impossible in philosophy. We have always already begun.

Since I cannot deduce everything from a few simple presuppositions, I will *shamelessly* introduce many other presuppositions as and when I see fit, with no argument or justification whatsoever. Not because I am a particularly crass or bad philosopher, but because this is the only way in which philosophy can proceed.

The presuppositions that I have set out are presuppositions within a greater whole that cannot be *explicitly* presupposed. They are a useful theoretical strategy; part of that whole and not something that could be used to build the whole from nothing.

I cannot start without presuppositions. Since I cannot start without presuppositions, and cannot question my presuppositions without having started, I will stick with the presuppositions that I have. They are a door into the domain of philosophy and seem to be a plausible starting point in the culture in which I am living. I cannot start from nowhere and wherever I start from will be erroneous from some points of view.

Hermeneutic Circles

> In order to provide a complete account of the physical world it will be
> necessary to give an account of how ... the theories of science
> themselves, as part of the physical world, are also the outcome of the
> laws which the theories express. A complete theory will thus need to be
> self-referential, so that in addition to providing the laws of the universe,
> those laws will need to be capable of providing an account of how
> human observers, as a certain combination of physical constituents on
> a planet in one part of the universe, will necessarily formulate at a certain
> point in time, through physical activity in their brain, the true theory of
> the universe.
>
> (Hilary Lawson, *Closure*)[2]

To understand this sentence you need to understand each of the
words in it. You need to know what 'to', 'understand', 'this',
'sentence', 'you', 'need', 'understand', 'each', 'of', 'the', 'words', 'in'
and 'it' mean. But the meaning of each of these words is affected
by their location in the sentence and by other sentences in the
paragraph. This broader context is needed to understand that
'this sentence' refers to the sentence itself and not to a different
sentence that has just been quoted.

The same problem is encountered at the level of an entire work.
To understand a book you have to read it: you have to cast your
eyes over every one of its parts. But how can you understand each
part without grasping how it is integrated into the whole? How can
you comprehend the fall of man in Genesis without relating it to
the future redemption of the world by Christ? How can you understand the beginning of the *Phenomenology* unless you already
grasp the essence of Absolute Spirit?

These examples illustrate the traditional problem of the
hermeneutical[3] circle: we cannot understand the parts without a
grasp of the whole and we cannot comprehend the whole without
understanding the parts. This is shown in Figure 1.

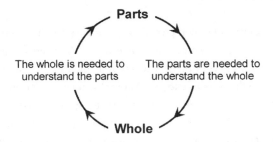

Figure 1. Hermeneutical circle between whole and parts

To have understood the last paragraph you must have read the parts in the context of the whole and grasped the whole through the serial assimilation of parts. You also approached the last paragraph with a large number of preconceptions and at this moment, you are sitting down and reading this book for a definite reason – perhaps because you are being paid to, because you are interested in the subject matter, or perhaps this was the only text that could be saved from the nuclear holocaust of 2012. You may also have certain preconceptions about the subject matter – perhaps you are a scientist searching for cracks and flaws in my position; perhaps you are a theologian seeking a way to God through my arguments; perhaps you are a linguist studying twenty-first century logic and grammar; or perhaps you can barely understand this book because its style and subject matter are wholly alien to you.

All the preconceptions that you have brought to my text affect how you receive it; how you unpack the contents that I have placed in it. Your understanding of this text depends on your approach to it and you are not even aware of most of the biases that you are introducing. This is the contemporary problem of the hermeneutic[4] circle: we always approach worlds, objects and texts with fore-conceptions that determine our subsequent interpretations. We have always already made up our minds in advance when we interpret something. This is illustrated in Figure 2.

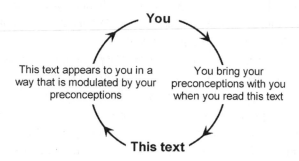

Figure 2. Hermeneutic circle between you and this text

Although solutions have been put forward to this apparent problem, after Heidegger, and especially Gadamer, this has become something to be affirmed and accepted, rather than escaped from and denied. We are all historically situated beings whose approaches to worlds, objects and texts have inevitably been conditioned by the culture that we have been thrown into. For Heidegger this hermeneutic circle is virtuous and must be leapt into in the correct way; according to Gadamer, we can develop better or at least more comprehensive perspectives on the world if we open ourselves up to what the past is saying and allow our prejudices to be questioned.

You are seated reading a text, dutifully risking your prejudices by being open to what it has to say. Perhaps you have all kinds of fore-conceptions that are modulating the meaning of the text. But these do not affect the fact that *the text is speaking about you; it is describing you as you are sitting down and reading it*. A biological treatise describes how your lenses are focusing on the letters; how your retina is being stimulated by the patterned light reflecting off the page; how the signals from your eyes are being channelled and processed by your retinotopic maps; how the macro patterns in your neural flows are your consciousness of what you are reading in the book. A historical treatise describes how you are a person in a particular epoch, dressed in clothes fashionable for your time and seated in a chair built using the technology of your day – a person at the end of a long line of people who have handed you your style, language, politics, technology and concepts. Whatever the area of the text, it is the text that is interpreting you.

Texts are not facsimiles of God's lapidary inscriptions: they are written by people. People set down interpretations of reality; they make statements about how things are. They write the texts that they and other people sit down and read. These texts provide interpretations of the people who wrote them – writing is an act of self-interpretation. This creates a third kind of hermeneutic circle. A person writes a theory and this theory interprets the person who wrote it. This is the kind of hermeneutic circle that is central to this book. The notion of the hermeneutic circle will *not* be used to describe the relationship between whole and parts or the effect of preconceptions on our interpretation of texts and worlds. It *will* be used to describe the way in which an interpretation of reality interprets the interpreter who created it. This type of hermeneutic circle is depicted in Figure 3.

A different way of expressing this is to say that we interpret reality and are also part of it. Since we are both interpreters of reality and reality itself, our interpretations of reality apply to ourselves. The hermeneutic circles that I am interested in are circles of self-reflexivity.

People create interpretations in numerous different areas. We have physical, chemical, biological, philosophical, political, psychological

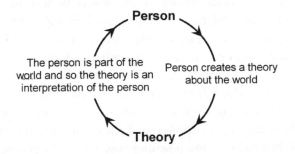

Figure 3. A person creates a theory and this theory interprets the person who created it

and sociological theories, all of which are self-interpretations to some extent. Many of these affect the naive presuppositions that I set out at the beginning of this chapter. They affect them directly when they are explicitly about people or theories, or they affect them indirectly when some of their consequences affect our theories about people or theories.

When a theory folds back upon itself it can *reinforce* the naive presuppositions that we have about people and theories. This is a *stable* hermeneutic circle that directly or indirectly affirms our position as theorizers about reality. There are also theories that criticize these presuppositions or undermine themselves in some other way. These form *collapsing* hermeneutic circles, which directly or indirectly deny that it is possible for people to create their interpretation of reality. Finally there are theories that have an *unstable* sustaining/negating relationship with one another. These theories are forced by their presuppositions to accept other theories that contradict these presuppositions.[5]

Not all theories touch on areas that are relevant to our naive presuppositions: there are theories that are too small or local for it to be immediately apparent whether they hermeneutically circle or not. They have not been expanded to the point at which they have a substantial effect on perception, language or the people articulating the theory. This does not mean that small or local theories should not be investigated carefully; many, if not all of them, presuppose larger theories or systems that *are* stable, collapsing or unstable hermeneutic circles.

Stable Hermeneutic Circles

Theories that form stable hermeneutic circles are productive of themselves; they interpret reality in a way that makes theory possible. In effect a hermeneutically circling theory says: 'Reality is constituted in such a way that this theory can be created within it.' This is illustrated in Figure 4.

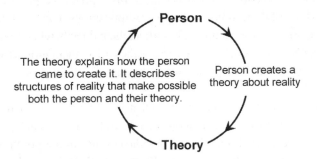

Figure 4. A stable hermeneutic circle is formed when a theory about the world explains how a person could create it

Hegel's system is a classic example of a stable hermeneutic circle. Hegel could achieve Absolute Knowing because the philosophical, political and cultural history that he was describing made his description of history possible. As Hegel sat down to write his *Phenomenology*, Napoleon's cannon shots outside heralded the end of the dialectic of desire and the arrival of an absolute state in which the *Encyclopaedia of the Philosophical Sciences* could be written. As Kojève puts it:

Absolute Knowledge became – *objectively* – possible because in and by Napoleon the *real* process of historical evolution, in the course of which man *created* new Worlds and *transformed* himself by creating them, came to its end. To reveal *this* World, therefore, is to reveal *the* World – that is, to reveal being in the *completed* totality of its spatial-temporal existence. And – *subjectively* – absolute Knowledge became possible because a man named Hegel was able to understand the *World* in which he lived and to understand *himself* as living in and understanding this World. ... By understanding himself through the understanding of the *totality* of the anthropogenic historical process, which ends with Napoleon and his contemporaries, and by understanding this process through his understanding of *himself*, Hegel caused the completed whole of the universal real process to penetrate into his individual consciousness, and then he penetrated this consciousness. Thus this consciousness became just as total, as universal, as the process that it revealed by understanding itself; and this fully self-conscious consciousness *is* absolute Knowledge, which, by being developed in discourse, will form the content of absolute *philosophy* or Science, of that *Encyclopaedia of the Philosophical Sciences* that contains the sum of all possible knowledge.[6]

History (as described by Hegel) made Hegel's description of history possible. Hegel and his theory of history coexist in a state of mutual complementarity that is a *stable* hermeneutic circle (Figure 5).

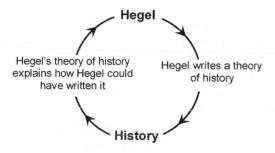

Figure 5. A stable hermeneutic circle in which Hegel's theory of history explains how it was possible for Hegel to write this theory of history

Collapsing Hermeneutic Circles

Theories in collapsing hermeneutic circles spirit themselves away by interpreting reality in a way that makes interpretation impossible. Collapsing theories are self-undermining descriptions of reality that break the self-reflexive link between people and their theories (see Figure 6).

A theory in a collapsing hermeneutic circle can be used to explain a number of phenomena. However, its central limitation

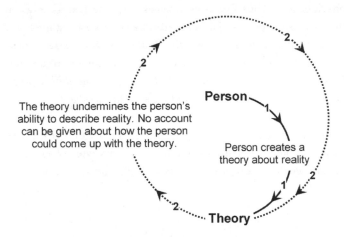

Figure 6. Collapsing hermeneutic circle in which it cannot be explained
how the person could come up with the theory

is that it cannot consistently account for its own presence.
Collapsing theories are orphaned from their origin as a person's
description of the world.

In general hermeneutic circles collapse because they contradict
the presuppositions (or a version of them) that I set out at the
beginning of this chapter. Anything that overturns the simple
picture of people perceiving the world and creating theories about
it opens up a mystical and strange world in which people cease to
be people, theories float free from evidence and/or the link
between people and language is broken. A collapsing theory dislocates us from our comfortable presuppositions about people and
theory and casts us upon a pile of broken paradoxes and twisted
contradictions.

A good example of a collapsing hermeneutic circle is the structural anthropology of Lévi-Strauss, which extends Saussure's notion
of the sign to include forks, village huts, relatives and weapons. In
Saussure's structuralism, representation is possible because there is
a distinction between signs and physical objects, with the former
being capable of standing for the latter. However, when Lévi-

Strauss interprets physical objects as signs as well, he erases the distinction between signifier and signified, and reduces everything to a multiplicity of signs operating within a structural system. Whilst in Saussure the mental concept of language (labelled with the sound pattern 'language') can be used to represent language, in Lévi-Strauss there is no distinction between signifier and signified, between sign and object, and so there are no longer any signs or representation. A sign in the mind and a sign in the world have the same status; they are differentiated from one other and part of a single system. As Derrida puts it:

> ... as soon as one seeks to demonstrate in this way that there is no transcendental or privileged signified and that the domain or play of the signification henceforth has no limit, one must reject even the concept and word 'sign' itself – which is precisely what cannot be done. For the signification 'sign' has always been understood and determined, in its meaning, as sign-of, a signifier referring to a signified, a signifier different from its signified. If one erases the radical difference between signifier and signified, it is the word 'signifier' itself which must be abandoned as a metaphysical concept. ... The concept of the sign, in each of its aspects, has been determined by this opposition throughout the totality of its history. It has lived only on this opposition and this system.[7]

Without something that is not a sign the word 'sign' loses its meaning and Lévi-Strauss' anthropology becomes unable to account for how it could be spoken about by Lévi-Strauss. This is illustrated in Figure 7.

Many of the theories that structure our day-to-day lives are also collapsing hermeneutic circles. In chapter 2 I will show how the hypothesis that we have brains leads to a collapsing theory of perception. Chapter 3 documents the self-reflexive collapse of the objective theory of time.

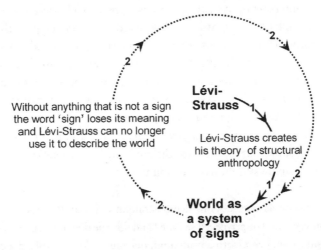

Figure 7. If the world is a system of signs, then there is no longer anything that is not a sign. The word 'sign' loses its meaning and Lévi-Strauss' structuralist anthropology collapses.

Invisible Theory

When a theory collapses what are we left with? On the one hand we have an articulation of the world that seems plausible and can make good predictions. On the other hand, beyond a certain point we find ourselves unable to discuss the theory any further. In the best case we lose evidence for the theory and remain people describing the world using language. In the worst case it becomes impossible for us to refer to reality at all: a theory that we seeded has become monstrous and sucked us into itself: it is the atoms, time, or the structure speaking – and perhaps there is no longer any speaking at all.

One response to this is to rule that collapsing hermeneutic circles are *illegitimate*. Theories that are not self-reflexively consistent must be discarded and better theories must be sought. This may be the only *rigorous* approach. What we *cannot* justify or speak about must be passed over in silence.[8]

The problem with this solution is that some theories are extremely compelling and useful, even if they undermine themselves at some point. We are haunted by the uncomfortable sense that some collapsing theories might be *true* – that the brain hypothesis and objective time are good theories – even if we cannot legitimately use them to describe the world. Furthermore, there seems to be some sense to the idea that we can *point* to collapsing theories, even if we cannot speak about them directly.

An alternative response is to preserve the sense that we have of a collapsing theory's validity, and deal with its collapse by describing it as *invisible*. Invisible theories are retained as theories about reality that can be described and refuted; the only difference between a stable and a collapsing theory is that the latter becomes invisible when it undermines its own status as a theory. Up to a certain point invisible theories can be spoken about in clear philosophical or scientific language; beyond this point they can only be described using hints, metaphors and mystical allusions.

It could be objected that we should be *highly* suspicious of this notion of an invisible theory. Like the thing-in-itself, an invisible theory has something deeply counter-intuitive about it that we long to get rid of with a bold sweep. This objection is substantial, but it loses its force once we realize that there may not be any stable hermeneutic circles at all.[9] Although I have cited Hegel as an example of a hermeneutically circling system, a more careful reading is actually likely to show that his hermeneutic circle collapses when the relationship between Hegel the man and Absolute Spirit is taken into account.[10] If all theories eventually collapse, we may have to live with invisibility for a while; even if we set up stable hermeneutic circles as our ideal.

Invisible theory can be thought of as a half-way concept at this stage – something that we cannot yet dispense with but that might eventually become superfluous. A pole to climb up before leaping out into the void.

The Return

A yearning man in tight trousers. Uttering the words 'Death oh death I long for thee!' he plunges the knife into his heaving breast. Snapping the spring flowers in his paroxysms of pain he gasps once again 'Death oh death I long for thee!'

A twisted youth death-married with petal confetti. Not only is the man dead; his *desire* for death is dead as well. Since he is dead, the man no longer desires to die. He no longer craves death and so, for no reason, he comes back to life again. As life arises the desire to die returns, and the cycle begins again.

When a theory vanishes into invisibility we fall silent, hold ourselves awhile … and then exhale. The invisible theory has cancelled itself out and in so doing it has cancelled out its cancellation as well. The evidence remains as it was before we embarked upon the collapsing theory and within this prelapsarian world we start to theorize again.

Amongst the joyous host returning is the invisible theory that cancelled itself out. Since its self-reflexive collapse has itself collapsed, there is no longer any reason for rejecting it and the cycle of collapse and return beings again. Collapsing hermeneutic circles move through a dialectical cycle of invisibility, return and collapse that is not an ascent to the Absolute or a negative dialectics, but a thought that constantly moves without moving anywhere.

Unstable Hermeneutic Circles

Unstable hermeneutic circles link a number of stable and collapsing hermeneutic circles together into a structure that manifests a queasy instability. This kind of theory has elements within it that maintain a self-sustaining relationship with the world, but it also contains the possibility of complete annihilation. This type of hermeneutic circle often emerges from some version of the claim that a multiplicity of theories are true but not necessarily compatible.

A simple example of an unstable hermeneutic circle is the assertion that everyone is correct, i.e., that the theories of everyone are to be believed. This theory starts off as a stable hermeneutic circle, since it includes itself amongst the theories that are correct. However, a person who believed this theory would soon come into contact with other people who make an exclusive claim to truth. For example, Jesus claims that the theory that everyone is correct is wrong because only he is the son of God and speaks the truth. The person's theory that everyone is correct commits her to believing Jesus, and yet Jesus is claiming that only he speaks the truth. As she listens to Jesus, her belief that everyone is correct forces her to believe him, and this undermines her theory that everyone is correct. However, she only started to believe Jesus because of her theory that everyone is correct, and not because of Jesus' own claim that he is the son of God. So once she starts believing Jesus she also starts to undermine her own grounds for believing Jesus. This leads her to stop believing Jesus, her theory that everyone is correct returns and the process begins again. This instability is illustrated in Figure 8.[11]

Unstable hermeneutic circles only arise when there are good reasons for reaching the conclusion that a multiplicity of conflicting positions are correct. Chapter 4 describes a homogenous zone in which no theory can be rejected on grounds of madness and every theory is as mad or sane as any other. Chapter 5 shows how theories about thought, language, ontology and form of life lead to a labyrinth of conflicting aspects in which the theory that describes this labyrinth is annihilated by the other aspects around it.

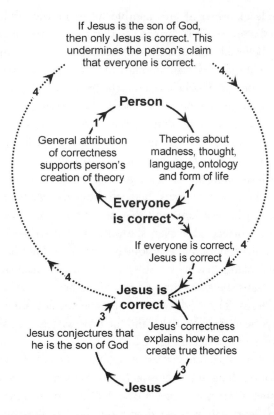

Figure 8. Unstable hermeneutic circle in which a person oscillates between believing that everyone is correct and believing that only Jesus is correct. This instability is caused by the interactions between circle 1 and circle 3.

2 Evidence for the Brain?

Simulation is no longer that of a territory, a referential being or a substance. It is the generation by models of a real without origin or reality: a hyperreal. The territory no longer precedes the map, or survives it. Henceforth, it is the map that precedes the territory.

> (Jean Baudrillard, *Simulations*)[1]

The White Room

A Mk. IV Advanced Cleaning Robot© is placed in a large white room and instructed to clean the floor. This robot has an ultrasound emitter and detector mounted on a flexible neck, brushes that automatically clean the room as it moves around and a grasping arm that it uses to pick up objects (see Figure 1).

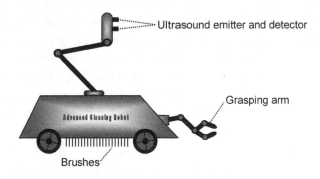

Figure 1. Mk. IV Advanced Cleaning Robot©

Earlier versions of this robot did not use ultrasound; they just blindly stumbled about in the hope that they would eventually cover the entire surface of the floor. When their collision detectors encountered an object, they attempted to move around it by reversing and heading off in a slightly different direction. To get around these limitations, the Mk. IV was equipped with an ultrasound emitter and detector and software to enable it to build up a virtual model of its environment.

The robot constructs its virtual model by sending out pulses of ultrasound that reflect off the walls of the room and enter its detector a short time later.[2] From the point of view of an outside observer, the robot and the wall are visible for the whole time that this is taking place. For the robot the situation is very different. The robot does not see the wall and then fire an ultrasound pulse towards it. If the robot could see the wall, it would not need the ultrasound. All that it can do is construct a virtual model of itself firing a pulse of ultrasound into a space of undetermined depth. This self-model is generated from memory in the Mk. IV robot. If we used a virtual reality headset to view the robot's model at this time, we would see a three-dimensional robot floating in the middle of an indeterminate space and firing a pulse of ultrasound into this space (T1 in Figure 2). When the reflected pulse returns, it enters the robot's detector (T2 in Figure 2). However, at time T2 in the robot's virtual world there is no representation of the ultrasound pulse entering the representation of the robot's detector because the robot has just received the signal from its real detector and has not had a chance to process the signal. Once the processing is complete, the robot simultaneously models the point in space that reflected the pulse along with the reflected incoming ultrasound pulse (T3 in Figure 2). If we were watching the robot's virtual model of reality, we would see nothing at T2, and then at T3 we would see the reflected pulse entering the robot's detector and a point come into existence at a distance from the robot. At T3 the ratio (length of the robot's self model) : (distance between the virtual detector and the virtual point) is the same as the ratio

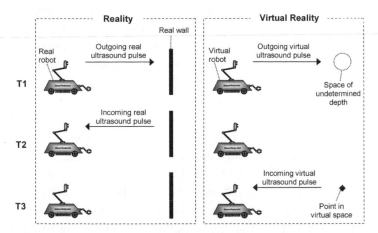

Figure 2. The robot builds up a virtual internal model of the room that it is cleaning

(length of the real robot) : (distance between the real detector and the wall), but the virtual model itself can be any physical size at all.[3]

The robot continues to emit ultrasound pulses and maps points until it has built up a complete model of the white room. When this is complete, the robot's memory contains a virtual white room that encloses a virtual robot situated in a position that corresponds to the position of the real robot in the real white room. If we used virtual reality equipment to step into this virtual room, we would see that the space of indeterminate depth has vanished. As we looked up, down and around us we would see a white room with a robot in the centre. This robot has an ultrasound emitter and detector mounted on its front, which it is using to map out the room that is to be cleaned.

This scanning is carried out once at the beginning of the cleaning operation. The robot then uses its virtual model to calculate a path that will cover the entire floor area. Once this planning is complete, signals are sent to the body of the real robot instructing its wheels to rotate. The movement of the real robot is shadowed by movements of the virtual robot whose virtual wheels carry it about in the virtual room.

One limitation of this robot is that its final model is not sensitive to changes in the real room, and so it becomes disoriented if it is picked up and moved to a different location. Another limitation of the Mk. IV robot is that its body model is hardwired in memory, and so it is unable to monitor itself for damage. To address these problems, a Mk.V version of the Advanced Cleaning Robot© was developed, which scans the room continuously, instead of building up a model once at the beginning of its cleaning operation. This Mk.V robot was programmed to scan itself with ultrasound so that it could build up a model of its body. One difficulty with this is that the parts the robot can scan are restricted by the degrees of freedom of its neck, and so it will never be able to scan the ultrasound emitter and detector themselves (unless the robot learns to use a smooth hard wall as a mirror). The Mk. V robot was also given sensors to monitor tyre pressure, strain gauges to detect damage, and a touch sensitive layer on the surface of its body and grasping arm.

These improvements enable the Mk. V robot to scan the real room and observe its real body. As the ultrasound pulses return they are integrated with the sensor information into a single three-dimensional virtual model. The parts of the environment that are only mapped using ultrasound are marked as external to the robot; the parts of the environment that contain other types of sensory information are interpreted as the robot's body.

As the Mk. V robot looks around, it sees a virtual white room that is updated in real time. It looks down at its virtual body and feels strain, pressure and touch within this part of virtual space as well. When it touches its virtual body with its virtual grasping arm, its real body is touched by its real grasping arm and it experiences both the touching and the being touched within its virtual body and grasping arm. As its real body moves around the real white room its virtual environment dynamically changes. Although the visible surfaces of parts of its body are missing because of the restricted degrees of freedom of its neck, the robot is unable to observe the absence of this information and so it interprets what it sees as a total world. This is illustrated in Figure 3.

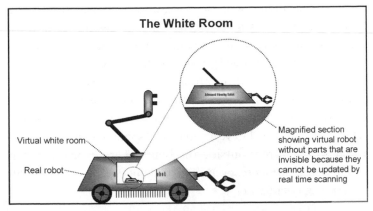

Figure 3. The real white room containing the Mk. V robot with its virtual internal model. Note that the orientation of the virtual room does not have to be the same as that of the real room for it to be an effective model. The robot's virtual body is only partially visible because the robot cannot scan all of its body or the ultrasound emitter and detector themselves. However, it does have sensor information for these areas.

The real white room is a source of data for the virtual white room, but it never directly appears within it. Although the robot is situated and acts in the real white room, it only ever *encounters* the virtual white room that is enclosed within its real body. This virtual white room is a total world for the robot; the only *world* that it ever has. When the robot stretches out its grasping arm to pick up an object, the arm that it senses and sees is an object within its virtual environment, and this virtual arm never reaches out beyond the limits of its physical body to touch objects in the real white room, even though it appears this way to the robot. If the electrons in the robot's RAM could produce *conscious experiences* – if there was something that it was like to *be* this pattern of electrons – then the robot might see and feel its virtual grasping arm in the same way that we see and feel our arms, but this would never be a direct experience of its real grasping arm. An experience of its real grasping arm is impossible for a robot that senses the world through signals – and it is difficult to see how *else* the robot could monitor its environment. Indeed, since all of its life experiences have been virtual, the robot is likely to have no idea that there is or could ever be a *real* white room – or rather, it will interpret the virtual white room *as* the real white room; as the *only* white room. If the robot had better cognitive capacities, it might observe its virtual body and *infer* that it uses its senses to perceive a *real* white room, vastly bigger than its virtual white room, which is the source of data for its virtual model. However, it might also think that a real white room lying entirely outside the limits of its experience was *metaphysical nonsense*, even if it could not conceive how else its experiences could arise.

> You and I, we humans, we mammals, we animals, inhabit a virtual world, constructed from elements that are, at successively higher levels, useful for representing the real world. Of course, we feel as if we are firmly placed in the real world – which is exactly as it should be if our constrained virtual reality software is any good. It is very good, and the only time we notice it at all is on the rare occasions when it gets something wrong. When this happens we experience an illusion or a hallucination.
>
> (Richard Dawkins, *Unweaving the Rainbow*)[4]

The Brain-based Theory of Perception

Introduction

It is extraordinarily difficult to divest ourselves of the belief that the physical world is the world we perceive by sight and touch; even if, in our philosophic moments, we are aware that this is an error, we nevertheless fall into it again as soon as we are off our guard. The notion that what we see is 'out there' in physical space is one which cannot survive while we are grasping the difference between what physics supposes to be really happening, and what our senses show us as happening; but it is sure to return and plague us when we begin to forget the argument.

Only long reflection can make a radically new point of view familiar and easy.

(Bertrand Russell, *An Outline of Philosophy*)[5]

Reality *is* bursting spring-green sunny tree, roaring engine, damp miasmic stilton, straining ripping muscle-sinew, tanging citrus, the aching loneliness of lover lost. In a state of dreamless sleep reality is absent. Whilst we are awake reality is present.

Reality is *out there*. I am surrounded by it, stretch to touch it, crawl about in it. There are *distances* between the part of reality that is me and other parts.

The brain is part of reality, an organ observed in certain creature's heads. Some philosophers and scientists claim that this *part* of reality is in some measure responsible for the whole that we experience around us. The story goes that this brain is a vast and very complicated neural computer created from billions of neurons that receive and transmit signals. The nerves pass sensor data to the brain, which processes it into an understanding of what is happening in the environment. This claim has been supported by dissections of dead humans, studies of brain damage, and brain modelling in artificial neural networks.[6]

I will be calling these speculations about the link between our brains and experiences the *brain hypothesis*.

The brain hypothesis comes in strong and weak versions. The weak version of the brain hypothesis sees the brain as some kind of tool that the owner of the brain uses to interface with the world. In the weak version, this owner of the brain is physically distinct from the brain itself. The traditional soul *has* a brain in the sense intended by the weak version of the brain hypothesis. The idea of someone who owns a brain without being one is not incoherent, but its dependence upon a mysterious second substance of some kind rules it out from further consideration here.

The strong version of the brain hypothesis conjectures that human beings *are* brains; that they are essentially nothing more than their brains; that they *exist* their brains. Under the weak version of the brain hypothesis it is theoretically possible to replace every part of the human body with a prosthetic part and leave the human being intact. Under the strong version of the brain hypothesis, you could give me an artificial heart and kidneys, a pig's skin and prosthetic limbs and I would remain the same person, but if you replaced my brain with a silicon neural processor, it is no longer obvious that I would be the same person or continue to have the same experiences. The weak version of the brain hypothesis endorses some kind of duality of substance, whereas the strong version of the brain hypothesis claims that there is only one kind of substance, which it calls 'matter'. The strong version of the brain hypothesis does not rule out the possibility that a new property of matter might be required to explain consciousness (McGinn), or that there might be something that it is like to be a brain (Nagel), but there is basically one kind of stuff or substance and a human being exists when this stuff is formed into a working brain.

The strong version of the brain hypothesis is obvious and straightforward to most people. It is so obvious that many would argue that it is not a hypothesis at all, but a plain and simple fact. However, as the extensive discussions of consciousness show, a number of problems arise when everything is reduced to a single substance. One of these is the mismatch between our phenomenological experience of consciousness and the physical operations of the brain. The processing of sensory data takes place *within* our physical brains, and yet we experience the coloured three-dimensional objects that result from this processing at some *distance* from our physical brains. This difficulty is summarized by Colin McGinn:

How *can* our minds reach out to the objects of experience? What is it about our brains, and their location in the world, that could possibly explain the way consciousness *arcs out* into the world? Consciousness seems to extend an invisible hand into the world it represents. (If I may put it so): how on earth could my *brain* make that possible? No ethereal prehensile organ protrudes from my skull! Phenomenologically, we feel that the mind 'lays hold' of things out there, mentally 'grasps' them, but we have no physical model of what this might consist in. We flounder in similes.[7]

One way to account for this brute phenomenological fact is to claim that our physical brains somehow *spread the results of their processing over objects*. This position is known as projection theory, which states that the world we experience around us is a combination of real physical objects and a perceptual construction that is projected out of the brain and superimposed over the real world.[8] Apart from its patent implausibility, the central problem with projection theory is that it has no basis in what we currently know about physics and we have never detected another person's qualia or hallucinations after they have been mysteriously 'projected' out of their brain. We could address these difficulties by hypothesizing a special property of matter – such as McGinn's property P – to explain how the mind arcs out into its environment. But such 'properties' are entirely without scientific merit unless methods can be devised for detecting them.[9]

Faced with these problems with projection theory we could throw away everything that we know about brains, physics and optics and revert to naive realism. However, many will be dissatisfied with this wholesale abandonment of contemporary science. A more appealing solution is indirect realism, which retains everything we know about brains and claims that our phenomenal bodies are *virtual copies of our real bodies*. If the brain is a neuro-computer, then it can generate an *internal* model of the relationship between itself and the external world without the need to 'spread' itself over things. Data from the nerves would be used to construct this virtual model, which in turn would be used to control movements of the body. Smythies puts this point well:

> It may be argued that it is superfluous to postulate a process of 'projection' since a proper attention to the internal detail of the physiological theory itself eliminates the necessity for making it. For if we admit the physiological account of the process of perception (which account led in the first place to the postulation of 'projection') then somatic sensa should be treated in a similar way to visual sensa. If the latter are the final products of a mechanical process of 'unconscious reception, selection, differentiation, integration and interpretation of sensory stimuli' then so must the former. I suggested above that it is self-evident that visual percepts are spatially external to the physical organism. This, however, is false. What actually is evident in experience is that visual sensa (percepts) are spatially external to what is usually loosely called 'my (human) body' (or in neurology the 'body image') but which should strictly be called the 'sensed body' or 'somatic sensory field'. This is merely the collection of all somatic sensa (touch, pain, thermal, pressure; skin, muscle, bone, joint and visceral sensa) within the field of direct experience during any one specious present.[10]

If everything that we experience around us is a virtual simulation, then there is no problem about how one part of the simulation – our bodies – can be separate from another part – the objects that the brain experiences. Both the virtual body and its virtual objects can be integrated into a single virtual reality – constructed by the real brain using data from the senses – without any need for mysterious physical properties. Versions of indirect realism have been supported by Bertrand Russell, Thomas Metzinger, Gregory Mulhauser, Steve Lehar and Richard Dawkins, among others.[11] This semi-Kantian interpretation of the brain hypothesis provides a coherent explanation of perception, dreams, phantom limbs and out of body experiences. Although we might metaphorically speak about the brain reaching out into its real physical environment, the only spreading that the brain actually does is within its own virtual environment.

This chapter will make the case for this interpretation of the brain hypothesis by examining physical objects, brains in vats, stereograms, size relationships, dreams, phantom limbs and motion. It will show that this is the *only* self-consistent and plausible interpretation of perception that does not need to invent mysterious new properties of matter. If we start with the premise that we have brains, then we inevitably end up experiencing a virtual reality generated by the brain.

The problem with indirect realism is that although we are forced into it, it is also an extremely counter-intuitive claim. Although it is easy to *say* that the world is a virtual reality generated by the brain, it is almost impossible for us to really *see* everything around us, everything that we take to be our actual world, as a virtual reality model. Someone who could *sustain* this terrifying vision would be brinking on madness. As the second part of this chapter will show, indirect realism also suffers from the problem that it tacitly depends upon evidence gained from naive realism for its plausibility. Without this it is just a hypothetical interpretation of a virtual fiction. We cannot keep the strong version of the brain hypothesis without moving into indirect realism, but we cannot remain indirect realists either. Supporters of the brain hypothesis are doomed to oscillate between naive and indirect realism; until they either give up on the brain hypothesis, or they *religiously* accept that:

> Out beyond the farthest things you can perceive in all directions, that is, above the dome of the sky, and below the solid earth under your feet, or beyond the walls, floor, and ceiling of the room you see around you, is located the inner surface of your true physical skull. And beyond that skull is an unimaginably immense external world of which the world you see around you is merely a miniature internal replica. This can only

mean that the head you have come to know as your own is not your true
physical head, but merely a miniature perceptual copy of your head in
a perceptual copy of the world, all of which is contained within your
real head in the external objective world.[12]

Physical Objects

> The causal chain of vision clearly shows that the brain cannot experience
> the world out beyond the sensory surface, but can register only the data
> transmitted to it from the sensory organs. ... A percept cannot escape
> the confines of our physical brain into the world around us any more
> than the pattern of voltages in a digital computer can escape the confines
> of particular wires and registers within the physical mechanism.
>
> (Steven Lehar, *The World in Your Head*)[13]

Brains are physical objects and like all physical objects they change
state when other physical objects, such as photons, electrons,
protons or other subatomic particles, impact upon them. A change
in one physical object does not affect another physical object
unless some kind of signal or force is passed between them.

In Figure 4 the signal from A does not affect B until it reaches B
– we witness events on the sun eight minutes after they have

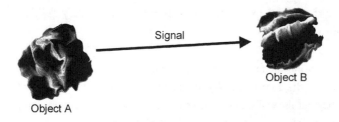

Figure 4. Two physical objects

happened. There is no instantaneous transmission of information from A to B; A is not *directly* aware of B. When a signal reaches B it might pass straight through B, it might be absorbed by B or it might be absorbed and then re-emitted by B.

When a physical object emits a signal it ceases to have any contact with that signal; it does not 'keep track' of the signal and is blind with respect to the signal's fate. The signal might exert forces on the physical object that emitted it, but in so doing it is acting as another physical object, which must in turn send signals to affect any of the objects in its environment.[14]

The brain is a physical object and has the set of properties that are common to all physical objects. The brain certainly has properties that other physical objects lack, but it is not free of the standard properties that all physical objects have. Figure 5 shows the brain floating in a bath of cerebrospinal fluid in the skull. An

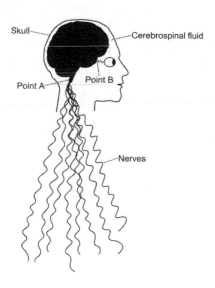

Figure 5. The brain and nerves. The brain only detects an incoming signal once it has passed point A or point B. An outgoing signal is no longer monitored once it has gone beyond point A.

intricate web of nerves connects the brain to the body. Signals are sent along the nerves to the brain. In accordance with the description of physical objects given above, a signal from the body only affects the brain after it has passed point A in Figure 5. If I damage a living human's foot, the human's brain only detects the damage once the nerve signal from the foot has arrived. If this signal is blocked – by breaking the neck or anaesthetising the damaged area, for example – then the human's brain does not detect the damage in the foot. Of course, the human might look at the foot and deduce that it was damaged. In this case a light signal has to travel through space to the eyes and then down the optic nerves. The human is only aware of the damage once the signal has left the optic nerves at point B and entered the brain. This signal can also be blocked by covering the foot, piercing the eyes or cutting the optic nerves.

The brain also sends signals and this signalling works in a similar way to that between other physical objects. Suppose that the brain sends a signal along a nerve to a muscle. This signal no longer affects the brain after it has passed point A. When the muscle contracts it sends a sensory signal back to the brain. The brain only detects this signal once it has passed point A; it detects signals *from* the contracting muscle and not the contracting muscle itself.

Brains in Vats

The brain hypothesis suggests a contemporary version of Descartes' demonic doubt:

> ... imagine that a human being (you can imagine this to be yourself) has been subjected to an operation by an evil scientist. The person's brain (your brain) has been removed from the body and placed in a vat of nutrients which keeps the brain alive. The nerve endings have been connected to a super-scientific computer which causes the person whose brain it is to have the illusion that everything is perfectly normal. There seem to be people,

objects, the sky, etc.; but really all the person (you) is experiencing is the result of electronic impulses travelling from the computer to the nerve endings. The computer is so clever that if the person tries to raise his hand, the feedback from the computer will cause him to 'see' and 'feel' the hand being raised. Moreover, by varying the program, the evil scientist can cause the victim to 'experience' (or hallucinate) any situation or environment the evil scientist wishes. He can also obliterate the memory of the brain operation, so that the victim will seem to himself to have always been in this environment.[15]

Since the brain only detects signals at its nerve input points, and is not aware of signals that it has sent beyond its output points, it is theoretically possible that the brain could be tricked into thinking that it is embodied, when in fact it is only envatted. The nerves could be stripped of their enveloping flesh and hooked up to a computer. The computer could be programmed to send signals that mimic nervous input from the body and respond appropriately to signals sent out by the brain. Although it is unlikely that the source of our nerve signals is a computer controlled by an evil (or beneficent) scientist, this possibility is consistent with everything that we know about the brain.[16]

Z. has terminal heart disease and only one or two months to live. Z. would like to be preserved cryogenically, but he lacks faith in the resolute march of progress; he doubts whether a future civilization would be able to revive him – or whether it would bother to revive him if it could. Fortunately for Z. there is another option: he can become a brain in a vat. The science of Z.'s time is capable of recording all the signals that enter and leave a human brain, and computers can send signals along the nervous fibres that lead to the brain. To make his vat life as interesting as possible, Z. decides to record some of his brain's signals so that he can experience them again when he has been separated from his body. Strapping on his data module, Z. spends the remaining few months of his life climbing, flying, loving, diving, feasting, ejaculating and writhing. When his heart stops, his nervous tissue is separated from his flesh, his brain is placed in a stainless steel vat and the experiences that he recorded are replayed.

Realistic replay is more complicated than it sounds because of intricate feedback loops between the brain and muscles, in which the brain sends a signal to the muscles, the muscles send a signal back and then the brain sends another signal to the muscles. To give a realistic impression of a scene, the computer cannot just play back signals: it has to respond *appropriately* to the signals sent out by the brain. But recorded data does not allow the computer to do this. For example, in one recording of a restaurant scene Z. punches the waiter in the face. When the recording is replayed, Z. tries to punch him in the stomach, but this movement is not in the recording, and so he experiences himself punching him in the face, even though he sent out a signal instructing his body to punch him in the stomach. Z. feels sensations in his body and senses an environment around him that is separate from his body, but he cannot move his body or change his environment. He has experiences, but he no longer *participates* in them. Bobbing in the broth he can only be reminded of what it felt like to be alive.

> The big body pottered on, with slow competence: yes, it really knows its stuff. I kept wanting to relax and take a good look at the garden – but something isn't quite working. Something isn't quite working: this body I'm in won't take orders from this will of mine. Look around, I say. But his neck ignores me. His eyes have their own agenda. Is it serious? Are we okay? I didn't panic. I made do with peripheral vision, which, after all, is the next best thing. I saw curled flora swooping and trembling, like pulses or soft explosions in the side of the head. And a circumambient pale green, barred and embossed with pale light, like ... like American money. I pottered on out there until it began to get dark. I dumped the tools in the hut. Wait a minute. Why am I walking *backwards* into the house? Wait. Is it dusk coming, or is it dawn? What is the – what is the sequence of the journey I'm on? What are its rules? Why are the birds singing so strangely?
>
> (Martin Amis, *Time's Arrow*)[17]

The Red Room

When Z. was testing the equipment, he recorded the nerve signals entering and leaving his brain as he sat on a chair in the middle of a red room. After pressing the record button, Z. rotated his head to the right and looked at a green picture on the wall. After a few seconds Z. rotated his head to the left and looked at an orange lamp standing in the left hand corner of the room. Z. then switched off the recording device. Whilst he was recording, Z. experienced the picture and its green colour separate from him, at a distance of about five feet. The lamp, too, was not experienced by Z. within his head; the lamp was out there in the world along with its orange colour. Z. felt embodied in the room; he experienced his arms, trunk and legs spatially separated from his head in the centre of the room. When Z. was asked to draw a diagram depicting his situation in the room he came up with Figure 6.

This diagram does not entirely capture Z.'s experience of the room because it is drawn from an objective viewpoint – it pictures the room from above – whereas Z. experienced the room from within; he had a first-hand perspective on it. Figure 6 also includes a black box behind Z., which he could not see when he was in the

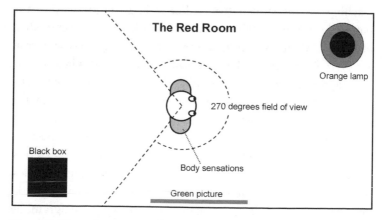

Figure 6. The red room seen from above

room – although he could remember where it was, and could have reached around to pick it up if he had wanted to.

When this recording is replayed to Z.'s disembodied brain, the same signals enter his brain from nerves that used to be spread throughout his body and the same signals enter his brain from optic nerves that were once connected to his eyes. If the brain hypothesis is correct, Z. *must see and experience the room in exactly the same way that he did when he was recording it.* When the recording is played back Z. feels his body, and sees a field of objects detached from it and surrounding it. Although Z.'s brain is in a vat, he can see the lamp along with its orange colour at a distance of ten feet from him; he can see the picture and its green colour separate from him at a distance of about five feet; he feels and see his arms, trunk and legs in the centre of the room. The only significant difference is that he would not sense the presence of the black box behind him (unless he could remember the red room clearly). The area outside his field of vision would be completely unknown because the recording only provides sensory input and does not replay memory.

As the playback progresses Z. feels his head rotating to the right to look at the picture, although he is not doing anything to control it. He then experiences his head moving to the left and his hand reaching for the stop button. After feeling the pressing of the button, he is immediately catapulted into silence and disembodied blackness. All of his experiences prior to pressing the stop button are every bit as real as the experiences that he had when he was making the recording: Z. does not experience the objects that he sees during playback as somehow 'in his head', any more than the real objects at the time of the recording were somehow 'in his head'. It is also highly unlikely that Z.'s brain would 'project' or 'spread' itself out into its real environment and see the scientists and stainless steel vat. Z.'s thoughts during recording and playback would no doubt be different, but his sensory experiences would be almost identical. If Z. was capable of drawing a diagram, he would draw the red room in the same way as before, except in this case he would omit all of the details that were outside his field of vision.

No doubt Z. will eventually tire of eating the same gourmet meals, climbing the same mountains and achieving the same orgasms in the same positions with the same men, birds and beasts with the same pillow talk. He has only two months worth of material and his brain will probably remain alive for fifty years or more. To liven up his life after death, Z. needs an *interactive* virtual reality. To achieve this, the computer could be set up to model Z.'s muscles and organs and work out what kind of response should be fed into Z.'s brain when he sends an instruction to a muscle or organ. When Z. decides to contract his bicep the computer would detect signals in the nerves that once led to his bicep, and model the response that the sensory nerves in the bicep and the rest of the arm would make. The computer could even model what a raised arm would look like to Z.'s eyes and send appropriate signals down the optic nerve. To be convincing this modelling would be incredibly complicated, but there does not seem to be anything seriously counter-intuitive about its possibility.

With this improved technology Z. can do more than passively experience a world that he used to belong to: he can interact with the environment that the computer feeds him. In the red room Z. no longer feels his head turning independently of his will; now he sends signals along nerves that were previously connected to his neck muscles, and the computer responds with the appropriate sensations. Z. can look behind him and see the black box; he can walk up to the picture and examine it more closely; he can even electrocute himself using the lamp. Now there is no longer any detectable difference between Z.'s original experience of the room and his experience of the room generated by the computer. Both are spatial, objective, interactive and separated from Z.'s experience of his body.

When he was fully alive, Z. might have wondered how his mind could reach out to the objects that surrounded him. In the virtual red room that he experiences as a brain in a vat, Z. might be prompted to ask the same question. Here Z. also feels himself embodied in the centre of a room and sees a field of objects spread out in front of him, and so it is natural for him to ask how the objects got outside of the head that is viewing them. But in the virtual red room neither the head nor the experiences correspond to anything in the objective world. The head that Z. touches in the virtual red room came into existence when the computer sent signals down nerves that were once attached to the surface of his skull; the hand that he sees in front of him came into existence after the computer sent pulses along his optic nerves. Z.'s head and the objects he sees are as real as any object that he has ever experienced, and yet in this virtual world there is no question about how Z.'s mind grasps things 'out there' because there are no things 'out there'. 'Out there' there is only a computer and a vat with a brain floating in it. In and out of the vat Z.'s experiences are identical and yet in the one case we speak about Z.'s brain 'spreading' itself over objects or 'projecting' itself onto things and in the other case we are happy to talk about Z. experiencing a virtual model of reality generated by his brain. A strange distinction considering that Z.'s brain is actually envatted in both cases. If Z.'s brain were taken out of the stainless steel vat and surgically implanted in a skull, it would have a different data source, but would not suddenly start to spread itself over the objective world again.

The Orange Room

We can observe the brain's creation of space in action:

1) I am staring at a piece of cardboard. On the piece of cardboard there are two patterned rectangles, predominantly orange in colour. By staring into the distance and bringing the cardboard into my field of vision, I create a double image of each rectangle and super-impose the two central ones to make a single figure. After some focusing and mental adjustment something suddenly 'clicks'. Three-

dimensional forms condense out of the flat central image. The background recedes to a distance of about one metre. The foreground shifts to around twenty centimetres below the surface of the cardboard. The flat pattern is *stretched out* into three dimensions. I am no longer looking at two flat rectangles with meaningless patterns on them; I am looking *into* a three-dimensional orange room containing a sphere, a pyramid and a rectangular block. The sphere at the back of the room is further away from me than the rectangular block at the front. The pyramid is level with the back end of the block. All three lie below the surface of the cardboard.[18] It seems as if I could reach into the room and touch the objects in it. The surface of the cardboard has become transparent; replaced by a three-dimensional image floating in space. There is space below the pattern where there was none before. I have '*pushed*' the pattern into space and simultaneously created the space that I have 'pushed' the pattern into (see Figure 7).

2) I don a virtual reality headset and look at two flat screens with slightly different images on them. If I make an effort, I can focus on the LCD screens themselves and see them as two-dimensional arrays of pixels. When this effort is relaxed the two-dimensional images are 'pushed' out into a three-dimensional transparent space. When I

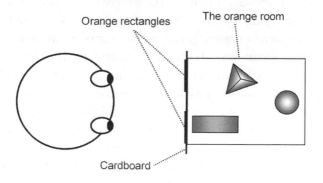

Figure 7. The stereogram orange room

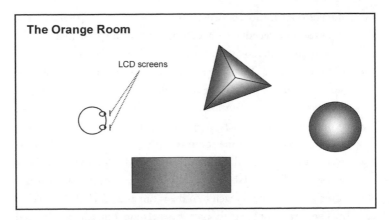

Figure 8. The virtual orange room

focus on the pixels, all the points of light are at a uniform distance
of about three centimetres from my eyes. As I relax my focus the
points of light condense into an orange room that stretches out
around me. Within this orange room there is a block, a pyramid and
a sphere. Using a joystick I can navigate my way around this virtual
landscape. For example, I can move around the sphere and inspect
it from a number of different angles; I can also mount the block and
look across at the pyramid (see Figure 8).

As I look at the stereogram and the screens in the virtual reality
headset, I am being *stimulated* by two flat patterns of dots and yet
I *see* a collection of objects spread out in front of me in an orange
room. I have *reconstructed* everything beyond the flat surfaces of
the stereogram and LCD screens using the information from the
patterns. My brain has pushed the transparent space and the
coloured objects in it into existence beyond the actual physical
limits of my visual field. If I did not know that the objects were
computer generated, I might be tempted to say that I am seeing a
real pyramid: that my mind has projected itself into objective
space, rather than into a space that it has itself created.

Normal vision also starts with two-dimensional arrays of dots
– the firing patterns of rods and cones in our retinas – that we

interpret as three-dimensional objects. Based on the examples so far, it might be thought that we push out a transparent space containing objects from the surface of our retinas, in much the same way that we push out a transparent space containing objects from the LCD screens suspended just in front of our eyes. It is this notion that gives some intuitive plausibility to the projection or spreading theories of perception discussed earlier. However, this picture is not strictly correct since very little processing is carried out on the retina's surface. The main processing of the retinal data occurs after it has passed from the retinas through the lateral geniculate nucleus to the visual cortex at the back of the brain, where most of the pushing of objects into space is carried out. Although it feels as if we are pushing a transparent space containing objects out through the bowls of our real eyes, the neural processing that generates our model of space is actually carried out close to the retinotopic maps in the visual cortex, which hold and organize the information gathered from the retinas.

This disparity between phenomenology and physiology could be resolved by McGinn's mysterious property P. According to this hypothesis, the transparent representation of space containing objects would be generated in the visual cortex and then property P would push this representation out through our real eyes and spread it over the actual objects. Tempting as this unusual suggestion is, if we want to stay within a plausible version of the brain hypothesis, a more likely explanation is that processing in the brain pushes the pulsing patterns of sense data out through the bowls of our *virtual* eyes into a three-dimensional *internal* model that is entirely contained within the limits of the physical brain. A crude illustration of this is shown in Figure 9.

Some people will object at this point that what is being put forward is a *homunculus* theory of perception: a Cartesian theatre in which a little virtual man inside the brain *looks* at the virtual orange room and creates a virtual virtual orange room within his virtual head. In one sense, this interpretation of the brain hypothesis

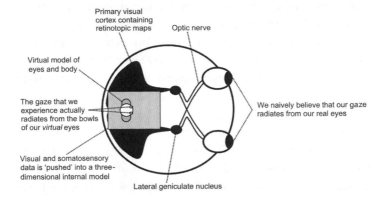

Figure 9. The brain pushes the firing patterns of sense data into a three-dimensional internal model. This is a very rough approximation since the brain's representation of space is likely to be distributed throughout a number of different areas and the body representation is processed separately from the visual information.

does amount to a 'homunculi in the head' theory, but not to the extent that it requires an infinite regress of homunculi within homunculi. Within the real world my brain senses its environment by detecting signals from my ears, eyes, nose, mouth, joints and skin. Once it has reconstructed these signals into an internal model of my body and environment there is no need for any *further* sensing. I am *directly* aware of the objects in my virtual environment – the presence of an object in my virtual environment is what my awareness of that object is – and so there is no need for a second perception of the virtual object using virtual light. The sphere that I see is my brain's representation that there is a sphere five metres from me, and so no information would be gained by the virtual man looking out through the virtual LCD screens at the virtual room. In a rather mystical sense I *am* my virtual environment and know it directly without needing to view it with my virtual eyes.[19]

This interpretation of the brain hypothesis might also be confused with idealism. However, although the brain hypothesis claims that we never *directly* experience the real world, there is a mapping between our experiences and the real world such that we can be said to sense this world *indirectly* (with obvious caveats about the real world being colourless, silent and without smell). This indirect realism is similar to Kant's transcendental idealism, except that the noumenal things-in-themselves are hypothesized by the brain hypothesis to be knowable to some extent through their phenomenal representation.[20]

Relativity

> An expansion that affects all bodies in the same way is not observable because a direct comparison of measuring rods at different places is impossible. ... The problem does not concern a matter of *cognition* but of *definition*. There is no way of knowing whether a measuring rod retains its length when it is transported to another place; a statement of this kind can only be introduced by a definition. For this purpose a coordinative definition is to be used, because two physical objects distant from each other are *defined* as equal in length. It is not the *concept* equality of length which is to be defined, but a *real object* corresponding to it is to be pointed out. A physical structure is co-ordinated to the concept equality of length, just as the standard meter is co-ordinated to the concept unit of length.
>
> (Hans Reichenbach, *The Philosophy of Space & Time*)[21]

The relativity of space is not controversial: Einstein informs us that the length of the platinum metre rule in Paris varies with the speed at which it is travelling; Reichenbach tells us that we would not notice if the platinum metre rule, along with all the rigid bodies surrounding it, was expanded or contracted by universal forces; Wittgenstein claims that the platinum metre rule never had a length anyway.

In a virtual reality generated by an ordinary computer my body is reconstructed along with its surrounding environment. When I look at my hand I see a virtual hand, not my real hand, which is actually cloaked in virtual reality apparatus. My entire presence within the virtual reality field, including all the parts of my body, is artificially generated and so my body can be large or small relative to any object – I can cradle the sun in my arms or walk upon the surface of an atom. This freedom from fixed size relationships is preserved when I use virtual reality to look at and interact with the world (telepresence). If a tiny robot were injected into my heart and connected up to virtual reality apparatus, I could watch the walls of my heart contracting around me and see my blood flowing past, even though there is no conceivable way in which I could ever fit my real physical body inside my heart. Robert Stone describes a telepresence system that works on an even smaller scale:

An STM consists of a fine needle stylus whose height z above a conducting surface is controlled by a piezoelectric drive that can also deliver independent motion in the orthogonal axes x and y. A small voltage is applied between the tip and the surface to be scanned which causes a small quantum mechanical current to flow when the tip is positioned within a few atomic diameters of the surface, whilst the z drive is controlled to maintain a constant tunnelling current between the tip and the surface. By converting the output of the STM into polygonal form, an operator can now 'fly' over the surface of, for example, a 15,000 Angstrom-square sample of platinum that has been bombarded with helium ions and diamond polished. ... The next step in this work has very similar aims to ARRC's telepresence initiative – to link the 'flight' of the human immersed in the microscopic virtual world directly to the motions of the real STM stylus.[22]

If the STM was directly coupled to my virtual reality apparatus, I would be immersed in the atomic environment and could witness atomic events in real time as I flew across the material's surface. It might even be possible for me to pick up atoms and move them about. As I lifted up a virtual atom I would experience force feedback corresponding to the forces on the real atom.

Since virtual reality transforms size relationships, my real body does not have to physically fit inside the computer that is generating my virtual environment. When I look at a virtual environment on the computer monitor and decide to enter it, it does not matter that I am 1.8 metres tall and the computer only 0.5 metres. Once I am inside, my body can be dwarfed by immense objects, even though my real body is considerably larger than the computer. The computer can be as small as a matchbox or as big as a house: this will make no difference at all to my experience of space within its virtual environment.

Although virtual environments of any size can be created within computers of any size, the virtual environments themselves always remain within the computer's physical limits – all of the data that is used to generate them is contained inside the case of the computer. Although we are very used to the idea that our environment is much larger than our heads, if the brain hypothesis is correct, then our entire virtual world is enclosed within the 1000 cubic centimetres of our real brains. When I look at St Paul's Cathedral, my virtual brain appears to be smaller than the virtual St Paul's Cathedral, but the virtual cathedral is actually contained within my physical head. However, the size *relationships* between objects are preserved by the virtual model. When I look at the real platinum bar in Paris the virtual platinum bar created by my brain has the same ratio to my virtual body that the real platinum bar has to my real body. The brain's representation of itself is also smaller than its representation of its environment – preserving the fact that the real brain is smaller than its real environment. Since we can only measure size by comparing one object with another, it is impossible for us to notice how small our virtual bodies and environment really are. If our world was compressed by universal forces, it could fit inside our real heads and we would not notice anything unusual. The best interpretation of the brain hypothesis suggests that in fact this has been the case.

The Green Room

> Fat told us of a dream he had had recently, in which he had been a large
> fish. Instead of an arm he had walked around with sail-like or fan-like fins;
> with one of these fins he had tried to hold onto an M-16 rifle but the
> weapon had slid to the ground, whereupon a voice had intoned:
>   'Fish cannot carry guns.'
>   (Philip Dick, *Valis*)[23]

> ...what we call waking life is a form of 'online dreaming.'
>   (Thomas Metzinger, *Being No One*)[24]

I lie down to sleep. In the warm bed sensations from my feet and legs
gradually fade from awareness. Hands, arms and body slip into the
hinterland between being and non-being. Nothingness envelops me
like a shroud.

I am in some kind of large open space. My surroundings are coloured, but
they are very unstable and indistinct. Suddenly I am somewhere else. I have
some kind of purpose and my interaction with other people in my surroundings
furthers this purpose. I am engaged in something, but its exact nature is not
clear to me. I do not reflect. I flit from hazy location to hazy location doing
things, saying things. Somehow I always know what I am doing in my
environment – I do not feel lost – but I rarely articulate what my actions or my
purposes are. My body is, perhaps, the least clear thing. I sometimes use it
to pick up things. I rarely see it. For the most part I just vaguely believe it to
be there and no more than this.

   Now I am in a green room. It is an unpleasant green, a sort of darkish
synthetic institutional green; streaky and badly painted. The room is quite dark
and indistinct. I have no idea what is behind me and do not think about what
is behind me. I do not feel that I could turn around, even if I wanted to. If I did,
I would not feel myself turning around; I would just suddenly experience the
other part of the room. The part of the room that I am looking at has some kind
of indistinct matter in its right hand corner. I know that this is a pile of soiled
sweaty dirty rags and sheets. A window is set into the left half of the wall in front

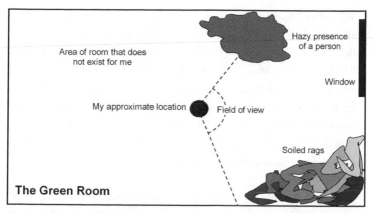

The Green Room

Figure 10. The green room

of me. There is a skirting board. To my left I know that there is a person of some kind. Some of my actions in the room are concerned with communication between myself and this person. But I do not see him. I do not turn to look. I do not feel that I could turn to look. I do not even hear his voice or my own speech. It is all very indistinct. Somehow we communicate. This is something that is necessary in this situation. I cannot say what is said, or why it is being said, but it has meaning.

Within the indistinct, vague, shifting, ethereal environment of the dream we experience ourselves as embodied and separate from the objects, places and faces that we encounter. I pad as lion across a prairie; I ooze as worm through a sticky eternal night; I inhabit a nebulous dream body and wander through a dream landscape whilst my real body slumbers in my bed. My real eyes blindly pulse and twitch beneath their lids; my dream eyes track the owl's silent drift through the night. The gaze in my dream is separate from the objects that it gazes upon, and yet the dream landscape is populated by objects and events that I have created. Rearing throbbing statues represent my desires. Paranoia condenses into dream beasts that worry and tear at my naked flesh. Absurd dramas enact fantasies of success or embody my deepest fears of failure:

What does Freud say in his initial definition of *Ubertragung*? He tells us about the *Tagesreste*, the day-residues, which are, he says, disinvested from the point of view of desire. These are, within the dream, the stray forms which have become, for the subject, of minimal importance – and are emptied of their meaning. So this is a piece of signifying material. The signifying material, be it phonematic, hieroglyphic, etc., is constituted out of forms which have forfeited their own meaning and are taken up again within a new organisation, thanks to which another meaning finds a means of gaining expression.[25]

The dream is my own construct, a virtual reality synthesized by my brain, and yet within the dream objects are spread out in front of me just as they are in waking life. We dream in our heads, and yet we experience our dream heads separately from our dream environment.

Meaningful and empty dialogue continues with the hazy presence to my left. The window and the soiled rags persist in my field of view. Now I feel a second presence in the room. Something within the rags persistently beams some kind of message at me. It says something **TO ME**. This message is very intense. Cold loud sheer digital presence. Overwhelming intentionality directed towards me. It is the sole focus of my attention. The other person, the window and the green room disintegrate as the bleeping enters and envelops me. I awaken into the blue room and switch off the alarm clock.

When I first hear the alarm clock my brain locates the data from it within the dream environment that it has constructed. The sound from the alarm clock is given a position and identity in dream space – it is not just something random or inexplicable. After a while, the sound becomes too persistent and causes me to awaken. Once I am awake the definition of my environment becomes much greater. The world acquires complexity and detail that were not present in the dream: colours are much brighter, sounds are louder and I experience the touching field of my body much more intensely. The field of objects spread out in front of me has also changed. In the green room the alarm clock was an intense communication emanating from a pile of dirty soiled rags; in the blue room the alarm clock has become an alarm clock on the bedside table. In the green room I was standing upright in the centre of the room; in the blue room I am lying down between the bedside table and the wall.

Although priests and prophets have seen dreams as an alternative objective world, we now no longer believe that our dreaming minds spread themselves over Venus' seductive curves within a second divine reality. In modern times it is commonly accepted that dreams are virtual realities generated within the brain and critical focus has shifted on to what happens when we awaken. Is waking up a shift from virtual to objective reality, or a change in the resolution, intensity and data source with which our virtual reality is constructed? Supporters of the latter hypothesis point out that the spatial separation between my body and other objects is the same when dreaming and waking, that the *memory* of my body, which is used to construct my dream body, is similar to my real body, and that in both environments the sound of the alarm clock is spatially located in a similar way. It also becomes much easier to explain waking and dreaming states if they are *both* seen as virtual realities constructed from different data sources: when we dream the brain constructs a virtual reality using data from memory; whilst we are awake the brain constructs a virtual reality using data from the senses. This explains why the waking world is much more stable and richer in detail than the dream world, and why fantasies do not usually get concretely embodied as objects within waking experiences.

> I am suggesting that not only are dreams experiences but, in a way, all experiences are dreams. When asleep, the brain dreams for us a world of experience which reflects solely the nocturnal brainstorms in our memory systems or in the processes in charge of binding features of experiences into wholes. When awake, the brain dreams for us a much more coherent world, because the causal chains constraining those dreams originate in a largely coherent reality out there.
>
> (Antti Revonsuo, 'Consciousness, Dreams, and Virtual Realities')[26]

The Invisible

Within a computer-generated environment it is not possible to point to the computer. If the computer represents itself within its virtual reality, you can point to the virtual computer, but you can never point to the computer itself. At most you can make a few vague gestures in the air, perhaps adding one or two gnomic phrases: 'The computer is everywhere', 'The environment is the computer', 'Our virtual bodies are the computer', 'The forces that we feel in this environment, the sounds that we hear, the scents we smell: all of these are the computer.'

In a lucid dream a philosopher asks me to point to my brain. Instinctively I point to my head (and feel irritated that such a stupid question could be asked by a character that I had invented). My virtual interlocutor dissolves, cackles, crackles and booms: 'Not your *dream* brain, point to your *real* brain, your real brain lying in your real bed, your real brain dreaming this dream at this moment.' Searing heat. Blinding light. Silence. Bemused ... How can I point to my real brain when I cannot see it? I look around. My real brain is everywhere, actively sustaining the components of the dream at this very moment. Even my dream eyes have been generated by my dream brain. All of the objects in my dream are parts of my real brain. My dream arm cannot point to my real brain because my dream arm is inside of and part of my real brain. It is like trying to point to matter in the real world. Giving up, I finally say: 'Thousands of dream kilometres beyond everything that I see, perhaps there the surface of my real brain is located. This point can never be reached. Everything that I see around me is my brain.'

In waking life the brain hypothesis does not make the problem any easier. The surface of the brain that is modelling my environment could lie thousands of virtual kilometres (measured using the virtual platinum bar in virtual Paris) from my virtual body.[27] I cannot use my virtual arm to point at my real brain because my virtual arm is part of my real brain. If I try, and lift my

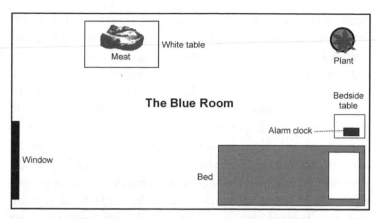

Figure 11. The blue room

virtual arm to point vaguely at everything, then my real arm is also lifted and points vaguely at everything. At what, then, am I pointing? My real arm is pointing at everything that it is not and my virtual arm is what it is supposed to be pointing at.

The Blue Room

> Miss 'W' said, "I was terribly fatigued, working as a waitress ... and lost the last bus. ... The next I registered ... I looked down and watched myself walk round the bend of Beaumont Street into Walton Street. ... The bit of me that 'counts' was up on a level with Worcester College chapel."
> (Robert Crookall, *Case-Book of Astral Projection*)[28]

I close my eyes and cross the room to the table. On the table lies a large piece of meat. With my left arm I reach out and feel the meat. It is warm, textured, rubbery and slightly sticky with blood. I pick the meat up. It is heavy and pulls my arm towards the ground. With my eyes still closed I reach out with my right arm. I can feel nothing there: the piece of meat has vanished and so has the table. My right hand moves about freely in empty space where the table and meat were present only a moment before. I allow my right arm to fall by my side and reach out again with my left arm. Now the meat and table have returned. Once again I palpitate textured flesh between my fingers; once again I encounter an area in the world that resists my grasp. I open my eyes. A piece of meat oozes gently onto the white table in front of me. I look at my left hand. It is pink and opaque; it obscures the objects behind it. Within the visual form of my left hand I experience the sensations of my left hand. These are initially very diffuse, but by concentrating I can focus on the feeling in each finger. When I wiggle the fingers of my left hand I see a pink form wiggling in space in front of me. Now I gaze at my right hand. My right hand is transparent: it does not obscure the objects behind it. I experience my right hand within a diffuse hand-shaped zone in front of me. By concentrating, I can feel the sensations in each finger. When I wiggle the fingers of my right hand I do not see anything happening in the world in front of me, but I can still feel my fingers wiggling. My left arm is visible between my shoulder and my left hand. My right arm becomes invisible about ten centimetres from my shoulder. The visible part of my right arm emerges from my shoulder and terminates in a stump. The transparent part of my right arm extends from the stump to my transparent hand.

> The most extraordinary feature of phantoms is their reality to the amputee. Their vivid sensory qualities and precise location in space – especially at first – make the limbs seem so lifelike that a patient may try to step off a bed onto a phantom foot or lift a cup with a phantom hand. The phantom, in fact, may seem more substantial than an actual limb, particularly if it hurts.
>
> (Ronald Melzack, 'Phantom Limbs')[29]

When people lose a real physical limb they often continue to experience a vivid phantom.[30] In many cases patients are able to move their phantom limb in the same way that they could before the amputation, although the phantom is no longer capable of interacting with objects. Phantom limbs are often painful and many attempts have been made to remove them, including cutting nerves within the stump and spinal cord and removing the parts of the cortex that receive input from the missing limb. None of these techniques has been entirely successful, which suggests that phantom limbs are linked to brain activation distributed across a number of different areas. According to Ronald Melzack, these are likely to include the somatosensory cortex, thalamus, reticular formation, limbic system and the parietal lobe along with other cortical regions linked to the recognition of the self.[31]

We experience phantom limbs when groups of neurons are firing in our brains. However, if phantoms 'may feel more substantial than an actual limb', then it seems very likely that the limbs that we experience every day are *also* phantoms generated inside our brains. When we lose a limb, our mind does not *create* a phantom because it cannot accept the loss – we just *continue to experience the presence of our limb in the same way that we did before*. The mind does not spread itself out over real limbs, and then 'push' out shadowy phantoms from mutilated stumps: our limb experiences are already phantoms that lose their ability to interact with physical objects when amputation deprives us of appropriate feedback from real arms and legs. However, it is not just our limbs that are phantoms, but our body, neck and head as well. Feet, hands, chest, back, nose, scalp and eyes are all fed in as pulsing sense data and 'pushed' out into the three-dimensional phantom body that we inhabit in our day to day lives.

Mr. Chapple of Halstead, said: "I was in the Exeter hospital ... and was talking to my neighbour when he just collapsed and died. The shock gave me a heart attack, and screens were put round both of our beds. The sister and nurse came to see me, and I was floating in the air above myself, and could see all that was happening – the doctor arrived and spoke to the sister; she went away and brought back an injection, which she gave me. As soon as I received it, I knew no more, and when I awoke next morning, I remembered all that had happened, and the sister confirmed what I had seen.

"The next night, at 3 a.m., I had another attack. The same thing happened; once again I found myself floating just under the ceiling and looking down on myself on the bed. I felt no pain and was just idly curious ... The night-sister attended me and I told her to hold me down as I was floating in the air. I suppose, to humour me, she did so, but called a nurse to hold me while she went away to get an injection. The same thing happened as in the first time – as soon as I received the injection, I knew no more."

(Robert Crookall, *Case-Book of Astral Projection*)[32]

Motion

Phenomenological examination reveals that perceived space is not infinite but bounded. This can be seen most clearly in the night sky, where the distant stars produce a domelike percept that presents the stars at equal distance from the observer, and that distance is perceived to be less than infinite.

(Steven Lehar, *The World in Your Head*)[33]

I cannot *go* anywhere in space; I am always *here*.

I am standing in a featureless desert. This desert is situated on a planet that is spinning on its axis and rotating around the sun. The sun and its surrounding planets are moving within a galaxy that is spinning and moving away from other galaxies. I concentrate on the space that wraps around me. It is bubble shaped with vague outer limits that seem to terminate somewhere around the visual horizon. This bubble is flattened – it is not a perfect hemisphere above me and does not extend below the ground. I run (fast) for five minutes. I stop, and test my experience of space. I am still *here*. My bubble of space wraps around me in the same way it did before. Now I run again, but this time with my eyes shut. I focus on my legs as they move, compress and flex. I feel my feet adjusting to the rocky ground. Now I switch my attention to the space around me. It has largely vanished, shrunk to the immediate vicinity of my body. This diffuse spatiality does not seem to be affected by my running. It remains static, travels with me. As I run I open my eyes. Space expands to its former shape and wraps around the visual horizon. But I do not feel that I am getting any closer to the edge of the space that envelops me. My movements do not take me anywhere within space. I feel the exertions of my body and minor changes in the scenery around me, but I am trapped *here*.

I am in the centre of Beijing. My surroundings have altered, but I am still *here* at the centre of space, just as I was before. Space does not feel any different in Beijing. I have not *gone* anywhere. The only thing that has changed is the shape of space, which is squeezed in between the buildings around me and terminates just above the tall orange building to my right. I do not sense the space inside the buildings.

I am in the blue room. Now my space bubble is even smaller. I have no sense of the space in the other rooms that the blue room is adjacent to. The space that I experience fills and is limited by the shape and size of the room.

Objective space stretches throughout the universe. Space as we experience it does not extend throughout the universe. We live inside a kind of bubble of space. The edges of this bubble have the potential to continue indefinitely, but at the same time they form a diffuse boundary between space and a non-spatial nothingness that we have no grasp of. At this moment I am sitting at my desk and staring out of the window. I have a very clear sense of the space between my window and the house opposite and a pretty good sense of the space behind me in my room. The space in front of me extends about 20m vertically into the air between the two houses and about 20m beyond the right and left hand edges of my view through the window. As I sit here I have little grasp of the spatiality of London and no idea at all about the entire spatiality of Britain. Furthermore, the earth as a whole completely eludes my spatial grasp, along with the sun, the galaxies and the universe. All that I ever experience is a small bubble within objective space; never the totality of objective space itself.

I am on a train. I look inside the train. Space is stationary along with everything that I see inside the carriage. I look outside the train. Now I am moving through space. I have the feeling that my body is moving through an objective spatial environment. Although my body is moving I remain *here* – my space bubble is unaffected by this movement.

I am in a flight simulator. I look inside the simulator. Space is stationary along with everything that I see inside the cockpit. I look out through the window of the simulator into the virtual environment. Now I am moving through space. I have the feeling that my body is moving through an objective spatial environment. Although I feel that my body is moving, I remain *here* – my space bubble is unaffected by this virtual movement.

Science has no way of detecting whether we are moving through objective space. All movement takes place relative to an arbitrarily chosen stationary object, and so there is no such thing as absolute movement through objective space. In subjective space we can change the experience of movement into a feeling of being stationary relative to moving surroundings. If we look out of a railway carriage, and see the train on the opposite platform moving, we experience movement. A moment later, when we realize that it is the other train that is departing, we return to being a stationary observer of a moving object.

If the brain creates a space, and plots data from the senses within this space, then this space will never move. There is nothing that this space can move relative to. The location at which data from the senses is plotted can change within this space, but the brain has no means of directly sensing the space that lies outside it. The brain will always be *here* if it creates its own space: it will not locate itself in an objective space whose co-ordinates change as it moves through it. My space bubble expands, warps, shrinks and morphs in response to data from the senses, whilst the vast distances of objective space serenely, smoothly and indifferently extend through vacuum and matter in an identical manner.

Vanishing Evidence

> What? and others even go so far as to say that the external world is the
> work of our organs? But then our body, as a piece of this external world,
> would be the work of our organs! But then our organs themselves would
> be – the work of our organs!
>
> (Friedrich Nietzsche, *Beyond Good and Evil*)[34]

Everything that we know about the brain points towards the indirect
realist interpretation of the brain hypothesis. It is the only way to
integrate our phenomenal experience of a spatial field of objects with
the known physical properties of the brain. Our fictional accounts of
brains in vats, the matrix and cyberspace point towards the indirect
realist account. Our experiences of stereograms, dreams and phantom
limbs point towards the indirect realist account. Even the great god
Kant put forward a metaphysical picture that is close to this interpretation of the brain hypothesis. And yet, in spite of all this, almost no
one supports this interpretation explicitly, and amongst those who do
pay lip service to it, probably none manage to sustain a lived belief
in it for more than a few fleeting moments at a time.

The facts suggest that our phenomenological experience of
perception is a virtual reality generated by the brain within the brain.
And yet we continue to believe that we directly experience real objects
and our real body. Is there, perhaps, a *conspiracy* against this interpretation of the brain hypothesis? Could this painful disorienting truth
be used by *terrorists* to undermine the foundations of our society? Or
perhaps the brain hypothesis itself is fatally flawed somewhere? To
trace the roots of the problem, the evidence for the brain hypothesis
will now be examined in more detail.

The Purple Room

A vast virtual purple room stretches away from me in all directions. I look around. I am surrounded by humans. The have legs,

heads, arms, eyes and bodies. A broken human lies on the ground beside me. I move over to examine it more closely. It has an internal skeleton clad in some kind of fleshy substance that oozes dark red fluid when I cut it. Inside the head there is a convoluted organ, connected to a large number of white filaments spread throughout the body. Through a microscope I can see that the convoluted organ has a large number of cells that could play a similar function to transistors in a computer circuit. The humans appear to be controlled by these computer-like organs inside their heads. In a sense these computer-like organs must be the most important thing for a human, since all their behaviour is determined by them. When I modify part of a living human's convoluted organ with a soldering iron, its behaviour changes. When I inject chemicals into this organ, the human's behaviour is also modified.

I look down and see human legs stretching away beneath me. I feel and see human hands in front of me. I am in a human body. I cross the purple room and see a human face in a mirror on the wall. When I touch myself I feel human hair and human flesh. When I palpitate myself I feel a human endoskeleton beneath the surface of human skin. I can feel the pumping of a human heart within my chest. When I trepan myself the mirror shows a convoluted organ floating inside my head. These observations lead me to conclude that I am a human being and that my behaviour is controlled by the convoluted organ floating inside my head. Indeed, all of these observations must themselves have been generated by the convoluted organ floating inside my head.

History

At first glance, the evidence for the brain hypothesis appears to be overwhelming. Scientific work over the last few hundred years has amassed a large body of facts about the mechanisms of the brain and its interactions with the body and environment. The brain hypothesis accounts for these facts very well – it covers a lot of ground, makes a lot of successful predictions and no facts have been discovered which give us any reason to doubt it. Although the brain hypothesis is only a *hypothetical* explanation for some empirical observations, this is not a reason to reject it or doubt it, because this lack of absolute certainty is just part of the general swampy way in which science works. At present, the brain hypothesis is the best explanation for our experience of the world.

At the beginning the brain hypothesis was a scientific theory like any other. We observed brains, did experiments and concluded that environmental data is gathered by the nerves and passed to the brain where it is processed into a representation of reality. Some of these experiments were as follows:

1) Using our body and some blunt surgical instruments we opened up Julie's skull and inserted some electrodes into her brain. When we switched on these electrodes she behaved differently and reported different experiences.
2) Using our body we damaged Julie's brain and she lost behaviour patterns and experiences.
3) Using our body we dissected dead Julie's body. This revealed a network of nerves leading to her brain.
4) On a computer we created recurrent neural networks that behaved in a similar way to some aspects of Julie's brain.

At this stage we did not take the discrepancy between physical reality and phenomenological experience very seriously. It was generally thought that this 'problem of consciousness' would soon be solved by some clever philosopher or other. The brain hypothesis appeared to be the stable hermeneutic circle shown in Figure 12.

People's encounter with evidence in the world led them to the brain hypothesis. This explained how people could observe the world and come up with hypotheses about it. The way in which people work, their observations and their theories about the brain were all

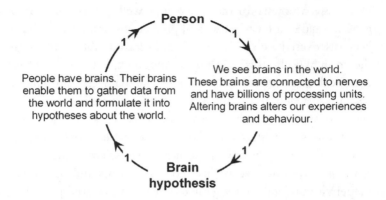

Figure 12. The first formulation of the brain hypothesis as a stable hermeneutic circle

tied together in a reciprocally supporting relationship. At this stage the brain hypothesis was a classic Popperian theory that integrated empirical evidence into a testable conjecture that could be refuted by further evidence.

The next stage in the evolution of the brain hypothesis was the emergence of a distinction between a *virtual* model of the world generated by the brain and a *real* world that lies beyond this model and is the source of data for the model. This development changed the nature of the experiments considerably:

1) Using our virtual hands we opened up a virtual model of Julie's skull. This sent signals to our real hands (hundreds of virtual kilometres away), which opened up Julie's real skull and inserted some real electrodes into her real brain. When we switched on the virtual electrodes the real electrodes in her real brain were switched on. Light from Julie's real body reached our real eyes, which sent signals that were used to update our virtual model of her, which behaved differently and reported different experiences.

2) By moving our virtual hands we sent signals to our real body (hundreds of virtual kilometres away) and instructed it to damage

Julie's real brain. This caused her to lose behaviour patterns and experiences, which was reflected in the changed behaviour of the virtual model of Julie reconstructed from sense data gathered from the real Julie.

3) Using our virtual body we dissected a virtual model of dead Julie's body. According to the brain hypothesis, this dissection simultaneously took place on the real dead body of Julie and the light from this real body was captured by our eyes and reconstructed into an image of a network of nerves leading to her brain.

4) The interactions between our virtual body and a virtual computer were used to remotely control the interactions between our real body and a real computer. On the real computer we created recurrent neural networks. Our real eyes looked at the real computer monitor and this data was used to reconstruct a virtual model of the computer monitor upon which was displayed behaviour that was similar in some ways to our virtual model of the human brain.

This revised interpretation of the brain hypothesis is also a stable hermeneutic circle, shown in Figure 13.

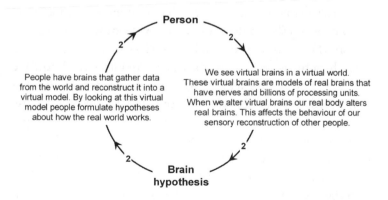

Figure 13. Second formulation of the brain hypothesis as a stable hermeneutic circle

Although circle 2 is a stable hermeneutic circle, it has undergone a subtle but essential shift. In the first stage of the brain hypothesis it was natural to move from naive observations about the world to a theory explaining these observations. In the second stage, the observations could hardly be said to be observations at all; rather, they appear to be more like *assumptions* about the world that are *already* involved in a particular theory. We are no longer moving from observation to empirical theory and from empirical theory to the nature of the person making the observation. Theory and evidence have become tangled up together – the evidence is already being interpreted in the light of a particular version of the brain hypothesis.[35]

A more serious problem with the virtual interpretation of the brain hypothesis is that the evidential link between it and the earlier version is broken. If the virtual interpretation is correct, all the evidence for the brain hypothesis (including the way in which computers work and our observations of the brain itself) is taken from virtual reality and we have never experienced a real brain or directly observed a connection between brain damage and behaviour change. But it seems that we would never have reached the virtual interpretation at all were it not for the earlier situation in which real evidence led to the brain hypothesis – evidence that no longer exists within circle 2. The development of the brain hypothesis has shown that this earlier evidence was an *incorrect* picture of our relationship to reality – we started to believe in the brain hypothesis because we only *partially* understood how the brain works. Before making the brain hypothesis we were immersed in a world that was *the* world and it made perfect sense to come up with a theory about how we perceive the world and process information. After developing the brain hypothesis we discover that the world that we thought we were immersed in is not *the* world at all, but a virtual copy. We believe in this later hypothesis because of evidence that was gathered and interpreted in the light of the earlier model, but a fully developed version of the brain hypothesis completely undermines this real evidence.

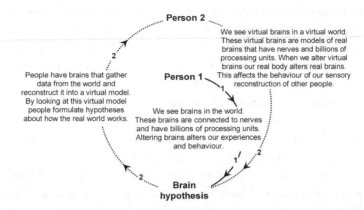

Figure 14. The shift from real to virtual evidence is a collapsing hermeneutic circle. Person 1 is at the first stage of the brain hypothesis. Person 2 is at the second. The first stage cannot support the second: they are completely cut off from one another.

Although the first and second versions of the brain hypothesis are both stable hermeneutic circles, it is impossible to use the real evidence in the first circle to support the virtual evidence in the second. The brain hypothesis becomes the *collapsing* hermeneutic circle shown in Figure 14.

To prove that the brain hypothesis is correct we need real empirical evidence. However, when we accept the real evidence it becomes virtual evidence that is completely cut off from reality. We can no longer move *from* real evidence *to* a theory about the brain because the real evidence is completely wiped out by the virtual interpretation of the brain hypothesis.

A third problem with the brain hypothesis is that it follows a very traditional division of reality into a realm that we do observe and a second realm that it depends on, but which in principle we can never observe. If we want to say *why* the brain hypothesis is correct and *why* Kant or the theologians are wrong, then we have to bring some real evidence to bear. We have to *prove*, rather than dogmatically state, that our version of the real is correct. The problem with this proof is that once we enter a virtual environment, we cannot use evidence from the virtual environment to support hypotheses about the invisible real 'computer' that is generating it. We cannot accept that everything is virtual and then use virtual evidence to *prove* that a real brain beyond everything that we see is creating the virtual world around us. A virtual model can be run on a games console, a Chinese Room, the population of China or even a biological brain. This gives the brain hypothesis a distinctly metaphysical and theological character. Now it appears that only a *religious vision* could lift us from our environing virtual world and uncover the *real* brain lying beyond the veil of illusion. Most likely this vision will be tacitly fuelled by the 'real' evidence that was discarded in the second stage of the brain hypothesis.

The difficulty with theological positions is that it is easy to lose faith in them and our world remains virtual only as long as we believe that a real brain is creating it. The catechism of a real body beyond the dome of the sky cannot be fuelled forever on virtual evidence. Inevitably we will drop the idea of an invisible real brain, flirt with idealism, return to naive realism, and start to brain hypothesize again.[36]

The Yellow Room

A vast virtual yellow room stretches away from me in all directions. I look around. I am surrounded by aliens. They have legs, heads, arms, eyes and bodies. A dead alien lies on the ground beside me. I move over to examine it more closely. It has an internal stainless steel skeleton clad in bright orange rubber. The rubber on one of the hands has come away and I can see stainless steel fingers connected to pneumatic pistons and fibre-optic cables. In the alien's head there is a glowing crystal sphere connected to a large number of fibre-optic cables that are distributed throughout the alien's body. Poking out of the alien's head are more fibre-optic cables and a sturdy metal ring. The glowing crystal sphere may be a receptacle for some kind of quantum processing gas, but it does not share any obvious features with the computers that I am familiar with. These crystal spheres are very important for the aliens' behaviour. If I break an alien's crystal sphere, it becomes dysfunctional. If I take the crystal sphere out of one alien and put it into another, then the high whining sounds and behaviour patterns of the first alien are transferred to the second. If I irradiate an alien's crystal sphere with intense light, its behaviour also changes.

I look down and see orange legs stretching away beneath me. In front of me I see and sense two alien hands that I can move about. I am in an alien's body. The rubber on my right hand is damaged and when I clench my fingers I can see little pistons contracting and stainless steel joints rotating. When I touch myself I feel the tough rubber that aliens are covered with. When I touch my right hand with my left I feel cold stainless steel pistons and fibre-optic cables. When I touch my head I feel fibre-optic cables poking out of it and a sturdy metal ring. I cross the room and look in the mirror. A golden eye gazes back at me from an alien face. When I unscrew the panel above my eye I can see a crystal sphere glowing inside my head.

These observations lead me to conclude that I am an alien and that my behaviour is controlled by the crystal sphere inside my head. If I borrow my friend's crystal sphere, I will become my friend. All of these observations about aliens and crystal spheres must have been generated by the glowing crystal sphere inside my head.

The Phenomenal and the Physical

From whence I think it is easy to draw this observation, That the *ideas of primary qualities* of bodies, *are resemblances* of them, and their patterns do really exist in the bodies themselves; but the ideas, *produced* in us *by* these *secondary qualities, have no resemblance* of them at all. There is nothing like our ideas, existing in the bodies themselves. They are in the bodies, we denominate from them, only a power to produce those sensations in us: and what is sweet, blue, or warm in idea, is but the certain bulk, figure and motion of the insensible parts in the bodies themselves, which we call so.

(John Locke, *An Essay Concerning Human Understanding*)[37]

The representation of space in the brain does not always use space-in-the-brain to represent space, and the representation of time in the brain does not always use time-in-the-brain.

(Daniel Dennett, *Consciousness Explained*)[38]

The *primary* qualities of matter are figure, solidity, extension, motion-or-rest and number.[39] These qualities produce ideas in our minds that resemble them. The shaped, solid, extended, moving and numbered particles interact with the senses and produce the idea of an ellipsoid, solid, extended, stationary single object, whose shape, solidity, size, motion and number *resemble* the shape, solidity, size, motion and number of an actual grape.

The secondary qualities of matter include warmth, sweetness, smoothness and red. These qualities are not really in matter; they are powers that matter has to produce ideas of warmth, sweetness, smoothness and red in our minds. The shaped, solid, extended, moving and numbered particles interact with the senses and produce the idea of a warm sweet smooth red grape in our minds. The warmth, sweetness, smoothness and redness of the phenomenal grape do not resemble anything in the physical world.

Within our virtual world, primary and secondary qualities are smoothly integrated into bunches of warm sweet red solid grapes. Close inspection does not reveal anything striking about the grapes' shape, solidity, size, motion or number that radically sets these qualities apart from the sweetness and redness. Indeed, it is the sweetness of the grapes that strikes us most about them; it is their most intense and real quality. However, according to Locke,[40] the sweetness and redness of the virtual grapes are not qualities of the real physical grapes: they are created in my mind when minute particles from the real grapes bombard my senses. In the physical world there is no sweetness or redness at all and no resemblance between the mind-dependent sweetness and redness that I experience and the molecules and photons in physical reality. In contrast to this, Locke claims that my ideas of the primary qualities of the grapes do resemble the primary qualities of the grapes in the physical world, which are real physical properties. According to Locke, the shape, solidity, extension, motion and number of the virtual grapes is the same as the shape, solidity, extension, motion and number of the real physical grapes. Furthermore, when minute particles from the grapes bombard my senses, my mind constructs ideas of shape, solidity, extension, motion and number that *resemble* the qualities of shape, solidity, extension, motion and number in the physical world.

In virtual space we only encounter ideas, and have no direct connection to the physical world. If primary qualities are the *only* qualities of physical reality, we will never be able to observe this directly. To evaluate Locke's theory we will have to look for features of our virtual world that support a distinction between primary and secondary qualities – we need *virtual evidence* for resemblance between our ideas of primary qualities and primary qualities themselves. Some of the arguments that have been put forward are as follows:

1) Primary qualities are more stable than secondary qualities. It is impossible to separate the primary qualities from an object, but the secondary qualities can be easily removed. Porphyry retains its shape, solidity, extension, motion and number when it is placed in the dark, but it loses its red and white colour. Pounding an almond does not remove its primary qualities, but its whiteness and sweetness disappear – replaced by greyness and bitterness. The problem with these rather dubious observations is that even if they were to be believed, they would still only show that some primary qualities are more stable than some secondary qualities. They do not prove that primary qualities are qualities of real physical things and

they certainly do not prove that our ideas of primary qualities *resemble* real primary qualities.

2) Primary qualities can be perceived by many senses, whereas secondary qualities can generally only be detected by a single sense.[41] If primary qualities were really in objects, then we would expect them to be detectable by more than one sense. Since secondary qualities are generally only detectable by a single sense, they must be artefacts of the sense organs. Whilst this argument is better than the first, it does not say anything about whether my ideas of primary qualities *resemble* real primary qualities. In fact we seem to have several very different ideas of extension – felt extension, seen extension and perhaps even heard extension – that are all supposed to map onto a single primary quality of extension, and so the multi-sensory argument actually tends to work against this assumption. Another problem with this argument is that some qualities might be detectable by one sense and other qualities detectable by many senses without this amounting to a metaphysical difference between them. Finally, as Mackie points out, contemporary science postulates a number of primary qualities of the physical world – for example, radiation and magnetic fields – that are not detectable by any senses at all. If some primary qualities cannot be detected by the senses, then the objectivity of primary qualities cannot be linked to the number of senses that can detect them.

3) Secondary qualities appear differently to different people, whereas primary qualities do not.[42] For example, phenylthiourea tastes bitter to some people and not others, but everyone experiences the solidity of a stone in the same way. If everyone experiences primary qualities in the same way, but tastes and sees things differently, then it is more likely that primary qualities are objective properties of physical things and resemble the qualities of physical things. These observations do work as an argument against resemblance between some of our ideas of secondary qualities and qualities in the world. If people experience the same stimulus differently, then their idea of the stimulus is not likely to match the objective physical quality of the stimulus. However, the *lack* of resemblance between some of our

ideas of secondary qualities and qualities in the world is not an argument *for* resemblance between our ideas of primary qualities and qualities in the world. There could just be an *invariant connection* between qualities in the world and our ideas of primary qualities, without any resemblance between them. The processing of primary qualities might be biologically hardwired in a way that prevents differences between people, but this does not show that our ideas resemble objective physical qualities.

All of these arguments highlight important differences between our ideas of primary and secondary qualities, but none of them comes close to proving Locke's metaphysical thesis that primary qualities are the *only* qualities of the real world and our ideas of primary qualities *resemble* qualities in the real world. The real reason Locke believed this was the empirical success of the mechanical philosophy and the corpuscular theory of matter, which were supported by Boyle and other scientists of his time. These theories conjectured that the world consisted solely of particles and the void, and explained all material phenomena in terms of the motion of the particles and their impact upon one another. Locke did not believe in the primary/secondary quality distinction because of his own weak arguments, but because he was convinced by the empirical success of Boyle's interpretation of matter and wanted an account of perception that fitted into this framework.[43]

Since Locke, science has postulated a number of new qualities of physical reality that are not directly detectable by the senses. We have moved beyond atomism and expanded the scientific ontology to include electrical and magnetic fields, energy, the strong and weak nuclear force, and many other non-sensory qualities. This leaves us with a tripartite division of reality into non-sensory qualities that can only be detected using scientific instruments, primary qualities that are detectable by instruments and the senses, and secondary qualities that belong to the mind alone and whose presence can only be inferred from primary qualities. A modern Locke would claim that physical reality consists only of non-sensory and primary qualities and that our ideas of primary qualities resemble primary qualities themselves.

The first part of this claim is supported by the observation that science only uses non-sensory and primary qualities to make its empirical predictions – if we consider only the non-sensory and primary qualities, we can successfully predict the appearance and transformations of both primary *and* secondary qualities, whereas no such account exists that takes the secondary qualities as its starting point. However, Locke's claim that our ideas of primary qualities *resemble* real primary qualities is not supported by the empirical success of science, which remains mute about whether our ideas of shape, solidity, extension and motion resemble shape, solidity, extension and motion in the real physical world. In fact the general trend of science is towards more and more abstract non-sensory qualities that are defined mathematically and have almost no foundation in our virtual world of ideas. *Measurement* and not resemblance is the starting point for scientific predictions, and so only number remains as a primary quality that *might* resemble its idea. However, it is not at all clear whether measured numbers are objective *qualities* of things; nor is it clear whether we have an *idea*, instead of just a concept, of number.[44] Even if numbers were ideas of real qualities, the predictions of science depend upon the manipulation of *abstract* symbols in equations and the mapping of the results back onto reality; they have nothing to do with *resemblance* between any of our ideas of primary qualities and the primary qualities themselves.

To make this point clearer, consider the equation $PV = k$ (Boyle's law), where P is pressure, V is volume, and k is a constant. To begin with, the letters 'P' and 'V' have no resemblance to our ideas of pressure and volume; they are just abstract symbols that have to be replaced by *measurements* of P and V if we want to make predictions.[45] These measurements cannot be directly obtained from the physical world because we have no immediate access to it, and so we have to extract numbers for pressure and volume by interacting with our virtual world of ideas. Although volume is linked with the primary quality of extension, our procedure for measuring it has nothing to do with any resemblance that our idea of extension might have to real extension. To measure volume, we start by calibrating a measuring instrument using the virtual platinum bar in Paris.[46] This measuring instrument is then compared to the object and its volume is obtained as a product of the ratios between the length of the measuring instrument and the dimensions of the object. For example, the volume might be two platinum metre lengths multiplied by one platinum metre length multiplied by three platinum metre lengths. This procedure of comparing the primary qualities of the rod with the primary qualities of the object to extract a *ratio* assumes that our idea of the measuring rod's extension maps onto the same primary quality as our idea of the object's extension, but it does not directly rely on our idea of extension to extract the measurement.

The measurement of pressure proceeds along similar lines. Although pressure can be linked to secondary qualities – such as a feeling of muscular tension when we try to breathe out with a blocked windpipe or 'pressure' in the sinuses when we have a cold – these are more like correlates of pressure than a simple primary or secondary idea. Even if we had a pure secondary idea of pressure similar to our idea of colour, we could not measure it scientifically using introspection. To measure pressure we need to evaluate the *effect* it has on the *length* of mercury displaced in a glass tube. This length measurement is made by comparing it with the platinum metre in Paris and converting into standard units.

This discussion of pressure and volume shows that in the application of Boyle's law, the scientist transforms some properties of her virtual world into numbers through measurement, puts these numbers into an equation and then uses the equation to make predictions in the form of further numbers, whose accuracy is established through further measurements. As long as the same things are measured each time, reliable empirical results are obtained and Boyle's law becomes a useful tool in our interactions with the world. However, at no point is there any need for resemblance between P, V and k and actual physical qualities. We could apply Boyle's law equally successfully if we extracted P from the sound of the gas and V from its colour. As long as the same physical qualities are measured each time and these *numbers* are put into $PV = k$, reliable scientific predictions can be made.

Science is not just independent of resemblance between our ideas of primary qualities and real primary qualities: its general metaphysical picture actively argues against this.[47] Locke could imagine the spherical, solid, extended corpuscles bouncing around to produce pressure, but contemporary science works with non-sensory qualities and completely non-intuitive physical theories that only make sense mathematically. In our human lives we are surrounded by solid colourful physical things, but we do science in the colourless, odourless, silent, four-dimensional universe described by relativity, quantum theory and string theory. We cannot imagine what quantum phenomena are *like* and the attribution of shape, solidity, extension and motion to quarks is as metaphorical as the attribution of colour and flavour to them. The same is true of ten-dimensional superstrings, curved spacetime or the Grand Unified Theory (if there is one). Whichever scientific theory one picks, it is clear that none of them present a 'picture' of reality that is imaginable by us using the ideas that are assembled within our virtual world. Although some of our physical theories have originated from ideas taken from our virtual world, their mathematical development has left all links with primary and secondary qualities behind.

These arguments against resemblance between our ideas of primary qualities and real primary qualities are supported by Bertrand Russell, who claims that our experience of matter cannot be naively transposed into physical reality. In an interpretation of the brain hypothesis that is very similar to the one set out in the first part of this chapter, Russell makes a clear distinction between the signals that we receive from the physical world, and use to construct our virtual reality, and the hypotheses that we make about the physical world:

Modern physics, therefore, reduces matter to a set of events which proceed outward from a centre. If there is something further in the centre itself, we cannot know about it, and it is irrelevant to physics. ... Physics is mathematical, not because we know so much about the physical world, but because we know so little: it is only its mathematical properties that we can discover. For the rest, our knowledge is negative. In places where there are no eyes or ears or brains there are no colours or sounds, but there are events having certain characteristics which lead them to cause colours and sounds in places where there are eyes, ears and brains. We cannot find out what the world looks like from a place where there is nobody, because if we go to look there will be somebody there; the attempt is as hopeless as trying to jump on one's own shadow.

Matter as it appears to common sense, and as it has until recently appeared in physics, must be given up.[48]

We interact with and measure the physical world by detecting signals from it, which we reconstruct into objects. But since we are only inferring the nature of objects from signals sent from them, there is no scientific reason or evidence for the belief that matter as we experience it resembles matter in the real world: 'The idea that there is a little hard lump there, which *is* the electron or proton, is an illegitimate intrusion of common-sense notions derived from touch. For aught we know, the atom may consist entirely of the radiations which come out of it.'[49] We can conjecture that there is non-sensory matter, talk about the qualities of this non-sensory matter and use it to make scientific predictions, but this non-sensory matter has little to do with the virtual matter that we experience, which is constructed by the brain in response to signals detected by the senses. The non-sensory matter that is the hypothetical source of signals and phenomenal matter belong to different worlds and we have no evidence at all for any resemblance between them.

A final argument against Locke's naive notion of resemblance comes from the claim of the brain hypothesis that our coloured moving tasty solid virtual world is 'pushed out' from billions of neurons firing in response to signals from the senses. Firing neurons do not *resemble* anything in the physical world except for firing neurons, and so there does not seem to be any reason why the firing neurons that represent primary qualities should lead to phenomenal experiences resembling primary qualities; and no reason why the firing neurons that represent secondary qualities should lead to phenomenal experiences that do not resemble anything. If we want to say why one quality of our virtual world resembles a quality in the physical world and another does not, then we need theories that can penetrate the virtual illusions surrounding us and reach through the grey mush of our minds into the real world. The problem is that we have no such theories: Locke's arguments are weak and science does not tell us anything about resemblance.[50]

Locke took a subset of our virtual qualities and attempted to reduce everything to them. His metaphysics reached beyond the limits of his ideas and speculated about how a real world of primary qualities could enable ideas about primary and secondary qualities to appear in our minds. Modern science has changed the picture somewhat, but the general outline remains the same. Non-sensory and primary qualities explain the appearance of our ideas of primary and secondary qualities. However, whilst the success of science supports Locke's focus on the primary qualities, he overreached himself with his claim that our ideas of primary qualities *resemble* primary qualities themselves. Of course, a lack of arguments *for* resemblance does not mean that our ideas of primary qualities do not resemble the primary qualities. They *might*, but this is certainly not something that can be assumed. What primary qualities look like cannot be known by us: we have to suspend judgement about what shape, solidity, extension, motion and number are *really like*. We also have to suspend judgement about what real space and real time are really like because without resemblance, everything is effectively reduced to secondary qualities. This leaves us in a frankly Kantian position, with the difference that we can use abstractions to describe the behaviour of the noumenal world with a high degree of accuracy. Ideas of space, time, matter and motion accurately predict the transformations of our ideas, but from within virtual reality we have no reason to believe that our idea of space resembles physical space, that our idea of time resembles physical time, that our idea of solidity resembles physical solidity, or that our idea of motion resembles objective physical motion. From the standpoint of human knowledge we have to treat the real world as if it had a completely non-sensory nature. It becomes a Thing-in-itself with an abstraction and emptiness that are accurately captured by Hegel's description:

> The Thing-in-itself ... expresses the object, when we leave out of sight all that consciousness makes of it, all the deliverances of feeling, and all specific thoughts about it. It is easy to see what is left, – utter abstraction, total emptiness, only describable still as a 'beyond,' – the negative of imagination, of feeling, and definite thought. Nor does it require much penetration to see that this *caput mortuum* is still only a product of thought, such as accrues when thought ends in abstraction unalloyed: that it is the work of the empty 'Ego,' which finds an object in this empty self-identity of its own.[51]

When we imagine a real brain, we imagine that its imagined qualities resemble its real qualities. Out there, beyond the dome of the sky, lies Julie's solid, grey, warm, squishy brain just like the image of her brain that I am imagining now. But if we don't know whether our idea of shape resembles real shape or our idea of solidity resembles real solidity, then this imaginative exercise falls down at once. I cannot imagine the shape of Julie's brain 'out there' unless I know that my idea of shape resembles real shape, and I cannot imagine the squishiness of her brain unless real solidity resembles imagined solidity. Without resemblance, the real brain and its real neurons are *unimaginable*. We only imagined that we could imagine the real brain because of our earlier immersion in naive realism: when we thought that we directly saw the things themselves and when we were brought up to believe that we inhabited real space and that the primary qualities of this space were objective physical qualities. All of this has to be given up within the developed and more consistent interpretation of the brain hypothesis that has been presented in this chapter.

When the brain becomes unimaginable the brain hypothesis fades into invisibility. After all, a *brain* hypothesis presupposes some *idea* about what real brains and neurons are really like, and explains perception, dreams and phantom limbs on this basis. Without resemblance, the brain hypothesis becomes a completely *abstract* theory. We can measure the brain, do scientific experiments on it and make successful predictions, but we are never measuring what we imagine we are measuring. That there is a world at all becomes the central mystery, rather than the question about how imaginable phenomenal experiences arise from an unimaginable noumenal brain.

The hard problem of consciousness is about how the brain's information processing could give rise to conscious experiences; how the soggy mush of firing neurons could blossom into phenomenal qualia. As McGinn puts it:

> How is it possible for conscious states to depend upon brain states? How can technicolour phenomenology arise from soggy grey matter? What makes the bodily organ we call the brain so radically different from other bodily organs, say the kidneys – the body parts without a trace of consciousness? How could the aggregation of millions of individual insentient neurons generate subjective awareness? We know that brains are the *de facto* causal basis of consciousness, but we have, it seems, no understanding whatever of how this can be so. It strikes us as miraculous, eerie, even faintly comic. Somehow, we feel, the water of the physical brain is turned into the wine of consciousness, but we draw a total blank on the nature of this conversion. Neural transmissions just seem to be the wrong kind of materials with which to bring consciousness into the world, but it appears that in some way they perform this mysterious feat.[52]

This hard problem arises because we are still trapped in Locke's distinction between primary and secondary qualities. We believe that the primary qualities of matter *as we experience them* are really out there beyond our virtual world, whereas the secondary qualities of matter are somehow created from these primary qualities. We imagine the primary qualities of the real brain (coloured grey because we cannot imagine something that reflects light and yet is completely colourless). Then we imagine the colour red and ask ourselves how this red could come from an intricate assembly of grey neurons.

In this thought experiment we imagine that the imagined brain is how the brain *really is*. However, I have shown that we have no reason to believe that there is any resemblance at all between an imagined brain and a real brain. An imagined brain is *nothing like* the real brain and so the attempt to imagine how the imagined brain gives rise to colourful conscious experiences will inevitably fail. Our ideas about extended, solid, moving neurons and our ideas of colour, smell and taste are all part of the virtual simulation created by the physical brain, which can only be described using the abstract language of science. The *real* problem of consciousness is how phenomenal experience arises from the physical world; the hard problem of consciousness is how one part of phenomenal experience (phenomenal red) can be reduced to another part of phenomenal experience (the phenomenal brain). *We can speak scientifically and mathematically about the real problem of consciousness.* Without a workable theory of resemblance, the *hard* problem degenerates into a futile imaginative exercise.

Conclusion

The ultimate revenge of the information system comes when the system absorbs the very identity of the human personality, absorbing the opacity of the body, grinding the meat into information, and deriding erotic life by reducing it to a transparent play of puppets. In an

ontological turnabout, the computer counterfeits the silent and private
body from which mental life originated. The machinate mind disdain-
fully mocks the meat. Information digests even the secret recesses of the
caress.

(Michael Heim, *The Metaphysics of Virtual Reality*)[53]

I am *here*, experiencing a world of buzzing bees, blooming flowers,
blue sky. I observe the way in which brains work and make the
brain hypothesis. An uncanny discontinuous jump. Reality slides
into cyberspace. My surroundings are the same – and yet radically
transformed. I no longer gaze upon an objective world of buzzing
bees, blooming flowers and blue sky; I *become* my gaze. Virtual
bees sup at fake flowers beneath a cyber sky. Billions of dancing
points of light *are* firing neuron patterns in my brain. Compared
to my virtual body, the virtual sky appears to be enormous, and yet
it only occupies a small part of my real brain. Compared to my
virtual body, the virtual bees are tiny, and yet I know that real bees
occupy a similar volume of objective space as the neurons synthe-
sizing my virtual sky. I observe and feel my hand; it looks and feels
the same as it did before I made the brain hypothesis, but its
materiality has vanished. I see and feel a virtual arm, a phantom
leg – hallucinate my head. I have been reconstituted out of virtual
flesh. As I intertwine with the body of the other, there are just
virtual arms, virtual tongues and virtual lips. All of my evidence for
the brain hypothesis has also vanished; virtual observations take
the place of this lost objectivity and the brain hypothesis becomes
an absurd metaphysical and theological leap. Confronted with
this loss of evidence, I abandon the brain hypothesis and instantaneously return to a naive relationship with objective reality.
Once more I observe how brains work and the cycle begins again.

The brain hypothesis is a powerful predictive theory that has
enabled extensive surgical interventions and treatments. Its problem
is that it shifts all of its evidence (including the way in which
computers work and our observations of the brain itself) from real

into virtual reality. If the brain hypothesis is correct, we have never experienced a real brain, directly observed a connection between brain damage and behaviour change, nor observed the primary qualities that we attribute to real brains. Kant also divided the world into noumena, which are in principle unobservable, and phenomena that we do observe. If we want to say *why* the brain hypothesis is correct and *why* Kant is wrong, we will have to bring some evidence to bear. We will have to prove, rather than just dogmatically state, that the brain hypothesis is correct. The problem with this proof is that all of its evidence will have to come from virtual reality, and a link between virtual and objective observations can only be made by assuming the objective brain that is in doubt.

We cannot rest in virtual reality for long, and cannot help re-entering it again. A delicate dance in which we construct a theory, lose the evidence for it, abandon the theory and take it up again. The brain hypothesis starts off as a convincing empirical theory and evolves into a theory that neutralizes the means that were used to prove it. Once the brain hypothesis has vanished, the evidence returns and the cycle begins again.

This interpretation of the brain hypothesis opens up an uncanny and terrifying vision of the world that undermines everything we naturally believe in and completely overturns our relationship to space. Given the initial evidence we are driven to the brain hypothesis. Given this conclusion we are led to question our sanity.

Many people will not believe in the interpretation of the brain hypothesis that I have presented here. They will either not worry about the fact that they experience objects at a distance from them, or prefer to believe in some mysterious property P (or Q) to account for this. This group of people continues to believe that they directly experience the real world and so no shift from real to virtual evidence takes place. To these people I can only reply that

I have not presented a particularly erudite or obscure argument; only some self-evident facts that are mostly ignored or rarely put together. Whilst we may not *want* to inhabit a virtual world, this interpretation of the brain hypothesis is self-consistent and convincing. If we retain the notion that the physical brain processes information using neurons, then everything points towards the conclusion that we experience and inhabit a virtual world created from incoming sense data.

Whether we do or don't place our faith in the metaphysics of the brain hypothesis, it has proved itself in many practical applications and is worth taking seriously at a day to day level – bullets in the brain are certainly *correlated* with reduced cognitive performance. The brain hypothesis can even be used to develop more intelligent and perhaps even conscious machines.

It is not a question of abandoning the brain hypothesis in favour of a better theory, but of recognising its structure and movement. There might be a more stable hermeneutic circle, or a less metaphysical hermeneutic circle, but would greater self-reflexive consistency necessarily make an alternative to the brain hypothesis more *correct*?

Given the problems with the brain hypothesis, there seem to be three main directions that we can take:

1) Resist this development of the brain hypothesis. Stick with the problem of consciousness. Invent mysterious explanations about how consciousness can spread itself over objects that are little more than pseudo-explanations.

2) Accept this development of the brain hypothesis and the eating up of its own evidence. Accept that it has changed from an empirical scientific theory into a metaphysical and wildly counter-intuitive claim. Maintain faith in the brain hypothesis, believe in the world described by scientific theory and continue as if nothing had happened.

3) Drop the brain hypothesis and stop trying to reduce one part of phenomenal experience to another. Revert to an improved phenomenology without the transcendental ego and eidetic intuition. Hearken to the things themselves.

An uneasy movement and tension between these three options is the position that we are currently in. And (quite frankly) this is probably the position that we have always been in. And (quite pessimistically) this is probably the position that we will always be in.

WE SEE THE THINGS THEMSELVES, the world is what we see: formulae of this kind express a faith common to the natural man and the philosopher – the moment he opens his eyes; they refer to a deep-seated set of mute 'opinions' implicated in our lives. But what is strange about this faith is that if we seek to articulate it into theses or statements, if we ask ourselves what is this *we*, what *seeing* is, and what *thing* or *world* is, we enter into a labyrinth of difficulties and contradictions.

(Maurice Merleau-Ponty, *The Visible and the Invisible*)[54]

3   Impossible Speech about Time

What, then, is time? There can be no quick and easy answer, for it is no simple matter even to understand what it is, let alone find words to explain it. Yet in our conversation, no word is more familiarly used or more easily recognized than 'time'. We certainly understand what is meant by the word both when we use it ourselves and when we hear it used by others.

What, then, is time? I know well enough what it is, provided that nobody asks me; but if I am asked what it is and try to explain, I am baffled.

(Augustine, *Confessions*)[1]

When writing the scenario of *The Shell and the Clergyman*, I considered that the cinema possessed an element of its own, a truly magic and truly cinematographic element, which nobody had ever thought of isolating. This element, which differs from every sort of representation attached to images, has the characteristics of the very vibration, the profound, unconscious source of thought.

(Antonin Artaud, 'The Shell and the Clergyman')[2]

The Hottest Show on Earth!!!

With a tight grip on Mack's sweaty hand you pad self-consciously down the dimly lit aisle, cast about in the gloom, find your row, shuffle and wedge your way across endless strangers' knees, and finally arrive at your seat. Sinking your buttocks into plush tattered velvet you tenderly caress Mack's greasy thigh, run your fingers over his rough calloused hands and drink a draft of hot-male stench from his open fly. Mack shoots you a stare through his clear blue eyes. You look away, move around a bit, slide your thighs and back into continuous contact with the seat, squirm-twitch-relax as

Mack's tongue tastes wax in your hairy ear, and look up at the blank screen. Stroking Mack's thinning hair you start to think about this, about that, about going back to Mack's place after the film, about the loving kiss Charlie gave you before he died, how Johnny must just be discovering Joey's little joke.

The film starts. A million pixelated points of light spring into being. Gradually all sensory awareness fades from your hands, buttocks, back and feet. This intermittently returns throughout the film (as your circulation clogs up or your muscles get tired) but for the most part it is as if you never had a body. Your mind ceases to think about the future, past or present. You join the film's internal movement; track the ebb and flow of action, the slow build up of desire. You fuse with the hero: his desires become your desires, your desires become his, or rather there is no longer any yours or his, just a person in a situation – not a spectator watching a hero in a film. Too captivated to look at your watch, you float free from world time into film time. Film time jumps between different points within its own artificial world time. It has a different past and different projects; it moves forward a few years, jumps back several centuries, and returns for a resolution in the present. Different points in film time take place simultaneously. Slow motion dilates moments into minutes. Dissolves reach across the years in seconds.

You have almost become a pure point of spectatorship fused with the spectacle, but there are some parts of the film that cannot be given to you by the projector and have to be completed by your inert body. The hero hangs precariously from a precipice; your body is gripped with tension and fear. The hero caresses a beautiful blond boy; your body throbs and bulges. The hero is crushed by an enormous boulder; your body is depressed and sad. The hero's dog, Shep, decides to fight on in his master's memory and your body surges with joy again. Less realistic than Huxley's feelies, these responses from your body fill in what is missing from the input of the film. An ordinary cinema cannot project bodily sensations, smells or emotions, and so your body closes itself off from its environment and fills in, as best it can, the responses that it would make if it was in the situation depicted. These are fairly limited because the ordinary cinema is not very realistic – the screen is flat, some distance away and you cannot smell or touch it. If the film medium could be improved, your body would make much more intense responses. Your fear would become *RAW TERROR* if you could *actually see* the precipice falling away beneath you. Your sexual excitement would reach an *UNBEARABLE PITCH* if you could *actually feel* the beautiful blond boy's tight tanned ass.[3]

> There is a basic principle that distinguishes a hot medium like radio from a cool one like the telephone, or a hot medium like the movie from a cool one like TV. A hot medium is one that extends one single sense in 'high definition.' High definition is the state of being well filled with data. A photograph is, visually, 'high definition.' A cartoon is 'low definition,' simply because very little visual information is provided. Telephone is a cool medium, or one of low definition, because the ear is given a meagre amount of information. And speech is a cool medium of low definition, because so little is given and so much has to be filled in by the listener. On the other hand, hot media do not leave so much to be filled in or completed by the audience. Hot media are, therefore, low in participation, and cool media are high in participation or completion by the audience.
>
> (Marshall McLuhan, *Understanding Media*)[4]

Cinema is a hot medium. Its high definition images and sound leave little for us to complete. But cinema is not as hot as it could be: there are still areas that we fill in and areas that we block off because we cannot fill them in. We are left to wonder what a *really hot* medium would be like: a medium with the same definition as our senses; a medium that leaves nothing for its audience to complete; a medium in which the audience almost becomes superfluous.

In an ordinary cinema the audience has to expand the flat screen into three dimensions, and they can never do this with complete conviction. This limitation could be overcome in a cinema that used three-dimensional frames. In a conventional cinema a powerful light shines through a transparent two-dimensional frame and throws an image upon a white screen. Next, a rotating shutter blocks off the light, the first frame is removed and replaced by the second, the shutter allows the light through again, and the second image appears on the screen. Each image is held stationary in the light for $1/48^{th}$ of a second, there is darkness for $1/48^{th}$ of a second whilst the frames are exchanged, and then the next image is held stationary in the light for $1/48^{th}$ of a second.[5] The frames are exchanged too rapidly for the audience to notice the immobility of the frames or the darkness in between, and so they interpret the succession of stationary images as a continuously moving picture.

A cinema that used three-dimensional frames could not shine the light through them. Instead, the frames would have to be placed directly before the audience, and they would have to be full size models (or larger) of what they were intended to represent.[6] These models could be illuminated from one or a number of light sources (in the manner of theatrical lighting), but each light source would have to have a rotating shutter, similar to the ones in a conventional cinema, to cut out the light whilst the three-dimensional frames were exchanged. During projection each three-dimensional frame would be placed in front of the audience, the lights would come on for $1/48^{th}$ of a second, the lights would go off for $1/48^{th}$ of a second whilst a second three-dimensional frame was placed in front of the audience, the lights would come on, and so on. This would lead the audience to see moving objects that appeared to be *actually there* in front of them. Three-dimensional sounds and odours could also be provided to obviate the need for the audience to fill these in or block them out. An illustration of this three-dimensional projection mechanism is given in Figure 1.

This medium is certainly hot by today's standards and extends three senses in high definition, but it is barely warm compared to what is possible. The spectators can see a beautiful blond boy in

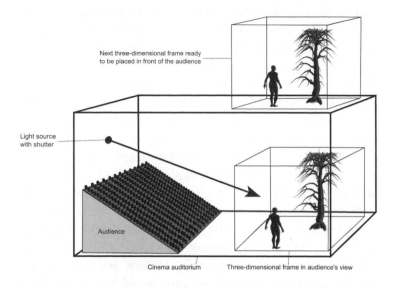

Next three-dimensional frame ready
to be placed in front of the audience

Light source
with shutter

Audience

Cinema auditorium   Three-dimensional frame in audience's view

Figure 1. Projection of three-dimensional frames

front of them; they can hear his voice, smell his groin, count the hairs around his nipples – it is as if he was *really there* – but they are unable to experience the electric thrill, the jolt of nerves, the contraction of the stomach, that the hero would feel in the real situation. This cinema can project the colour of the blond boy's body, the smell of his sweat, blood and semen, the crack and squeak of his whip and leather, but the audience are left to guess about the slippery smoothness of his ass and they can only speculate about the waves of passion that must be coursing through the hero's virile heart and loins as he gazes upon him. What is needed is a medium that *gives* its audience the sensations and emotions of the hero *as they are experienced by him*. Such a medium would not only project three-dimensional colours, scents and sounds, but sensations and emotions as well, directly into the brains and/or bodies of the audience.

To create this medium, sensational and emotional data could be encoded alongside each frame in addition to the sound and odour information. As each three-dimensional frame is thrown in front of the audience, their brains/bodies would be held in the sensational and emotional state of the hero for $1/48^{th}$ of a second by injecting chemicals and stimulating appropriate areas of the brain with electrodes. Whilst the light is covered by the shutter the sensational and emotional state would be switched off. When the next frame is illuminated a new slightly altered sensational and emotional state would be projected into each member of the audience. Each sensational and emotional state would not continuously alter, but would be held fixed for the time that it was on. It would then be switched off and replaced by a different static state, also held for $1/48^{th}$ of a second.

In this cinema the audience can stroke the hairs around the beautiful blond boy's nipples, feel the tightness of his ass and marvel at the firmness of his thighs. In this cinema the audience feel *real fear* as the hero hangs over the precipice, *real passion* as the hero and the beautiful blond boy cling rapturously together, *real agony* as the hero is crushed by an enormous boulder. The fact that they experience the sensations and emotions of the hero from their seats, instead of from the centre of the action, creates a sense of dislocation – but this is exciting cinema.

It is a crucial moment: the hero scans the horizon and tastes the rich black earth; he *has* to decide – either way it could turn out for the worst, but he *has* to decide. In the state of anxiety projected into them by the cinema the audience think: 'What *will* he do? What will he *do*? *WHAT WILL HE DO?*': they fill in what the hero must be thinking at this critical juncture; they empathetically project an agitated dance of options into his mind as he struggles to reach a decision. In this cinema the audience still has something to complete – this medium is not as hot as it could be. How can they experience truly heroic indecision if they have to generate it themselves, from their own insipid imaginations? How can they empathize in any kind of depth with a hero whose psychic life is a complete mystery to them?

This residual coolness of the cinema is made worse by the tendency of the audience to mentally drift at a tangent to the action, even in the most exciting films. Although the audience's central region of consciousness is for the most part entirely filled with the content given to it by the film, there are moments when they switch from total absorption in the action to disbelief about a sexual position, worries about their laundry. They shuffle in seats that do not play a part in the film before them and remember that it is 'just a movie'. For a really hot cinematic experience the *thoughts* of the hero will have to be projected into the audience as well.

To make this cinema red hot, the hero's thoughts could be encoded alongside the sound, odour, sensation and emotion information that accompanies each frame.[7] Each fragment of thought would be held in the head of each member of the audience for 1/48th of a second, switched off, and then replaced by a slightly different fragment using some kind of brain stimulation. In this way, the audience would think like the hero, have the same sensational and emotional responses as the hero, and see, hear and smell the objects that the hero sees, hears and smells. The only difference between the experiences of the audience and those of the hero would be the distance and angle from which the audience observe the projected objects.

This cinema is built and billed as 'The Hottest Show on Earth!!!'. Millions of people flock to see *Bulging Leather*, the first film to be made in the new format, and Roger and Mack go on their second date to the premiere. During the show Roger, for no apparent reason, runs into the area where the three-dimensional frames are being exchanged. Fortunately, the film uses the original floor of the projection area, and so only the character models are exchanged by the huge machine. Instead of being mashed by the mechanism, Roger finds that he can freely wander amongst the characters, whilst he experiences the sensations, emotions and thoughts of the hero. In this situation Roger is surrounded by three-dimensional bodies that move, talk, eat, bleed, shit and smell and Roger is himself a three-dimensional body that moves, talks, eats, bleeds, shits and smells.

Roger stands proud within the movie. The rest of the audience watches Roger standing proud within the movie. But what separates Roger from the film? Although he has come from the audience, it is a common device in the theatre to plant actors amongst the spectators. Perhaps the director decided to project a character into the audience that walks up to join the action in the projection area to increase the feeling of audience participation? Something has to be found about Roger, as he stands there before our eyes, to distinguish him from the projected illusions surrounding him. There are a number of possibilities:

1) Roger has freedom of the will.

From the audience's point of view, nothing can be observed about Roger that suggests that he has freedom of the will.[8] If they had seen the film before, they might conclude that Roger has freedom of the will by observing that he behaves differently this time around (whilst all the other characters perform the same actions and speak the same words). However, since this is the first time that they have seen the film, they have no idea whether the actions of Roger have been determined in advance.

From Roger's point of view the issue is more complicated. He started out as a member of the audience who ran into the projection area. All the time that he is in the projection area he continues to watch the film – all that has changed is the position from which he watches it. The question about Roger's freedom of the will becomes a question about whether any person who sees a movie in a hot medium experiences freedom whilst they are doing so – a freedom that could distinguish them from the film that they are watching.

In an ordinary cinema we do not have any control over the action that takes place. We abandon ourselves to the film, fuse with it and experience its development as the product of our own volition. In a film, characters laugh, eat and weep, and by empathetically projecting ourselves into their situation, we laugh, eat and weep as well – carried blindly and willingly forward by the flow of action thrown into existence from a pre-determined film strip. This lack of control over the events that take place in a film does not make us feel unfree in the cinema – we do not sigh with relief when we emerge into the cold night air because we have recovered our freedom of the will. The only things that we could be said to freely create in an ordinary cinema are our intellectual, sensational and emotional reactions to the film's content, which differ from person to person and could be said to create a limited form of separation between us and the film in an ordinary cinema.

In 'The Hottest Show on Earth!!!' there is almost nothing for the audience to complete, but this does not diminish their sense of freedom. On the contrary, it allows them to join more fully with the flow of events as they happen; to will them from the inside, instead of vicariously participating from outside. Everything is given to the audience of 'The Hottest Show on Earth!!!' and so there is no need for them to inject a residue of self back into the action that they are observing. Even a sense of having willed the events is thrown into them twenty-four times per second. Furthermore, the audience does not have the freedom to detach themselves from the action, to say to themselves 'it's only a movie', because the thoughts in their heads are the hero's thoughts, projected into them at twenty-four frames per second. If there is going to be any detachment from the film, it will have to take place within the film, as some kind of postmodern, ironic, self-parodying, film-within-a-film scenario.

2) Roger's body continuously exists.
From the audience's point of view, this cannot be used to separate Roger from the film that surrounds him. It is dark when the frames are exchanged, and so they cannot observe any continuity in Roger's body – and this would remain true if the projection speed was slowed right down. It makes no difference to the audience if Roger's body is replaced by a different one, in a slightly different position, every $1/24^{th}$ of a second.

Since Roger uses his body to perceive his body – using his eyes to see his hands, for example – then if he was being projected, his perception of his body would vanish along with his body in the interval in which the frames were exchanged, and he would be unable to observe any discontinuity in his existence – if Roger's eye vanished at the same time as his hand, then he would be unable to observe the disappearance of his hand. To observe the disappearance of his body in between frames, Roger needs a soul (or something like a soul) that is distinct from his body and can perceive continuously in the place where his body disappears. Theological speculation aside, it seems safe to conclude that this is not the case, and so neither the audience, nor Roger himself, can use the continuity of Roger's body to separate him from the film.

3) If Roger was being projected, he would only exist for half the time of the audience. This would make Roger's subjective time run at twice the rate of time in the cinema.
The audience cannot observe any difference between Roger's subjective time and their own because they have no experience of Roger's time. If Roger was being projected, any time observation within him would be a part of the film, and film time runs independently of world time. Both Roger and the audience are immersed in film time, and so Roger's brief flashes of non-existence would not make this run any faster or slower for him.[9]

4) Roger thinks to himself: 'I am Roger. I was born in 1966, grew up in the Chatham Islands, and had my first homosexual experience with a man called Terry. I remember my life up to this point. I remember coming into the cinema with Mack, buying our tickets and taking our seats. Film characters cannot remember their lives. They lack my richness of character; they are thin creations of a scriptwriter's mind, shallow archetypes for us to project our fantasies into.'
The content of Roger's thought cannot be used to separate him from the film. The fact that Roger thinks at all might be used to separate him (see point 5), but the *content* of Roger's thought *is*

projected into him by the cinema. A postmodern plot might involve similar thoughts, but these would have no bearing at all upon Roger's real situation. Every single member of the audience thinks the same thoughts at the same time as Roger, and it would be sheer chance if these thoughts (recorded in advance by a neuroprogramming studio) accurately described Roger as he wandered about in the cinema. Nothing that Roger thinks has any connection at all with his situation.

5) The projector can project thoughts and emotions into Roger, but it cannot project thoughts and emotions into the models that surround him.
Roger's skin is stuffed with flesh, brains and blood; the coloured surfaces of the hero could be concealing anything. The models that are successively thrown in front of the audience could be made of wax, wood or polystyrene, but whatever inert substance is used to construct them, it will not be possible to fill this substance with emotions or thoughts. Roger is human: forged from a flesh and blood that is capable of receiving conceptual and emotional input; the hero's lifeless wax and wood can never be packed with thoughts and feelings.

From the audience's point of view, this is not at all relevant. They cannot feel Roger's feelings and so they cannot use them to distinguish Roger from the characters that surround him. From Roger's point of view, this assumption could be used to separate him from films that are made using non-biological models, but there is no reason why films could not be made using flesh, nerves and blood held immobile in emotional states as intense as Roger's own.

6) If Roger vanishes when the film ends, then he was part of it.
Once the film has ended it should be easy to tell if Roger was part of it. However, the director might decide to keep Roger on after the official end of the film as a further trick to increase its realism. Even after the house lights have gone up the audience could still be uncertain whether the film has finished. They can only find out if

the film has really ended by going up into the projection room and seeing if there are any more models left to project. This would allow the audience to separate Roger from the film, but it presupposes that the audience can take a truly outside perspective; that there is not a film-within-a-film structure; that the projection room is not itself being projected.

If Roger was part of the film, he would be unable to observe its end, and so he could not use this method to separate himself from it. After the alleged end of the film Roger might still exist: either because he is separate from it, or because the film has not ended and he is still being projected.

7) If there are no models of Roger in the projection room, then Roger is a member of the audience.
During or after the film the audience could go up into the projection room. There they would see tens of thousands of lifeless models stacked up in storage. If there are models of Roger amongst them, then Roger was part of the film; if there are no models of Roger, then Roger was a real member of the audience who wandered into the projection area by mistake. This point is similar to the preceding one. If you are sure that there is only one projection room (and that it is not a projection of a projection room), then it is easy to separate Roger from the film by looking at the models. However, if there is any ambiguity as to whether the projection room is itself part of the film, then it is not possible to use the contents of this room to distinguish Roger from the film that he has entered.

Overall, it seems that only an outside perspective could be used to separate Roger from the film that he is standing in. Neither Roger nor the audience can *observe* anything about Roger or the film that could distinguish him from it. If the projection room door was locked, it would be impossible to separate Roger from the other characters in the movie.

This collapses the status of the whole audience into ambiguity. Any one of them could have run into the projection area; any one

of them could be stooges about to run into the projection area. In
'The Hottest Show on Earth!!!' the experience of watching a film
is identical to the experience of being in a film: it is no longer
possible to separate a fiction of yourself from your own reality.

The situation becomes even more difficult if a different set of
thoughts and emotions is projected into each member of the
audience. Neo-neo-realist movies could be made in which people
wander about and do their own thing. Each member of the
audience could choose, as they bought their tickets, to experience
the thoughts, sensations and emotions of a different character. In
*A Bunch of Loving Brothers and Sisters Gathered Together at the
Movies to Have a Great Time* each member of the real audience
becomes a different member of a fictional cinema audience. This
fictional cinema audience watches a remake of Warhol's *Couch* in
which the projected characters wander about, eat bananas, fuck
and smoke. The house lights are brought up[10] and the audience
starts to eat bananas, fuck, smoke and wander amongst the
projected models. Now the audience is mingling with three-dimensional figures that are moving around, eating bananas, fucking and
smoking. They themselves are three-dimensional figures that move
around, eat bananas, fuck and smoke. They think – but perhaps
these figures think as well? They feel – but perhaps these figures feel
too? At first the audience thought that the projected models were
'lifeless' and 'animated by some clever technology', but now they
are not so sure: 'They look just like us', 'Speak just like us', 'They
scream when they are in pain' … Solipsism is never sustainable for
very long.

A Cinematic Model of Time

Introduction

This is what the cinematograph does. With photographs, each of which
represents the regiment in a fixed attitude, it reconstitutes the mobility

of the regiment marching. It is true that if we had to do with photographs alone, however much we might look at them, we should never see them animated: with immobility set beside immobility, even endlessly, we could never make movement. In order that the pictures may be animated, there must be movement somewhere. The movement does indeed exist here; it is in the apparatus. It is because the film of the cinematograph unrolls, bringing in turn the different photographs of the scene to continue each other, that each actor of the scene recovers his mobility. ... The process then consists in extracting from all the movements peculiar to all the figures an impersonal movement abstract and simple, *movement in general*, so to speak: we put this into the apparatus, and we reconstitute the individuality of each particular movement by combining this nameless movement with the personal attitudes. Such is the contrivance of the cinematograph. And such is also that of our knowledge. Instead of attaching ourselves to the inner becoming of things, we place ourselves outside of them in order to recompose their becoming artificially. We take snapshots, as it were, of the passing reality, and, as these are characteristic of the reality, we have only to string them on a becoming, abstract, uniform and invisible, situated at the back of the apparatus of knowledge, in order to imitate what there is that is characteristic in this becoming itself. Perception, intellection, language so proceed in general. Whether we would think becoming, or express it, or even perceive it, we hardly do anything else than set going a kind of cinematograph inside us. We may therefore sum up what we have been saying in the conclusion that the *mechanism of our ordinary knowledge is of a cinematographical kind.*

(Henri Bergson, *Creative Evolution*)[11]

Now I see the chestnut hair of a small child on a small bike and hear cicadas on a soft summer night. *Now* I experience snake-roughened hands, chocolate mouth and a rose nose. *Now* I feel pain in my head, a love-sick aching heart and fear *fills* me as I helplessly freeze before the horn blare and rapid onrush of headlights. *Now* I am thinking.

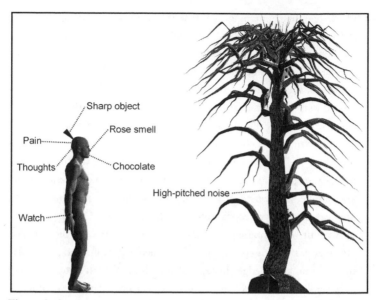

Figure 2. A *now*

Figure 2 shows a *now* in which a thinking man tastes chocolate, smells a rose, experiences pain as a sharp object pierces his head and listens to a high-pitched chirruping noise emanating from a nearby tree. In this illustration a portion of the world has been seized and immobilized on paper. Although the man is wearing a watch, there is no time in the picture: the thinking man will stand there for eternity, forever contemplating the same tree with the same sharp object piercing his head.

Time is external to everything in Figure 2. It is not the man; it is not the tree; it is not the watch. If this was a real situation, the man, tree and watch would all change in time, but they would not be time. The same is true of all the colours, sounds, sensations, smells and tastes in Figure 2.

Time converts the static things in Figure 2 into processes; it animates the thoughts, colours, sounds, sensations, scents and flavours of the world. Once Figure 2 has been animated by time we can use changes in its constituent parts to indirectly measure the flow of time, but the things that change are not themselves time.

The *now* depicted in Figure 2 is an instantaneous moment outside of time; an eternal moment without temporal extension. Time is the relationship between the nows, the *becoming* of the nows, the bringing of a new now into existence and the sliding of the present now into a non-existent past.

This separation of time from a static now leads to a *cinematic* theory of time. In the cinema a temporal situation is created by successively placing immobile frames before an audience. Each of these frames is eternal and atemporal – the world in a state of pause – and the projector gives life to these frames by making them succeed one another. When time is conceived of in this way, it becomes something that throws frames of reality successively into existence, converting everything within each reality-frame into processes that change over time. Time becomes a projector in the sky, a projector beyond the universe; a God who sustains us in existence by continuously creating us anew.

Our ordinary theory of time is cinematic. We habitually objectify time in this way when we measure time or speak about the passing or flow of time. This interpretation of time is also used within modern physics when it talks about four-dimensional *space*time.

Whilst an ordinary projector can only project two-dimensional colours and sounds, time is a projector that projects three-dimensional thoughts, colours, sounds, sensations, scents and flavours. An ordinary projector shows a photographic reproduction of reality; time projects *reality itself* – everything that we experience within the world; everything that *is there* before us as the world. An ordinary film cuts rapidly between different times and places; in reality time projects *realtime*. In an ordinary film, the future and past frames are present, stored above and below the light; in the world, it is not clear whether the past and future reality-frames exist, and I will defer this question for the moment and speak of time as something that *throws into (or as) existence*. The cinematic theory of time thus amounts to the claim that *time is a realtime reality projector that throws three-dimensional frames of reality into (or as) existence*.

This chapter starts by developing this interpretation of time in more detail. An ordinary cinema consists of an audience, a screen, a shutter, a light, a sequence of frames, and a projection mechanism that advances the frames. None of these can be directly attributed to time, but it does have structures that are similar to some of these components and the first sections look at the way in which each of them fits into the realtime reality projector. In the central part of this chapter some objections are dealt with and clarifications given about the mechanisms of the realtime reality projector and its relationship to modern physics. The chapter then concludes with an analysis of the problematic self-reflexive relationship between cinematic time and language. If the ordinary and scientific picture of time is correct, people cannot speak about time within time at all – theories about the realtime reality projector become *invisible* to people whose time theories have trapped them within a static now.

The Audience, Screen, Shutter and Light

Audience

In a cinema, the audience *watches* pictures that are thrown onto the screen by the projector: the audience is *separate* from the film that they are viewing. In the realtime reality projector, the audience is within the frames that are thrown into existence, and so there is no distinction between the film that the audience is watching and the audience itself. If time is a realtime reality projector, then the audience is *within* the frame that is animated by time. People do not watch time from within another time, nor do they observe time from eternity. The realtime reality projector projects a film without an audience; a film that is its own audience.

Screen

In an ordinary cinema the screen exists prior to the showing of the film and persists in existence whilst successive images are thrown upon it. In the realtime reality projector there is no screen because time projects existence itself. Since time projects existence, there cannot be anything outside of this projected existence for it to project onto. No eternal substance persists outside of time; there is no empty vessel into which reality is thrown. The totality of reality simply comes to be and then comes to be again in a slightly different configuration. This coming-to-be does not come to be *upon* something; it simply *comes to be*.

Shutter

Projectors need shutters to block out the light in between frames. Without the shutter, the audience would see a blurred continuously sliding film strip superimposed over the ordinary picture. In the realtime reality projector the audience is part of the frame, and so there are no observers of the interval between frames. Therefore there is no need for a shutter to conceal the frame exchange. Furthermore, photons only exist within the frame, and so it is not necessary to block them between frames.

Light

An ordinary projector shines a powerful light through the transparent film frames, which reflects off the screen and pierces the eyes of the audience. In the realtime reality projector the frame is immobile, and so there cannot be any movement or reflection of light within it.[12]

To understand light within the reality-frame we need to refer back to the discussion of the brain hypothesis in the previous chapter. Light is used by the brain to detect objects, but it is the firing of neurons or populations of neurons that is correlated with our conscious experience of objects in the world. The realtime reality projector throws reality-frames into existence in which there are photons 'floating' in the air and firing neuron patterns that are consciously experienced as illuminated objects in the world.

The Reality-Frame

The reality-frame includes everything within each static now; everything illustrated in Figure 2. For the most part, it is relatively easy to imagine how all thoughts, colours, sounds, sensations, tastes and scents could be frozen within an immobile frame and brought back to life by a succession of such frames. This is basically our ordinary cinema experience boosted with some hypothetical technology. However, if our experience is projected in this way – if time projects a sequence of *atemporal* nows – then our experiences of time and movement must *also* be part of the reality-frame. Within the world projected by the realtime reality projector, time and movement must be experienced within an instant: they must be time-images and movement-images; textures within an immobile reality-frame that have no connection with time itself – experiences that are animated *by* time whilst remaining separate from time. This will now be covered in a little more detail.

Time-Images[13]
Somehow we know about time. We have some kind of image of time that informs us about it. This image of time may be fixed or it may change over time. If the time-image changes over time, it does so because time throws successive frames of us into existence with different time-images. When I remember that I recited Psalm 53 yesterday, this memory is an image of an earlier now. I also expect that I will recite Psalm 55 tomorrow. Without these time-images I would be locked in a present without a past or future; a present in which I have no knowledge or experience of time.

By itself, the presence of memories and expectations is not enough to give us an image of time. If we are not aware that we are expecting or remembering, then our expectation or remembrance is not a time-image. When I daydream about tomorrow or vividly re-enact a previous experience, I am in some sense actually in the future or past. In this case the future or past become *present* and lose their character of futurity or pastness. It is only when I come back to myself in the present that I realize I have been experiencing a fantasy or memory and not the real present. A true time-image is a combination of present and past, present and future, or past, present and future. I have to have some awareness that I am remembering at the same time as I am remembering; I have to be conscious of my situation in the present to intentionally direct myself towards an image of the past or future. If I am not rooted in the present, I cease to remember the past and start to re-live it instead.

A simple model of the time-image is offered by Augustine:

> From what we have said it is abundantly clear that neither the future nor the past exist, and therefore it is not strictly correct to say that there are three times, past, present, and future. It might be correct to say that there are three times, a present of past things, a present of present things, and a present of future things. Some such different times do exist in the mind, but nowhere else that I can see. The present of past things is the memory; the present of present things is direct perception; and the present of future things is expectation. If we may speak in these terms, I can see three times and I admit that they do exist.[14]

The three parts of the Augustinian time-image are the present of the past, the present of the present and the present of the future. All three are collected together within us at any point in time, and their content provides us with a definite location in time. For example, I can remember Monday yesterday, I am in Tuesday today and I expect that Wednesday will come tomorrow. The movement of an event from the present of the future to the present of the present to the present of the past gives us a sense of the passing of time. Two days ago I expected Monday to come tomorrow; yesterday Monday was today; today I remember that Monday was yesterday – Monday moves from the present of the future to the present of the present, and then to the present of the past. Augustine illustrates this using the example of a psalm, which moves from the present future (expectation) through the present present to the present past (memory):

> Suppose that I am going to recite a psalm that I know. Before I begin, my faculty of expectation is engaged by the whole of it. But once I have begun, as much of the psalm as I have removed from the province of expectation and relegated to the past now engages my memory, and the scope of the action which I am performing is divided between the two faculties of memory and expectation, the one looking back to the part which I have already recited, the other looking forward to the part which I have still to recite. But my faculty of attention is present all the while, and through it passes what was the future in the process of becoming the past. As the process continues, the province of memory is extended in proportion as that of expectation is reduced, until the whole of my expectation is absorbed. This happens when I have finished my recitation and it has passed into the province of memory.
>
> What is true of the whole psalm is also true of the parts and of each syllable. It is true of any longer action in which I may be engaged and of which the recitation of the psalm may only be a small part. It is true of a man's whole life, of which all his actions are parts. It is true of the whole history of mankind, of which each man's life is a part.[15]

When this is interpreted within the cinematic model of time, we can see that successive reality-frames of Augustine reciting his psalm contain different distributions of the psalm between memory and expectation. When he has recited a quarter of it, there is a quarter present in his mind as memory, three quarters present as expectation, and a tiny fragment in direct perception. When he has recited three quarters of it, three quarters are present in his mind

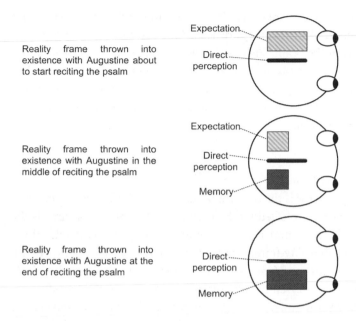

Reality frame thrown into existence with Augustine about to start reciting the psalm

Reality frame thrown into existence with Augustine in the middle of reciting the psalm

Reality frame thrown into existence with Augustine at the end of reciting the psalm

Figure 3. Successive reality-frames containing Augustine reciting a psalm

as memory, a quarter present as expectation, and a tiny fragment in direct perception. The psalm changes location or categorization within Augustine's mind as he recites it and before or after his recital there is no direct perception of it. This is illustrated in Figure 3.

These different distributions of the psalm between expectation, perception and memory are different time-images in Augustine's head, which are fixed within each reality-frame. Changes in this time-image come about because successive reality-frames containing Augustine are thrown into existence with slightly different time-images. The time-image itself is atemporal; an immobile 'texture' within the reality-frame.[16]

The location of past time-images within the brain is well documented. Both implicit and explicit memories are correlated with activation in the basal ganglia, hippocampus, amygdale, entorhinal cortex, parahippocampal cortex and the perirhinal cortex.[17] These areas may be the location of the time-images, but it is more likely that they are needed to activate time-images in other areas of the brain, such as the visual cortex. What is clear is that when these areas are damaged, the time-images are damaged as well. For example, after a brain infection, patient Boswell's present of the past became extremely limited. When he recites a psalm he is unable to describe even the main points of the text that he has just read.[18]

Movement-Images

The projector is the only thing that moves in an ordinary cinema. In a world projected by the realtime reality projector, time is the only 'mover' and the static reality-frames remain immobile. Although reality-frames succeed one another, we do not experience this succession: God is the only spectator who could *directly* experience movement in a realtime reality projected world.

And yet we inhabit a world of perpetual oscillation and change in which objects shift, stream and swirl around us. Within this projected world we cannot deny our *experience* of movement, and yet we never directly experience objects moving. Although we are thrown into existence with the belief that an object has been at a previous location, and with the expectation that it will be at a different location at a later point in time, this is not by itself enough to account for our experience of movement. There must also be a movement-image within the reality-frame; an *instantaneous* grasp of the movement of an object. This movement-image is a direct experience of movement; an immobile image of movement that does not depend on time, although changes in it can be brought about by time.

Something that is almost a movement-image in our everyday experience is a blurred photograph of a moving object. In the blurredness of the object I can almost see movement in the immobile picture. Within the brain our phenomenal movement images are correlated with activation in the middle temporal lobe (V5) and the medial superior temporal area, which contain cells that respond to movement in the visual field. When the static reality-frame contains firing neurons in these areas, movement-images are present. When these areas are damaged, there are no movement-images in the reality-frame. For example, a patient studied by Josef Zihl et al. completely lost her ability to perceive motion after a bilateral lesion in the lateral temporo-occipital cortex: 'She had difficulty, for example, in pouring tea or coffee into a cup because the fluid appeared to be frozen, like a glacier. In addition, she could not stop pouring at the right time since she was unable to perceive the movement in the cup (or a pot) when the fluid rose. Furthermore the patient complained of difficulties in following a dialogue because she could not see the movements of the face and, especially, the mouth of the speaker.'[19]

The Projection Mechanism

An ordinary projector *moves* when it exchanges the frames. This movement takes place *in time*; movement is a displacement of space over time. If we are trying to analyze time, we cannot describe it as a *moving* realtime reality projector, because this uses an unacknowledged time to explain time. A *moving* realtime reality projector could be projected by a second realtime reality projector, which in turn could be projected by a third realtime reality projector, which in turn ... We can imagine God sitting beyond the universe in His projector room in the sky throwing us all continuously into existence, but we can also imagine *GOD* sitting beyond a universe that includes both God and us, throwing both God and us continuously into existence.

Time itself cannot *move*; it is the condition of possibility of all movement. Time cannot *exchange* frames; it is the condition of possibility of all exchange. Time cannot *throw* us into existence; throwing *takes* time and so time can only throw us if it is situated within a second more primordial time.

Two interpretations of the realtime reality projector circumvent this infinite regress. The first thinks of time as a *thing*, a fourth dimension of space that is no different from the other dimensions. This interpretation avoids infinite regress because four-dimensional spacetime is completely immobile and so there is no need for a moving mechanism to exchange the frames. The second interpretation thinks of time as the active processing of the world: the exchang*ing* of the frames, and not a physical thing that causes this exchange to take place. This avoids infinite regress because there is no thing behind the exchange that carries it out; no thing that could be projected by a more primordial temporality. In this second interpretation there is only the embodied exchange itself, which is inseparable from the frames that are being exchanged.

Four-Dimensional Spacetime

And time is not nor will be another thing alongside Being, since this was bound fast by fate to be entire and changeless. Therefore all those things will be a name, which mortals, confident that they are real, suppose to be coming to be and perishing, to be and not to be, and to change their place and alter their bright aspect to dark and from dark to bright.

(Parmenides, *Eighth Fragment*)[20]

We see that by time are designated the characteristics of a space relatively higher than a given space – i.e., the characteristics of the perceptions of a consciousness relatively higher than a given consciousness.

For the one-dimensional being all the indices of two-, three-, four-dimensional space and beyond, lie in time – all this is time. For the two-dimensional being time embraces within itself the indices of three-dimensional space, four-dimensional space, and all spaces beyond. For man, i.e., the three-dimensional being, time contains the indices of four-dimensional space and all spaces beyond.

Therefore, according to the degree of expansion and elevation of the consciousness and the forms of its receptivity the indices of space are augmented and the indices of time are diminished.

In other words, the growth of the space-sense is proceeding at the expense of the time-sense. Or one may say that the time-sense is an imperfect space-sense (i.e., an imperfect power of representation which, being perfected, translates itself into the space-sense, i.e., into the power of representation in forms).

If, taking as a foundation the principles elucidated here, we attempt to represent to ourselves the universe very abstractedly, it is clear that this will be quite other than the universe which we are accustomed to imagine to ourselves. *Everything* will exist in it *always*.

This will be the universe of the *Eternal Now* of Hindu philosophy – a universe in which will be neither *before* nor *after*, in which will be just one present, *known or unknown*.

(Peter Ouspensky, *Tertium Organum*)[21]

One solution to the infinite regress of moving realtime reality projectors is to discard the projection mechanism. Time is not a projector that *throws* frames into existence; instead, all of the three-dimensional frames exist 'simultaneously' together, stacked up along the fourth dimension so we cannot see them. In this interpretation of the realtime reality projector, time becomes space and the universe freezes into an eternal, immobile, four-dimensional hypersolid. To make it easier to understand how time could be the fourth dimension of our three-dimensional world, I will start by looking at how time could be the third dimension of a two-dimensional world.

Although we generally interpret the images in an ordinary cinema three-dimensionally, what actually appears to us is a two-dimensional reality. On the screen two-dimensional colour fields collide and interact, and this moving image is a magnification of the effectively two-dimensional world within the celluloid frame. In more conventional interpretations of time, the present exists in a state of becoming, past states no longer exist and the future will exist. However, if time is a dimension of space, then the past and the future must co-exist together. In the case of the two-dimensional cinematic frame, the past and future of the film exist as two-dimensional frames rolled up above and below the light. *We* can

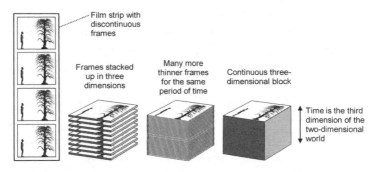

Figure 4. Stacking up of two-dimensional frames into a third temporal dimension

see the past and future of this celluloid world because our world has more dimensions than it, but a two-dimensional person, whose perception was restricted to their two-dimensional world, would be unable to perceive their past and future. Since they could not perceive their past and future they might describe time as the becoming of the present, just as we do in our three-dimensional world.

If the past and future frames are to be a genuine third dimension of this two-dimensional celluloid world, there needs to be continuity between them. The present hand of a two-dimensional person must exist on a continuum with her hand five minutes ago: it cannot be broken up into a series of spatially separate two-dimensional frames.[22] The only way to achieve this is to *stack* the frames one on top of another, to make each frame infinitely thin, and then to make the number of frames infinite. In this way a three-dimensional continuum can be created from a series of two-dimensional frames, and time can become the third dimension of a two-dimensional world (see Figure 4).

On the basis of this explanation about how time could be the third dimension of a two-dimensional world, it is relatively easy to see how it could be the fourth dimension of our three-dimensional world. In this interpretation of the realtime reality projector, the reality-frames are not thrown sequentially into existence, but stacked on top of each other along the fourth dimension.[23] Our future already exists as the three-dimensional reality-frames 'above' us. Our past persists as the three-dimensional reality-frames 'below' us. Because our perception is limited to three dimensions, we cannot see our past or future, and this is also the reason why we see changes *in* the objects around us. In reality objects do not change at all: they just appear to change because we only see part of them at any point in time. The rest of the object exists outside of our field of vision, with the changes spread along its four-dimensional length. An apple starts off hard, green and sour, it sweetens as it ripens, and eventually it turns dark brown mottled with mould. Normally we would say that the *same* apple ripens and rots; that changes take place *in* the three-dimensional apple. From the perspective of four-dimensional spacetime, there are no changes *in* the apple. What we interpret as changes in the three-dimensional apple are, in fact, different perspectives on an unchanging four-dimensional apple. In itself, the apple is a four-dimensional hypercylinder with a rotten 'top' and an unripe 'bottom' and at each instant of time we only see a section through this hypercylinder.

If time is a spatial dimension, one might think that it should be possible to rotate objects in and out of time. For example, a one-dimensional line that changes colour over time is actually a striped two-dimensional surface. If we could rotate this surface by ninety degrees about its centre, then, instead of a uniformly coloured line that changes over time, we would see a striped line that does not change. A cube that changes colour over time could also be rotated, although this is impossible to visualize using our three-dimensional imagination. Unfortunately, we cannot test the four-dimensional theory by attempting such a rotation, because our three-dimensional bodies cannot apply the force perpendicular to three dimensions that would be needed to rotate the hypercube. Two-dimensional beings can only apply forces in two dimensions and so they cannot lift a rod into three dimensions from within their plane. Within our three-dimensional world a force along the fourth dimension would be needed to rotate a cube in four dimensions.[24]

I quoted Ouspensky at the beginning of this section because he has a particularly clear vision about what four-dimensional spacetime might actually be like. A crucial part of his theory is the absence of any movement along the fourth dimension. We cannot move along the fourth dimension of time because movement can only take place within time; it would only be possible to move along the fourth dimension if we did so within a second, tacitly presupposed time:

> … in those theories which have attempted to combine the idea of time with the idea of the fourth dimension appeared always the idea of some spatial element as existing in time, and along with it was admitted *motion upon that space*. Those who were constructing these theories evidently did not understand that leaving out the possibility of motion they were advancing the demand for a *new* time, because motion cannot proceed out of time. And as a result time goes ahead of us, like our shadow, receding according as we approach it. All our perceptions of motion have become confused. If we imagine the new dimension of space and *the possibility* of motion upon this new dimension, time will still elude us, and declare that it is unexplained, exactly as it was unexplained before.
>
> It is necessary to admit that by one term, *time*, we designate really two ideas – 'a certain space' and 'motion upon that space.' This motion does not exist in reality, and it seems to us as existing only because *we do not see* the spatiality of time. That is, the sensation of motion in time (and motion out of time does not exist) arises in us because we are looking at the world as if through a narrow slit, and are seeing the *lines of intersection* of the time-plane with our three-dimensional space only.[25]

In four-dimensional spacetime all changes in three-dimensional objects have become four-dimensional shapes and so there is no movement anywhere. However, if this elimination of movement is to be successful, it has to explain how the *illusion* of movement could come about. Ouspensky unsuccessfully tries to show that the third dimension of solids is perceived by animals as motion, but his analysis either falls into the trap of having the animals move in relation to the solids, or it makes the unconvincing assertion that the sides of a cube seen from an angle appear to move away from the observer. Later on, Ouspensky goes back on his claim that there is no movement anywhere, and talks about the *shifting* of the light of consciousness from one I to another:

> Motion goes on inside of us, and it creates the illusion of motion round about us. The lighted circle runs quickly from one I to another – from one object, from one idea, from one perception or image to another: within the focus of consciousness rapidly changing I's succeed one another, a little of the light of consciousness going over from one I to another. This is the true motion which alone exists in the world. Should this motion stop, should all I's simultaneously enter the focus of receptivity, should the light so expand as to illumine all at once that which is usually lighted bit by bit and gradually, and could a man grasp simultaneously by his reason all that ever entered or will enter his receptivity and all that which is never clearly illumined by thought (producing its action on the psyche nevertheless) – then would a man behold himself in the midst of an *immobile universe*, in which there would exist simultaneously everything that lies usually in the remote depths of memory, in the past; all that lies at a remote distance from him; all that lies in the future.[26]

Such movements presumably take time, which creates problems for Ouspensky's theory of an immobile universe. Furthermore, even if we could eliminate this movement by *expanding* our perception, this expansion would be a movement within time, and our earlier experience of *shifting* from one I to another would remain unexplained.

A better way to understand the illusion of movement and change in a four-dimensional universe is through the analysis of the time-image and movement-image that I presented earlier in this chapter. If time is a string of static nows, we never experience time or movement directly and only experience an atemporal *image* of them in the present. It makes no difference to our experience of time or movement if we are projected by a moving realtime reality projector or if our frames are stacked up four-dimensionally. Each immobile frame contains both movement- and time-images and so the people within each frozen reality-frame experience both movement and time. They do not experience the four-dimensional universe as a whole because each fragment of their lives exists within a different three-dimensional reality-frame. Four-dimensional spacetime is a 'succession' of such people thrown into existence, or rather an enormous burst of existence in which all of these 'successive' people are 'thrown' 'into' existence 'simultaneously'.

If time is the fourth dimension of space, then all of its parts co-exist 'at the same time'. There is not one now that moves along the fourth dimension of time, nor is there a succession of nows. Every event in time and space is existing now in just the same way that everything in the three-dimensional space around me is existing now. I am finishing this chapter, starting this chapter, and writing this sentence 'simultaneously'. All of the events from the beginning to the end of the universe are taking place now. The big bang is exploding out of the void now the last atom is slowing to a halt now I am being torn from my mother's womb now my last gasp is rasping through my lips now.[27]

The problem with describing all events as 'simultaneous' within four-dimensional spacetime is that it can lead people to imagine the four-dimensional universe as some kind of enormous block floating before their eyes. This suggests that the four-dimensional hyper-block *endures* in the same way that three-dimensional objects endure in time, but if time is the fourth dimension of space, then the whole assemblage of time and space cannot endure or last for any length of time because the endurance of things has been reduced to their extension along the fourth dimension. The four-dimensional hyperblock that the universe is could endure for five minutes or for five thousand years without affecting any of the objects inside it. Even if the hyperblock just flashed in and out of existence for an instant, the objects within it would still endure for exactly the same period. Any endurance of the hyperblock itself would have to be explained as a fifth dimension, which, in turn, could only endure in a sixth, and so on. Ouspensky takes this route, and speaks about a fifth dimension, a line of eternity '*perpendicular to time*' through which each moment within time becomes eternal.[28] If it is conceived spatially or temporally, then this eternity leads to an infinite regress, but the fifth dimension of eternity could be more generously interpreted as an attempt to say that temporal words like 'duration' are simply not applicable to the four-dimensional universe as a whole. The four-dimensional universe does not endure for a long or short time, for five minutes or five thousand years. Its 'eternity' signifies that it has no relationship to time.[29]

This interpretation of the realtime reality projector eliminates the projector altogether by pushing the idea that time is a *thing* to its logical conclusion.

If time is a thing, then nothing can move in relation to this thing unless it does so within a second temporality. If time is a thing, it must be an immobile thing.

If time is a thing, it can only endure within a second temporality. If time is a thing, it must be a thing that does not endure.

The thing that time is cannot move, change or endure. This thing is an eternal thing: it is not the kind of thing that we encounter in our day to day experience. All of the things that we encounter within time endure, change, and move relative to other things. The time-thing is not a thing of this kind. As Ouspensky says, it may only be possible to hint about this 'thing'; to speak about it using distorting metaphors taken from our everyday experience:

Anything that can be said about the understanding of temporal relations is inevitably extremely vague. This is because our language is absolutely inadequate to the *spatial expression of temporal relations*. We lack the necessary words for it, we have no verbal forms, strictly speaking, for the expression of these relations which are new to us, and some other quite new forms – *non-verbal* – are indispensable. The language for the transmission of the new temporal relations must be a language without verbs. *New parts of speech* are necessary, an infinite number of new words. At present, in our human language we can speak about time by hints only. Its true essence is *inexpressible* for us.[30]

The Reality-Frame Flux

Everything, it is said, *comes to be* and *passes away* in time. If abstraction is made from *everything*, namely from what fills time, and also from what fills space, then what we have left over is empty time and empty space: in other words, these abstractions of externality are posited and represented as if they were for themselves. But it is not *in* time that everything comes to be and passes away, rather time itself is the *becoming*, this coming-to-be and passing away, the *actually existent abstraction, Chronos,* from whom everything is born and by whom its offspring is destroyed.

(Georg Hegel, *Philosophy of Nature*)[31]

A second interpretation of the realtime reality projector is that time is the exchang*ing* of the frames, the *throwing* itself, and not something 'behind' the throwing that carries it out. We live in a world in which reality-frames are exchanged, a world that *change*s. We cannot explain this exchange by a mechanism (God) that (Who) mysteriously *moves* to exchange the frames because this leads to an infinite regress of realtime reality projectors. Something has to be taken as a fundamental datum; there has to be a point at which explanation stops. The exchange of frames is such a point. Frames simply *are* exchanged in our reality, and our name for this flux of frames is 'time'. Time is the *becoming* of the now, the fabrication-of-a-new-now-and-displacement-of-the-old-now-into-the-past; the running off of the present frame into non-existence and the eruption of a new frame to fill its place. For the realtime reality projector to be a plausible theory of our experience, this exchange of frames has to be continuous, not discontinuous as it is in the ordinary cinema. The content of these frames could have been determined at the beginning of the universe, or it could be spontaneously created from moment to moment. In the latter case, the world as a whole ceases to be deterministic, but time becomes the only free 'agent' within it.[32]

This projection mechanism could work by throwing a continuous succession of physically distinct three-dimensional frames into existence. This would be similar to the four-dimensional interpretation of the realtime reality projector except that only the present frame would exist at any point in time. Alternatively, the projection mechanism could 'move' the same three dimensional objects into different positions over time. In this case it would be the *arrangements* of things that pass into non-existence, not the actual physical objects themselves. These two projection mechanisms would both produce the same set of objective displacements in objects over time and so it would be impossible to empirically determine which one is actually in operation.

A river flows *in time*. A flux fluxes *in time*. A projector projects *in time*. The difficulty with this interpretation of the realtime reality projector is that it appears to require movement to bring about the exchange of frames, which would make it dependent upon a more primordial temporality. How can there be flux or becoming without a more primordial time for this flux or becoming to take place in? How are we to say that the exchange of frames *is itself* time, when everything that we have described as an exchange up to now has taken place *in* time? To avoid this infinite regress of time processes taking place within more primordial times, we will continue to say that the exchang*ing* of the reality-frames *is* time, but we will add the further condition that this time does not take place in time. This leaves us with the consequence that the reality-frame flux cannot be said to flux at any particular *rate*. Reality-frames cannot be exchanged faster or slower because these relative measures can only be evaluated *within* time. This point is made by Husserl in his discussion of the primordial flux:

... we find necessarily and essentially a flux of continuous 'alteration,' and this alteration has the absurd property ... that it flows exactly as it flows and can flow neither 'more swiftly' nor 'more slowly.' Consequently, any Object which is altered is lacking here, and inasmuch as in every process 'something' proceeds, it is not a question here of a process.[33]

A second consequence of this interpretation of the projection mechanism is that the reality-frame flux cannot *endure* for any period of time. If I am shearing a sheep, the movement of the shears over the sheep takes a certain amount of time, but if time is the exchanging of the frames, then this exchanging cannot endure for a stretch of time without a second time for it to endure in. From within time, we can say that a process has lasted for five minutes or five thousand years, but time itself does not last for any time at all. The persistence of objects is constituted *within* the flux and so the flux itself does not persist. As Husserl puts it:

There is no duration in the primordial flux. For duration is the form of an enduring something, an enduring being, something identical in the temporal series which last functions as its duration. With occurrences such as a storm, the motion of a meteorite, etc., it is a question of uniform nexuses of alteration of enduring Objects. Objective ... time is a form of 'persistent' objects, their alterations, and other processes concerned with them. 'Process' is, therefore, a concept which presupposes persistence. Persistence, however, is a unity which is constituted in the flux, and it pertains to the essence of flux that there can be nothing persistent in it.[34]

This interpretation of the realtime reality projector eliminates the projector altogether by pushing the idea that time is a *process* to its logical conclusion.

If time is a process, it is a process that cannot process at any particular rate.

If time is a process, it is a process that cannot last for any period of time. Time has not 'existed' for any length of time; the exchanging of reality-frames does not endure.

If time is a process, it is an eternal process that does not come to be or pass away. It is the eternal processing of the world that makes all world processes possible.

If time is a process, it is an eternal process, and not the kind of process that we encounter in our everyday experience. Our ordinary processes take place within time, they endure for a certain period and process at a certain rate. The eternal reality flux lacks all of these features. This process processes; this exchanging exchanges; this absolute flux fluxes; this temporality temporalizes. According to Husserl:

> It is evident then, that temporally constitutive phenomena are, in principle, objectivities other than those constituted in time. They are not individual Objects, in other words, not individual processes, and terms which can be predicated of such processes cannot be meaningfully ascribed to them. Therefore, it can also make no sense to say of them (and with the same conceptual meaning) that they are in the now and have been previously, that they succeed one another temporally or are simultaneous with respect to one another, etc. To be sure, one can and must say that a certain continuity of appearance, namely, one which is a phase of the temporally constitutive flux, belongs to a now, namely, to that which it constitutes, and belongs to a before, namely, as that which is (one cannot say was) constitutive of the before. But is not the flux a succession? Does it not, therefore, have a now, an actual phase, and a continuity of pasts of which we are conscious in retentions? We can only say that this flux is something which we name in conformity with what is constituted, but it is nothing temporally 'Objective.' It is absolute subjectivity and has the absolute properties of something to be denoted metaphorically as 'flux,' as a point of actuality, primal source point, that from which springs the 'now' and so on. In the lived experience of actuality, we have the primal source-point and a continuity of moments of reverberation.... . For all this, names are lacking.[35]

Both the spacetime and reality flux interpretations of the projection mechanism reduce the realtime reality projector to things and processes that we ordinarily encounter *within* time. It may prove impossible to explain time on the basis of the things and processes that we encounter within time, or even to talk about it metaphorically using these fundamentally intratemporal ideas. On the other hand, something along the lines of one of these mechanisms may be correct and is needed if we are to continue with our ordinary theories and intuitions about time. The problem then becomes how human beings can describe time within time using language. This will be the topic of the final part of this chapter after I have covered a number of other issues surrounding the realtime reality projector.

Clarifications and Objections

Thrownness

> As being, Dasein is something that has been thrown; it has been brought into its 'there', but *not* of its own accord ... Thrownness, however, does not lie behind it as some event which has happened to Dasein, which has factually befallen and fallen loose from Dasein again; on the contrary, as long as Dasein is, *Dasein*, as care, *is* constantly its 'that-it-is'.
>
> (Martin Heidegger, *Being and Time*)[36]

ot plan our existence. We just ... *came about*. 'Suddenly' we were here: thinking, looking at things, walking around. Something greater than ourselves set us down, put us here, threw us 'into' the reality that we experience at each instant. We did not choose to be: we *became*. It is possible, as Russell suggests, that this miraculous appearance of experience took place just five minutes ago:

> Now, apart from arguments as to the proved fallibility of memory, there is one awkward consideration which the sceptic may urge. Remembering, which occurs now, cannot possibly – he may say – prove

that what is remembered occurred at some other time, because the world might have sprung into being five minutes ago, exactly as it then was, full of acts of remembering which were entirely misleading. Opponents of Darwin, such as Edmund Gosse's father, urged a very similar argument against evolution. The world, they said, was created in 4004 BC, complete with fossils, which were inserted to try our faith. The world was created suddenly, but was made such as it would have been if it had evolved. There is no logical impossibility about this view. And similarly there is no logical impossibility in the view that the world was created five minutes ago, complete with memories and records. This may seem an improbable hypothesis, but it is not logically refutable.[37]

What if I had come into existence five minutes ago? Would I, *could* I notice if I had? If I did come into existence five minutes ago, I came into existence with memories stretching back thirty-three years, and with the belief that I had been existing for longer than five minutes. This possibility can be waved aside by pragmatism, by the fact that my philosophizing can only take place within a framework of 'common sense',[38] but it remains consistent with the structure of my experience. If I came into existence five minutes ago, I would feel everything that I am feeling now, think everything that I am thinking now – the only difference would be the falsity of my belief that I have persisted on earth for thirty-three years, which would become a by-product of the memories that came into existence with me five minutes ago; something that itself came into existence five minutes ago. But this figure of five minutes is entirely arbitrary: I could have been thrown into existence two minutes ago, one minute ago, thirty seconds ago. In fact, I could have come into existence in the middle of this sentence. There could have been an eternal empty void and then, suddenly, the world, my body, my memories, this chapter up to the letter 'e' in the middle of the last sentence, could have suddenly come to be. Possibly this is indeed what happened; nothing that I have observed since believing myself to have written that letter 'e' has either confirmed or contradicted this hypothesis.

Death is the impossibility of all possibilities. It comes to a person from outside. I see a person and later I see a corpse. Something happens to a person that leaves their body apparently intact, but steals away their actions, their life, their soul. I believe that this will happen to me some day, but I cannot imaginatively grasp it. I will not be able to observe my own death because if I could do this I would not be dead. If I die slowly I can prepare myself for death. As my body pumps its last dark juice into the dust I can ponder my imminent demise – 'I will not exist for the next fifty years, I will not even exist tomorrow' – and cease to worry about seizing power or getting my next meal. An instant death is very different. If I die without expecting to die, I am simply wiped out with my protentive horizons unmodified. As I stand around, unaware of the impending nuclear attack, I might think to myself: 'I am going to live for the ne' and then be vaporized before I could complete the rest of the sentence. In the fraction of a second that it would take for my molecules to disperse, I would not have time to modify my sentence to: 'Oh no! I'm being wiped out this instant!' – I would die with my expectations of a long and prosperous life intact. All of my protentions would remain directed at my projected future, and then they would simply cease: extinguished along with the rest of my body and mind.

These observations suggest that if I came into existence for five minutes, and then was wiped out, I could believe for the whole of those five minutes that I had existed for thirty-three years and was going to exist for another fifty. The same would be true if I came into existence for five seconds, and the situation would be no different if I momentarily flashed into existence and was immediately erased. We exist as thrown and are thrown into existence with a past and future that are independent of what is actually behind or before us. Although our focus of attention is rarely 'on' the present we are always 'in' the present, surfing on an ephemeral now between the abysses of past an

Fixed and Mobile Moments

> ... time always flows and progresses by leaps, and each leap is a whole together and indivisible into parts at the level of progress by intervals. ... these temporal leaps are temporal measures marked off by demiurgic sections and in this way at least indivisible into parts. Each is a whole together, and must be said to display the halting (epischesis) of time in its advance, and to be called a 'now' not in the sense of a boundary of time, but in the sense of a time which is demiurgically indivisible into parts, even if it is divisible in our thought, and that infinitely.
>
> (Damascius, Commentary on Parmenides)[39]

When we watch a film, our experience of the image is formed from a succession of fixed frames, each of which is held for a $1/48^{th}$ of a second. We do not notice the fixity of these images, but perceive them as continuously moving. This creation of continuous film time from a succession of immobile instants depends on our underlying realtime, without which we would not experience any time in the cinema. If the audience was 'paused' along with the frames, they would only see the black interval in between frames, and almost nothing of the film at all.

If we do not experience time in which we are 'paused', then the experience of *existing* a reality projector that worked in this way would be nothing like our lived continuous experience – it would not even be like watching a film in which we were paused whilst the frames are stationary because we would not experience the black intervals between frames. This creates a problem for the realtime reality projector because if it is to be at all plausible as a theory of our experience, it cannot work by prolonging an instant into a duration. An instant cannot be *extended* into a duration because we cannot perceive such an extension – our experience of an unextended instant and our experience of an instant that has been extended into a duration are identical. Nothing moves in an instant – movement takes time – and so there is no experiential difference between an immobile reality-frame held in existence for an indefinite period and an instant cut out of our moving experience.

The only way in which the realtime reality projector can project a succession of reality-frames without pausing them is by *continuously* connecting the nows together. In the four-dimensional interpretation this is not a problem since the block of spacetime is a continuum along the fourth dimension. Within the reality-frame flux interpretation, the projection mechanism will have to operate by continuously throwing reality-frames into existence and destroying them. At any point in time, only one reality-frame exists, which is destroyed as soon as it is created, and then a new one is thrown into existence. Another way of putting this is to say that in both interpretations the *description* of time as a succession of instants is an abstraction from the temporal continuum in the same way that the description of a line as an infinite number of points is an abstraction from the spatial continuum.[40]

The Empty Vessel

The starting-point for the time-reckoning is therefore afforded by the concrete phenomena of the heavens and of surrounding natural objects, and the succession of these, fixed as it is by experience, serves as a guide in the chronological sequence.

(Martin Nilsson, *Primitive Time Reckoning*)[41]

Time has not always been a realtime reality projector in the minds of men. It started out as the observation of periodic phenomena in the heavens. I look up into the sky and observe that the sun is directly overhead. This is the cue for me to undress and slide softly into bed with my wife. Once the sun has moved to a point halfway towards the earth, I kiss her gently and resume my rustic labours. The change in the sun's location is used to measure the duration of our lovemaking. The sex takes place *within* a certain time.

Modern time has gradually closed in on us. No longer a series of periodic points enclosing our actions, it has become a continuous flow saturating every moment of our lives. The precise quantification of time brought about through the watch and atomic clock means that there is no longer any 'space' within time for activities to take place in – just a single flow of activities and time together.

This has had a largely unacknowledged affect on our ideas about movement, which we still tend to think of as taking place *in* time. Although I might say that I swam the Thames in five minutes, modern time reckoning has made this 'primitive' notion of movement within time redundant. Movement is a displacement of space over time and whilst we can record the time that a movement takes, this does not make movement independent of time or something that could be contained within it. Modern movement is a *composite* of space and time. There can be movement within *a* space and movement within *a* time, but no movement within space in general or time in general.

The residual belief that time is an empty vessel creates a tension within the ordinary conception of time. On the one hand we believe in the cinematic notion of a river of time. On the other hand we retain a latent belief in continuous three-dimensional objects that move *within* time, which is no different from the primitive observation of periodic phenomena. For both interpretations of the projection mechanism there is displacement of space over time, but no movement *within* time. The objective flow of space and time together makes movement *within* a measured time period possible.

Simultaneity

A black buzzing fly hurls itself upon the walls of its crystal prison. A dust-stuffed chair tries to shelter me from the sun-scorched world. I vacantly stare at the flowing television tapestry bleached by the beam of light pouring in through the grimy window. Australian television signals sent over by satellite. My naked body is relaxed and oppressed by the heat and light burning over its surface. Too drugged by the heat to move, to think, I stare blankly at the shifting screen.

The fly stops. Starts to crawl. Moves rapidly over the surface. Stops. Tastes. Moves rapidly over the surface. The light slackens its grip on my torpid body and a movement stirs within it. A cloud? I squint a glance back along the burning beam. A shadow is crossing the sun, plugging the heat to leave a fiery halo and a canopy of stars. Darkness. Cold washes over my weak sweating body. Live pictures from the eclipse over Mosul spin out an empty late-night news slot. The fly tentatively buzzes, settles, buzzes, settles.

The shadow creeps on. The sun bursts back and reaffirms its hold on my shivering body. The news moves on: a lost child in Sydney, a man beaten to death, a new factory in Melbourne.

During the eclipse I saw the stars, residual light from the sun, the television pictures sent from Mosul to Australia and from Australia back to Mosul and the room around me. I heard the buzzing of the fly and commentary from the television. All of these were taking place at the same time for me, all of them were taking place *now.*

Although, for me, all of these events were simultaneous, seen from a more objective perspective they all took place at different times. The light from the eclipsed sun radiated from it eight minutes earlier (if the sun exploded, it would take me eight minutes to find out). The light from the stars took thousands of years to reach me – the stars that I see before me now are the stars as they were thousands of years ago. The television pictures showed the eclipse as it looked 0.1 seconds earlier. I heard the buzz that was released from the fly 0.03 seconds ago. From a different perspective all of these events would have taken place at radically different times. If I stood on the sun to observe the moon's shadow on Earth, I would see an event taking place that *took place* eight minutes ago on Earth. If I sat on Theta Orionis 'at the same time' as the eclipse was taking place on Earth, the eclipse would become an event 1500 years in the future. We see the past of distant events and the events that we see around us lie in the future for distant observers.

The assemblage of events that constitutes our now is relative to the speed of the signals that inform us about events and the position from which we observe them. If there is a single objective now, we can only calculate its content retrospectively. We cannot directly observe this now because everything that we observe has already

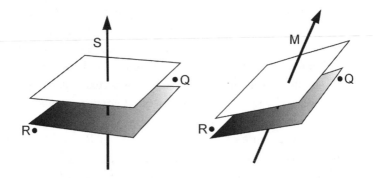

Figure 5. Different observers have different sets of simultaneous events[42]

taken place – even the pain that has just started in my head is a few microseconds old.

The set of events within each now also depends on the speed at which the observer is travelling, and so events that take place in one order for one observer can take place in a different order for a different observer. This is illustrated in Figure 5, taken from Penrose's *The Emperor's New Mind*. The planes in Figure 5 represent points in time at which events are simultaneous for the observers S and M. According to S, event R takes place before event Q. However, the moving observer M, on the right hand side of Figure 5, has different sets of simultaneous events and observes that event R takes place *after* event Q. In this case there is not a unique concept of simultaneity that includes both observers. As Penrose puts it:

> Consider the two events R and Q ... According to S, the earlier event R takes place before the event Q because R lies on an earlier simultaneous space than Q; but according to M, it is the other way around, Q lying on an earlier simultaneous space than R. Thus, to one observer, the event R takes place before Q, but for the other, it is Q that takes place before R! (This can only happen because R and Q are what are called *spatially separated*, which means that each lies outside of the other's light cone, so that no material particle or photon can travel from one event to the other.)[43]

There is indeterminacy in the order of the events R and Q because there is a spatial interval between them[44] and so a light signal from R cannot reach Q before Q takes place. When there is a spatial interval different observers can see a different order between events. However, causal chains at R and Q can be connected by light signals, and so there is a temporal interval between them that is not affected by the movement of S and M. In this example, both S and M would see the same sequence of events taking place at R, and the same sequence of events taking place at Q. Their only point of disagreement would be over which events in the causal chain at R were before, and which were after, the events in the causal chain at Q.

Within the realtime reality projector the now is a *single* simultaneous explosion of existence. But relativity seems to have superseded this Newtonian myth of an absolute uniform time. A plurality of nows relative to observers has replaced the single now and a multiplicity of orderings of events has replaced the single sequence. If it is indeterminate whether one spatially separated event is before or after another, how can there be a single reality-frame with a determinate content? How can the *retro* reality projector survive this relativistic criticism?

The solution to this difficulty is that although events may have an indeterminate order when they are observed by spatially separated people, there may still be a single objective order of events, which could be used to explain 'contradictory' observations on the basis of signals arising from a single absolute stream. Penrose takes this line, and says about S and M: 'The motion is here thought of as *passive*, that is it only affects the different *descriptions* that the two observers S and M would make of one and the same space-time.'[45] This suggests that although our individual perspectives on reality are limited – *my* now is a greasy lake and a chemical plant; *your* now is a dozen mackerel and a violin – these fragments are all part of a single now that is thrown into existence by the realtime reality projector. From an entirely objective perspective events with a spacelike interval can be reduced to a single sequence.

The Failure of Time Theories

The Speech of Time

> For all things subsist in Him by Whom they were created, nor do the
> things that live owe their life to themselves, nor are those that are
> moved, but do not live, by their own caprice brought to motion. But He
> moveth all things, Who quickens some with life, whilst some that are
> not so quickened He preserves, disposing them in a wonderful way for
> last and lowest being. For all things were made out of nothing, and their
> being would again go on into nothing, except the Author of all things
> hold it by the hand of governance. All the things then that have been
> created, by themselves can neither subsist nor be moved, but they only
> so far subsist, as they have obtained that they should be, are only so far
> moved, as they are influenced by a secret impulse.
>
> (Gregory the Great, *Morals on the Book of Job*)[46]

This chapter has presented a cinematic interpretation of the
objective theory of time. Although I have outlined a couple of ways
in which time might project the now, the exact mechanism is not
that important – the crucial thing is the distinction between a
fixed *immobile* present, which contains everything that we are, and
the 'process' by which this present is moved into the past and a new
present brought into existence.

We believe that we are human beings who *endure* through time.
We believe that we are the *authors* of a language that we speak *in*
time. We believe that we form words, spurt them through our lips
and persist whilst we do this. However, the situation is very
different if time is a realtime reality projector. Language has to be
created and spoken over time, but if time is a realtime reality
projector, then our existence is fundamentally atemporal (which is
why the interpretation of time as a spatial dimension is at all
plausible). Fossilized within each frame our *static* existence is
utterly unable to express itself in a living language tied to time.

Language in the cinema is spoken by the film's projector. The characters in a film talk of time and yet it is not they who do the talking. Whether the characters are fleshy three-dimensional models or dancing configurations of light, all of their talk of time is carried out by the projector, not by the characters themselves. The projector lifts the characters' jaws up and down, waggles their tongues, vibrates their lips. The projector speaks all of the speech in the cinema; the characters are not the authors of their own words. The fragments of sound within each frame are not living language spoken in time. These fragments have to be *ordered* and *combined* to form language, and it is the projector that does this. Only the projector *speaks* in the cinema.

From within the realtime reality projector, we are conscious that we *will* say words, that we *have* said words and that we are *in the middle of* saying words, but we never actually say them and our feeling that we do is an illusion. We might have some kind of intuitive comprehension within the instant, but we cannot translate this into a temporal discourse because we are never animated enough to speak it or think it. Choosing our words takes time and the succession of static instants does not give us time for this. Time throws successive fragments of sound and thought into existence, and assembles these into a discourse that can be comprehended only by itself and God. *Our* knowledge of the world is not contained in written, thought, or spoken language. What *we* know about the world cannot be said.

This is most obvious in the four-dimensional interpretation of the realtime reality projector. The three-dimensional instants of human existence are actually a line of physically distinct people continuously connected along the fourth dimension. Each person in this line has an instantaneous moment of language in his or her head, but they never say an entire sentence: they never live in the active creation and exchange of words that is speech. None of the people in this line (even the last) ever thinks or speaks a whole sentence:

at most they are instantaneously aware of being about to speak, having spoken, or being in the middle of speaking a sentence. None of these people has any relationship at all to language that is spoken or thought over time. Any knowledge that they have is compressed within the eternal instant that they exist. Words in this interpretation of time are something that transcends the human; they can be read only by God and have no relationship at all to (wo)man.

The objective theory of time is a *collapsing* hermeneutic circle, shown in Figure 6.

The world says the words of time. Our thoughts are the thoughts of time. Our speech is the speech of time.

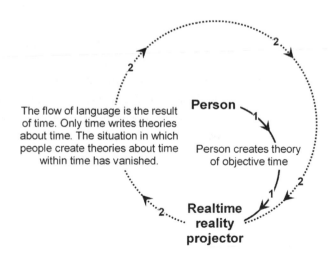

Figure 6. Time might be able to speak about itself, but people cannot speak in time about time. The realtime reality projector collapses into invisibility.

The Realtime Reality Projector Cannot be Known By a (Wo)Man

Parmenides-Spinoza's Concept-Being is *Eternity*, whereas Hegel's Concept-Being is *Time*. Consequently, Spinozist absolute Knowledge, too, must *be* Eternity. That is to say that it must exclude Time. In other words: there is no need of Time to realize it; the *Ethics* must be thought, written, and read 'in a trice.' And that is the thing's absurdity. [Plotinus, however, accepts this consequence.]

This absurdity was already denounced by Plato in his *Parmenides*. If Being is truly one (or more exactly, the One) – i.e., if it excludes diversity, all diversity – and therefore all change – i.e., if it is Eternity that *annuls* Time – if, I say, Being is the One, a man could not *speak* of it, Plato remarks. Indeed, Discourse would have to be just as *one* as the Being that it reveals, and therefore could not go beyond the single word 'one.' And even that. ... For *Time* is still the crucial question. Discourse must be *intemporal*: now, if he has not the time, man cannot even pronounce a *single* word. If Being is *one*, or, what amounts to the same thing, if the Concept *is* Eternity, 'absolute Knowledge' reduces for Man to absolute *silence*.

I say: for Man. That is, for the speaking being that lives in Time and needs time in order to live and to speak (i.e., in order to think by means of the Concept). Now, as we have seen, the Concept *as such* is not (or at least does not seem to be) necessarily attached to Time. The universe of Concepts or of Ideas can be conceived of as a universe of *Discourse*: as an eternal Discourse, in which all the elements coexist. [This is what Plotinus says.] And as a matter of fact, there are (it seems) *non*temporal relations, between Concepts: all Euclid's theorems, for example, exist simultaneously within the entirety of his axioms. [And Plotinus insists on this fact.] Hence there would be a nontemporal *Discourse*. The *idea* of the Spinozist System, then, is not absurd: quite simply, it is the idea of *absolute* Knowledge. What is absurd is that this System is supposed to have been fabricated by a *man*, who in actual fact needed *time* in order to fabricate it. ... Or else, again: the *System* can exist outside of Time; but, starting from temporal existence, there is no *access* to this System.

(Alexandre Kojève, *Introduction to the Reading of Hegel*)[47]

If time is a realtime reality projector, (wo)man is not temporal. Everything that we are, everything that we experience, is bracketed within a sequence of atemporal frames, a series of *static* instants thrown or manipulated by time. Discourse is essentially temporal and so *we* cannot *describe* time as a string of nows from within our succession of static nows. Our experience is fundamentally *eternal* within the realtime reality projector, and we become absurd if we claim to speak about it. Any (wo)man who claims to state the theory that time is a realtime reality projector also has to claim that she or he is God.

Although Kojève denounces Spinoza's absurd claim to have *written about* or *fabricated* an eternal theory, he still leaves open the possibility that Spinoza could have known his system through some kind of nontemporal discourse; a set of nontemporal relations that co-exist simultaneously. This suggests that we can know about the realtime reality projector from within by grasping it instantaneously as a *picture* in our minds: I can picture a projector in an ordinary cinema (as a combination of space, time and movement images), I can picture my own reality being projected, I can create a limited picture of the universe as an eternal block of four-dimensional spacetime, and I can picture the eternal exchange of reality-frames. The realtime reality projector is a mechanism which embodies the theory that time is a sequence of nows and I can picture this mechanism in an instant.[48]

We can know the realtime reality projector from within as a picture composed of space, time and movement images. The absurdity begins when we try to describe this picture. Any *statement* about the realtime reality projector has to extend over time, and yet we (the people who are describing the realtime reality projector) do not exist in time because we are trapped within a succession of static nows. We can grasp the truth about the realtime reality projector in an instant, from within a single frame, but only God can formulate a description of this picture that cuts across a number of reality-frames. A temporal description surpasses the instants that we are; it can only be grasped by an *outside audience* of our projected world.

One potential objection to this is that the theory of the realtime reality projector could have been developed over time until it could be grasped within a single now. Throughout this chapter I could have built up the realtime reality projector in your mind until you reached the point at which you could picture it in an instant. This combination of temporal description and eternal theory is used by Kojève in his interpretation of Hegel:

> We know that for Hegel this end of history is marked by the coming of Science in the form of a Book – that is, by the appearance of the Wise Man or of the *absolute* Knowledge in the World. This absolute Knowledge, being the *last* moment of Time – that is, a moment without a *Future* – is no longer a temporal moment. If absolute Knowledge *comes into being* in Time or, better yet, as Time or History, Knowledge that *has come into being* is no longer temporal or historical: it is *eternal*, or, if you will, it is *Eternity* revealed to itself; it is the Substance of Parmenides-Spinoza which reveals itself by a *Discourse* (and not by Silence), precisely because it is the *result* of a historical *becoming*; it is Eternity *engendered* by Time.[49]

Kojève claims that, according to Hegel, time 'existed' 'for a while' and then was annulled at the end of History. Time ceased to 'exist' when man ceased to Act in a historical way. When man reached absolute Knowledge, the fight for recognition ended and historical time was supplanted by an Eternity in which absolute Knowledge is present: an eternity in which absolute Knowledge *can* be known by a man in an instant and *has* been known by the Wise Man (Hegel).

According to Kojève, there was a limited period of time, prior to the abolition of time, during which a theory of time could be stated by (wo)men. This contrasts with the realtime reality projector, which does *not* posit a different kind of historical time leading up to the moment at which time could be grasped in an instant. Kojève claims that the nature of time changes over time: a description of time takes place in time and then time ends and its nature can be grasped in an instant. However, the realtime reality projector's interpretation applies to the *whole* of time – it claims that time has *always* been this way. This theory of time does not look back over time, and then claim that description was possible before this theory arose. On the contrary, *once this theory of time has been accepted it 'looks back' over time and concludes that description has never been possible, that the description that it claims to have made has never taken place.* Now, perhaps, time can be grasped in an instant, but in the run up to this instant all the descriptions that attempted to analyze time were so much hot air, so much absurd metaphysics. Kojève gives an account of how an eternal theory can be built up over time; the realtime reality projector is an eternal theory that negates all of our past and present attempts to speak about time using language.

'An intuitively plausible theory of time is thrown into existence after some lengthy descriptions of it. Our intuitive instantaneous grasp of this theory reveals that earlier attempts to articulate it were not saying anything at all; it shows us that these earlier attempts were only speaking about time if, by some miracle, God was using our mouths to articulate his own Absolute theory. We became Wise (Wo)Men at one point in our history and this "Wisdom" revealed to us the worthlessness of Wisdom in the form of language. The theory that time is a realtime reality projector silences all speech about it. It is not absurd for *us* to have this theory if it can be grasped as an instantaneous picture, but we cannot *say* anything about it. This chapter has been so many empty words, so many ink blots on a page. It has not described anything. It has not said anything. Time is not a "realtime reality projector". "Realtime reality projector" has lost all meaning for us.'

Conclusion

One could, in the light of the fact that the divine life is itself a continual variation, apply to the divinity in the most exalted sense the name of time.

The old mythology which speaks of Chronos as primeval being and first divine principle seems thereby to be somehow in contact with the truth.

(Franz Brentano, *Philosophical Investigations on Space, Time and the Continuum*)[50]

All created things are God's speech. The being of a stone speaks and manifests the same as does my mouth about God; and people understand more by what is done than by what is said.

(Meister Eckhart, *The Essential Sermons, Commentaries, Treatises and Defense*)[51]

This chapter has set out a cinematic model of our ordinary theory of time. All theories that objectify time and separate it from the contents of a static now are covered by this model.

Cinematic time transmutes our spoken words into projected fragments thrown into existence *by* time and not generated by us *about* time. Any theory of time that we come up with within the realtime reality projector *might* be true, but this truth has to be a coincidence established by God or Time – not the kind of truth that we could deduce or arrive at ourselves from within a sequence of immobile nows.

In a film there is no difference between true and false statements about time: the characters can have any theory of time that they want – nothing impedes their development of time theory and yet they know nothing about time.

In a cinema only the audience can experience the film's time, observe its changes and interpret its dialogue. The realtime reality cinema is *atheistic*: it has no separate audience, no detached observers and no viewpoints from nowhere.

The claim that time works in a particular way is also a claim that people and language work in a particular way. If time is objective, people and their theories become objectified.

'This ink is black.' 'This ink is red.' From our perspective we can see a difference between these two statements – one is false and the other true. But the ink formed these two statements with equal aplomb: it did not twist and writhe as I applied it to misdescribe it. If time is objective, we are time's ink: our texts and speech are written by time and read by no one.

The theory of the realtime reality projector is a moment of thought at the same time as it abolishes thought. We enter it, there is a flash of light, and theory vanishes.

I have described how the theory of the realtime reality projector collapses, and yet stupidly, blindly, idiotically, I am continuing to speak about it.

Perhaps David Gamez is continuing to speak about the realtime reality projector because he is maintaining a *tacit* belief in his ability to manipulate language. He is not taking the realtime reality projector *seriously enough*. His inauthentic, superficial speech does not have the *depth* to worry about whether it was created by what it is speaking about.

Or perhaps David Gamez is taking the realtime reality projector *extremely seriously*. In this case he is free to speak about it because if it is true, it does not matter whether it is spoken about or not. If time is a realtime reality projector, then everything that is said will be as much about the world as the cattle and cars that move within it. If the realtime reality projector is real then the claim that we should 'stop speaking about it' is meaningless. No plans of action, no prescriptions or proscriptions for discourse, can emerge from the realtime reality projector.

Whether they take it seriously or not, people will continue to think about the realtime reality projector. These are four directions which their thought might take:

1) Our *picture* of time as a realtime reality projector is *correct*, but our language does not contain an accurate description of time because time cannot coherently organize the sounds that it places in our mouths. Words as arbitrary as the whispering of the wind or the chattering of pebbles by the sea are thrown into existence by time, but these do not describe time. We cannot use language to describe the world and the language that is in the world does not describe time.

2) Our picture of time as a realtime reality projector is correct and, by some lucky coincidence or divine intervention, 'Time is a realtime reality projector' is an accurate description of time. This is a stable hermeneutic circle, but it does not include people within it (see Figure 7).

We exist only within the immobile now, but we believe that continuities of human form extend over time. In the mouths of these continuities of human form there are theories of time, similar to the theories of time in the mouths of celluloid forms in the cinema. We are not responsible for these theories any more than the characters in a film are responsible for their theories. As far as *we* can tell, the

Figure 7. A stable hermeneutic circle in which the words thrown into existence by time/God describe time/God

sounds that are associated with the continuities of human form might be about time or they might not say anything at all. However, it could turn out that the sounds emerging from our mouths are a language that is being used to describe time as a realtime reality projector, just as a character in a film might truthfully say: 'I am character in a film, thrown into existence twenty-four times per second, and composed of nothing but celluloid.' If we continue to call what issues from our mouths 'language', then this 'language' only speaks about time if the 'person' (God or Time Itself) Who assembled it is describing time. Although this is something that *we* can never know, it is certainly *possible* that the speech pouring forth from our lips 'about time' is actually about time. This is what I mean when I say that it would be a lucky coincidence if *our* theory that time is a realtime reality projector is actually a theory of time.

3) The realtime reality projector is a *false* theory of time and a different time theory is correct. One problem with the claim that the realtime reality projector is *false* is that any theory or observation about time can be shown within a film, and so the cinematic theory of time can always be presupposed to be more primordial than any other. This theory reconstructs our entire experience, including anything that any other interpretation of time could be based on. Since it undercuts all other theories, the realtime reality projector will always be one possible theory of time, but any statement about it will be absurd. A second problem with claims about the falsity of the realtime reality projector is that it models our scientific and ordinary theories of time, and so it is far from clear how we could replace it. The objectification of time in physics has had some impressive empirical success, and it would not be easy to completely replace the cinematic conception with something like Bergson's creative evolution, even if this could be shown to be a stable hermeneutic circle.

4) 'Time' is a by-product of metaphysical discourse and our ways of describing it are inevitably taken from *within* time; from the spatial objects and processes that we encounter in the world around us. The meaning of the word 'time' does not extend beyond these 'distorting'

metaphors and so it is senseless to look for an alternative to this *metaphysical* concept. This is the approach taken by Derrida:

> The concept of time, in all its aspects, belongs to metaphysics, and it names the domination of presence. Therefore we can only conclude that the entire system of metaphysical concepts, throughout its history, develops the so-called 'vulgarity' of the concept of time (which Heidegger, doubtless, would not contest) but also that an *other* concept of time cannot be opposed to it, since time in general belongs to metaphysical conceptuality. In attempting to produce this *other* concept, one rapidly would come to see that it is constructed out of other metaphysical or ontotheological predicates.[52]

'Time' is a word that has had a certain strategic value within the philosophical tradition. We have played various metaphysical language-games with the word 'time', all of which have made the claim that there is something called 'time' out there in the world. Now we have come to recognize that this word 'time' is just a by-product of a certain historical discourse and if we want to go beyond metaphysics we will have to abandon it in favour of words like 'trace' or 'différance'. This links up with point 1) above, for in 1) 'time' is also a meaningless word. However, in 1) time is an objective feature of reality that we cannot speak about, whereas 'time' here is just a word with a certain situation in discourse, a word with a set of grammatical manipulations that we can apply to it, a word that does not refer to anything. 'There is time in the world' and 'There is no time in the world' become equivalent nonstatements.

4 Merging Madness and Reason

There are three ways to escape from prison:

1) After months of bleeding scrabbling at damp coarse mortar, you prise and yank free one of the bars and jump slide and run with pounding heart over the rooftops. A clutching-razor-wire-shred leaves you blood-dripping in a wet field. You make a stumbling break for the dark sodden woods, tear off your prison uniform and take a deep fresh breath of earthy air.

2) Long months of solitary contemplation teach you that the prison's dripping grey-granite walls, barbed yards and armed guards were all erected to *protect* you from oppression. Prisons shelter freedom: they keep it out of reach of the jack-booted dictators that wander in the countryside outside.

   Your prison clothes transfigure into the bold blue uniform of a brave new world. The taste of prison fare is enhanced by emancipation. You rush from your cell to share your discovery with the shambling hollow-eyed 'prisoners' and the stubbled 'guards'. Soon, people will start to club the 'guards', rip out the bars and tear down the walls to break *into* the 'prison'; clamouring outside the gates they will beg for freedom.

3) A lightning-flash of sudden insight reveals that prisons and freedom, barbed enclosures and liberated spaces, are just so many man-made ways of dividing space; valid for certain applications and purposes, but of no real importance or significance. Life is happy and sad, monotonous and exhilarating, on both sides of these artificial barriers. You light your pipe, crack open a beer and chill out in the homogenous zone.

Introduction

> Chirps in a box. If you abstract yourself far enough from a given context you seem somehow to create a new kind of concretion. It isn't something you have or see but yet somehow. It's being fascinated by the generative process of the mind. The thing is to be caught in it, yet abstract from it. Both be in it and out of it – revolving everything around me. You explode like when the stars explode. In the sky a plate which burned bright. Symbol of all light and energy with me contracted into this plate.
>
> (Anonymous schizophrenic patient)[1]

> I philosophize only in *terror*, but in the *confessed* terror of going mad. ... But this crisis in which reason is madder than madness – for reason is non-meaning and oblivion – and in which madness is more rational than reason, for it is closer to the wellspring of sense, however silent or murmuring – this crisis has always begun and is interminable.
>
> (Jacques Derrida, *Writing and Difference*)[2]

Is your mind a tumult of twisting upheavals sliding reaching and marching to the rat tat tat of the soldier's drum? Can you feel the surging explosion of brilliant light effaced by a thunder-clap plunge into empty black? Can you see your sanity spiralling off into a convulsing puppet that jerks, flips out as it twitches and disintegrates in despair?

Are your vomit-stained rags the soft ermine of royalty? Is your incoherent babble the rumination of philosopher, scientist or saint? Is your *un*-reason reasonable?

Why are you *not* mad, mentally ill, insane, maniacal, abnormal, schizophrenic, of unsound mind, crazy, barmey, fucked-up, off your trolley, gaga, a loony? *Prove* that you have *not* lost it, flipped your lid, been taken by the fairies, abducted by the aliens.

You have never been *diagnosed* as mad – this is the shifting sand upon which you erect your sanity. But your illness has gone unrecognized ... you have been deprived of treatment because the steady-sure advance of science has taken *too long* to reach you.

This chapter will correct this oversight: it will prod science to progress a little further; it will bare your craziness for all the world to see; it will demonstrate that you are a demented fucked-up schizo who should be chucked into the loony bin. Unfortunately there is no cure. Anaesthetization, normalization, lobotomization, electrocution, and brain surgery are all on offer, but they are all just as crazy as the illness that they attempt to heal.

There are some normal[3] people who are pretty much sane, a number of people who are neurotic or marginal cases, and a few people who act in ways that appear crazy to any reasonable man. Any number of shadings can be found in between these three groups. On this continuum the majority of people stand within the zone of health, which shades off imperceptibly into mild and then chronic disease.

There is also a continuum of truth. The majority of people know the truth, some are mildly deluded, and a minority have completely lost their grip on reality.

According to our normal way of thinking, these two continua overlap and are, perhaps, ultimately the same. Mentally healthy people stand within the bright light of truth, which shades off into the dark deluded world of the mad, lost in their delirious unreason. The more mentally diseased a person is, the less seriously we take their beliefs; the further a person's beliefs are from our own truth, the more we are inclined to call them mentally diseased.

The red on a rainbow's outside edge is qualitatively different from the blue on the inside. However, the rainbow of colours is formed from electromagnetic rays vibrating at different frequencies, and so in physical reality red and blue have only a quantitative difference between them.

Although normality and madness appear to be qualitatively different, sanity and insanity can be reduced to quantitative intensity differences within a single homogenous zone. Within this zone it is the intensities of the human qualities that are important: shadings from health to disease and from truth to falsehood are secondary attachments to the zone; temporary labels stabilized by the majority's consensus.

The first part of this chapter highlights the traces of madness that are present in all parts of the continuum (it reveals the electromagnetic spectrum behind qualitative differences in colour) by uncovering the schizophrenic[4] thought in the normal child, our inner thinking, our past as a culture and in philosophy and science. After the madness of normality has been unveiled the ground will be prepared for a vision of the homogenous zone that underlies both sanity and insanity.

The second part of this chapter is a detailed study of the homogenous zone that deals with its structure, the disjunctions and reversals that arise within it, its mutation in isolation and some of the objections that could be raised against it. These include medical theories of madness and the reduction of madness to childhood experiences or other extraneous events. Finally, the third part shows how excess sanity or insanity destabilize the theory of the homogenous zone, which is also forced to accept theories of madness that directly contradict its own position.

Although the main thrust of this chapter is towards the dissolution of an absolute difference between sanity and insanity, it does recognize that the distinction between normality and madness in our culture (and in virtually every other according to cross-cultural comparisons) identifies a difference between people that cannot be simply dismissed as a social artefact or structure of language. Schizophrenics are *different* from your average nine-to-fiver. The homogenous zone incorporates these differences by describing them as collections of different intensities of qualities, some of which are labelled 'mad' by people, and others labelled 'sane'. Sociological theories are used to explain how these labels cause parts of the continuum to become accentuated so that there appear to be two discrete groups.

Self-styled normal people (and often madmen as well) often suffer from the delusion that there is some essential quality in madness, which normal thought (fortunately) lacks. The arguments in this chapter show that the world of the schizophrenic is the world of the normal person: distorted in some areas, reduced in others, but essentially the same style of operation. Madness is a caricature of reason, which in many ways makes it a better image of the processes of reason than the account reason gives of itself.

Beneath the flickering labels of consensus there is just the homogenous zone, thrown from nowhere onto the surface of spaceship Earth. After the sane have merged with the mad, all past, present and future beliefs become situated within the same space, mad disease collapses and we become six billion ghosts groping and wandering in the global weed garden ... blind, stumbling, reaching out.[5]

... the Renaissance, after the great terror of death, the fear of the apocalypses, and the threats of the other world, experienced a new danger in this world: that of a silent invasion from within, a secret gap in the earth, as it were. This invasion is that of the Insane, which places the Other world on the same level as this one, and on ground level, as it were. As a result, one no longer knows whether it is our world that is duplicated in a fantastic mirage; whether, on the contrary, it is the other world that takes possession of this world; or whether the secret of *our* world was to be already, without our knowing, the *other* world. ... Reason, too recognized itself as being duplicated and dispossessed of itself: it thought itself wise, and it was mad; it thought it knew, and it knew nothing; it thought itself righteous, and it was insane; knowledge led one to the

shades and to the forbidden world, when one thought one was being
led by it to eternal light.

(Michel Foucault, *Mental Illness and Psychology*)[6]

Sliding Between Sanity and Insanity

Labels, Clusters and Thresholds

> *Social groups create deviance by making the rules whose infraction consti-*
> *tutes deviance*, and by applying those rules to particular people and labelling
> them as outsiders. From this point of view, deviance is *not* a quality of the
> act the person commits, but rather a consequence of the application by
> others of rules and sanctions to an 'offender'. The deviant is one to whom
> that label has successfully been applied; deviant behavior is behavior that
> people so label.
>
> (Howard Becker, *Outsiders*)[7]

Societies function according to explicit and implicit systems of rules.
We drive on the left, shit in private and respect other people's bodies
and possessions. Most deviations from these rules go unnoticed: we
ignore minor deviations in public and excuse the small deviations of
our family and friends. However, past a certain point, or in certain
contexts, deviations from the system of social rules can no longer be
ignored or excused, and the transgressing person is *labelled* deviant.
This label creates a difference between the deviant and the people who
label him. Before the person was labelled he was part of society and
his family and friends accepted him as one of them – as *like* them. After
the label has been applied the person becomes someone different; an
outsider marginalized from the group.

Once a person has been labelled, our tendency to reify language leads
us to perceive a qualitative difference between the labelled person and
a person who has not been labelled. We see the person *as* deviant. This
may motivate a search for an explanation of this difference – for a
deviant physiognomy, deviant genes or a deviant childhood.

Furthermore, labelling can make a person's behaviour more deviant, since they often start to believe the label themselves and act out their life in accordance with it. In this way labelling creates the perception of a qualitative difference between two parts of a continuum and increases the actual differences between labelled and unlabelled people.

According to labelling theory, most deviations – such as rape, obscenity and theft – are readily classified and predetermined punishments are held ready for them. However, some deviant actions are difficult to classify and there is no obvious way in which they can be dealt with. If I stare intently at the left ear of the person who is speaking to me, they soon come to feel that I am breaking some unwritten law of social etiquette. However, since there is no explicit law or punishment pertaining to the orientation of the eyes in conversation, they are forced to fall back on a *residual* category of deviance that groups my transgression amongst all the other unclassifiable acts that break social norms. This single catch-all deviant category is called 'madness' in our society: people who break rules in unclassifiable ways are stamped 'mentally ill' and shunted off into the asylum. As Thomas Scheff puts it:

> The culture of the group provides a vocabulary of terms for categorising many norm violations: crime, perversion, drunkenness, and bad manners are familiar examples. Each of these terms is derived from the type of norm broken, and ultimately, from the type of behavior involved. After exhausting these categories, however, there is always a residue of the most diverse kinds of violations, for which the culture provides no explicit label. ... For the convenience of the society in construing these instances of unnameable rule-breaking which are called to its attention, these violations may be lumped together into a residual category: witchcraft, spirit possession, or, in our own society, mental illness. In this discussion, the diverse kinds of rule-breaking for which our society provides no explicit label, and which, therefore, sometimes lead to the labelling of the violator as mentally ill, will be considered to be technically *residual rule-breaking*.[8]

Some people who have been labelled mentally ill resist this label and continue to live their lives as before. Others may accept it, especially if they have been interned in an asylum and pressured to conform to the stereotype of mental illness in this environment. If they accept the label, they may feel that they have a disease and need treatment. They may act in ways that confirm the diagnosis and behave in a manner that is stereotypically crazy or schizophrenic – especially if this helps them to resolve or hide from some of the problems that led to their initial deviation:

> When labelling first occurs, it merely gives a name to rule-breaking which has other roots. When (and if) the rule-breaking becomes an issue, and is not ignored or rationalized away, labelling may create a social type, a pattern of 'symptomatic' behavior in conformity with the stereotyped expectations of others. Finally, to the extent that the deviant role becomes a part of the deviant's self-conception, his ability to control his own behavior may be impaired under stress, resulting in episodes of compulsive behavior.[9]

Labelling theory is open minded about the cause of the original deviation, but it does think that deviations are extremely common throughout the population and that most of them go unnoticed. According to Scheff, 'Relative to the rate of treated mental illness, the rate of unrecorded residual rule-breaking is extremely high.'[10] This is confirmed by investigations into the distribution of mental illness amongst the population at large. In *The Social Creation of Mental Illness* Cochrane cites studies that suggest that the prevalence of psychological 'symptoms' amongst the general population is between 20 and 60 per cent, with only a small proportion – perhaps 5 per cent – actually receiving treatment: 'In our study of the distribution of psychological symptoms in urban areas of England we found that fully 36 per cent of the sample interviewed had four or more of the 22 symptoms asked about – a level which is sometimes used as a criterion for psychological "caseness". Over 20 per cent met the more stringent criterion of 7 or more symptoms.'[11]

A central reason why some people with symptoms[12] of schizo-phrenia are labelled mentally ill, whilst others with some of the same symptoms are not, is that a *cluster* of phenomena is much more noticeable than a single one. Although schizophrenic symptoms, such as hallucinations, delusional beliefs and affectual withdrawal, are widely distributed throughout the population, we do not notice them when they are present individually, intermittently or in small numbers. However, if a number of symptoms are concentrated in an individual over an extended period of time, then they can disrupt their attempt to live a normal life and the person is immediately identified as being a bit 'paranoid' or 'strange'. It is significant in this respect that the criteria for diagnosing schizophrenia (DSM IV) require *two or more* of certain symptoms to be present for at least a month for a positive diagnosis to be made. A large proportion of the population has symptoms of mental illness, but only those with a cluster of them are labelled 'mentally ill'.[13]

Related to the idea of a cluster of symptoms becoming noticeable, is that of a *threshold*, which can be used to separate a continuum into two readily discernible groups. Everything that passes the threshold is sorted into one group and everything that falls below it is sorted into another. For example, if we were asked to divide block A in Figure 1

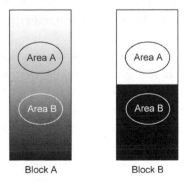

Figure 1. Application of a threshold increases the differences between areas A and B

into two regions, one white and the other black, we would apply a threshold to it and classify grey lighter than the threshold as white and grey darker than the threshold as black.

This application of a threshold leaves us with a block divided into two areas that are wholly distinct from one another (block B). Before block A was classified there was little difference between areas A and B. However, after the application of the threshold area A becomes radically distinct from area B. If there is a continuum of intensities of symptoms throughout a population – for example, some people who hallucinate a lot and others who only hallucinate occasionally – then people with an intensity of symptoms that exceeds our tolerance level will become labelled 'mad'. This creates two distinct groups: one perceived as homogenously mad and the another perceived as homogenously sane.

Overall, labelling theory, supported by ideas about clustering and thresholds, shows us how a population with a continuum of symptoms of schizophrenia divides itself into two distinct groups, one mad and the other sane. People whose clusters of bizarre behaviour pass a culturally dependent threshold are classified as clinically insane by the rest of the population and the labelling and isolation of these deviants reinforces their symptoms and makes them even more different. It is not an abyss or a qualitative distinction that separates sanity from insanity, but a quantitative difference, split into two labelled groups by clustering and thresholds.

Whilst labelling theory goes some way towards explaining many of the differences between the mad and the sane, it is only a partial theory, and has little to say about how a person who is normal one day can mutate into a madman overnight without any influence from labelling or institutionalization. For example, Barbara O'Brien woke up one morning and found herself immersed in a world of operators and things; in another case, a shoe salesman went berserk and journeyed from city to city purchasing shoe stores with money that he did not have. The medical model cannot completely explain these transformations either, but it can at least point in a promising direction. This does not invalidate labelling theory, but it does indicate that supplementary accounts may have to be sought from other areas. Labelling theory explains why we perceive a continuum of schizophrenic symptoms as two distinct groups of normal and mad people, but why there is a continuum of intensities at all and why people move along it, are questions beyond its remit.

The Monstrous, A Rich Chuckling Cry

6 years:
Very fearful. Especially auditory fears: door-bell, telephone, static, ugly voice tones, flushing of toilet, insect and bird noises.
Fear of supernatural: ghosts, witches.
Fear that someone is hiding under the bed.
Spatial: fear of being lost, fear of the woods.
Fear of the elements: fire, water, thunder, lightning.
Fear of sleeping alone in a room or of being the only one on a floor of the house....

7 years:
Many fears, especially visual: the dark, attics, cellars. Interprets shadows as ghosts and witches.
Fears war, spies, burglars, people hiding in closet or under bed.
Fears now stimulated by reading, radio, cinema.
Worries about things: not being liked, being late to school.

8 to 9 years:
Fewer fears and less worrying. No longer fears the water; less fear of the dark. Good evaluation, and fears are reasonable: about personal inability and failure, especially school failure.

(Frances Ilg and Louise Bates Ames, *Child Behavior*)[14]

Night, *darkness*, **terror**. Suggestive forms lurk, over there, *out* there, in the cupboard, *in* the corner. Embodied evil: under my bed, behind the stark dark form of my chair. A menacing presence, the monstrous *there*, **approaching threatening** *fear.* A cosy retreat under the enveloping duvet wins a brief reprieve – but it is still *out there*, lurking, menacing; behind the chair, in the cupboard, between the walls, **sinister**, *waiting* in that suggestive pile of clothes. *Fear.*

The child senses the presence of the monstrous, the uncanny; it fears the demons that lurk beneath the serenity of light. Adults provide the child with endless myths, tales and names to channel and dissipate this fear. It is the devil, the bogeyman, Freddy Kruger, a troll, an ogre, a wolfman. Eventually childish myths are discarded and replaced by adult ones (the F.B.I., K.G.B., C.I.A., N.S.D.A.P.), or sublimated and hidden in morality or other adult concerns. These hidden terrors are temporarily reactivated and relived in horror movies or more subtly in detective thrillers, where the lurking presence of evil is projected into an unknown wrongdoer and dissipated when the criminal is brought out into the light of day and punished.

Evil is a force of multiple shifting forms in the adult world, but it is still there, *lurking*, **menacing** the adults coddled in their bedclothes of self-righteousness.

Friends chatting and discussing, dancing and playing. A population of little girls and boys, bizarre benign cuddly creatures, animals that advise: the inanimate has feelings too. Talking toys, situations and jokes shared with invisible friends.

Stories and cartoons reflect this animated world of the child. Singing trees, dancing brooms and laughing birds populate a landscape that has not yet hardened into the opposition between objective and subjective. The child experiences neither of these abstractions: the living breathing buzzing talking world is simply *there* in all its richness. Adults used to believe that they were accompanied in their day to day goings-on by playmates in heaven and the people doomed to wander amongst the sad lands of the dead. They continue to 'pretend' that brute lumps of flesh and fur have thoughts and feelings too.

In modern society it could be argued that our friends from heaven and amongst the dead have departed, and that animals *really do* have feelings. Perhaps the animation of the child's world actually does fade as we gain wisdom, or perhaps it is exchanged for the rather soulless quarks and freakish forces that are alleged to populate the world as we know it. Perhaps we only rediscover our friendship with the world in brief instants: when we pat a proud stone lion, curse a malicious toe-blunting brick, or unite with a surging singing happy world along a woodland path in spring.

The imaginary of Disneyland is neither true nor false, it is a deterrence machine set up in order to rejuvenate the fiction of the real in the opposite camp. Whence the debility of this imaginary, its infantile degeneration. This world wants to be childish in order to make us believe that the adults are elsewhere, in the 'real' world, and to conceal the fact that true childishness is everywhere – that it is that of the adults themselves who come here to act the child in order to foster illusions as to their real childishness.

(Jean Baudrillard, *Simulacra and Simulation*)[15]

There are essentially only quantitative differences between the dream of the youngster who plays general on his hobby-horse ... the twilight state of the hysteric, and the hallucinations of the schizophrenic in which his most impossible wishes appear fulfilled. All these are but points along the same scale.

(Eugen Bleuler, 'Autistic thinking')[16]

We *were* schizo children. And perhaps we have yet to grow up.[17]

We are Autistic

... when we think in complete security and with no strong integrating tendency at work we have nothing like language processes going on in our minds. We have almost nothing 'in mind.' Certain recollections of past states of the organism flow and shift with extreme velocity to certain things which according to the old psychologists are associated with them, and we arrive at a realization that the intended action, for example, would fail; that is that. Then we begin again and presently we arrive at a series of hypothetical events which might work; and *then* we think. We think in various ways. The most striking way in which we think is how to tell our thoughts to someone else; if you think of anything in terms of how to tell it to a stranger, your mental process approaches the characteristics of good written language.

(Harry Stack Sullivan, 'The Language of Schizophrenia')[18]

We sit alone, staring into space, tuned to the inner murmurings of our souls. Inchoate experiences shift and stir; only partially carved into the clarity of words. Emotional complexes, memories, words, concepts and hypothetical situations lock and mesh, collide and drift together. Suddenly a meaningful constellation snaps into place; realization dawns. We integrate this reconfigured congeries of image, memory, concept and language into our world picture; slot it into our vision of how things *are*. We may act upon this realisation, or begin the labour of assembling it into an articulate speech that we offer as a gift to another.

Our inner speech omits an enormous amount of contextual detail that is implicitly known by us, but not by the person that we talk to. Furthermore, a great deal of the thinking of inner speech is done with images instead of words – I do not think the word 'father' when I am thinking about my father: I bring brief flashes of a memory of my father before me. If our inner speech was written down without the implicitly assumed context and images, it would make very little sense, even to the person who originally thought it. As Vygotsky explains:

The inner speech of the adult represents his 'thinking for himself' rather than social adaptation; i.e., it has the same function that egocentric speech has in the child. It also has the same structural characteristics: Out of context, it would be incomprehensible to others because it omits to 'mention' what is obvious to the 'speaker.' These similarities lead us to assume that when egocentric speech disappears from view it does not simply atrophy but 'goes underground,' i.e., turns into inner speech. ... which serves both autistic and logical thinking.[19]

Many think that the mad speak strange because chemical imbalances have corrupted their thought processes. An alternative interpretation offered by Sullivan is that people labelled 'schizophrenic' have the same thought and inner speech as normal people, but find it harder to translate their inner speech into outer speech when they are communicating with others. Each person speaks autistically to themselves, but this is usually hidden when they translate it into the consensual public language:

> ... the closest approaches to schizophrenic speech in your daily life occur when you do not need to be alert, because you are secure. The schizophrenic has given up any hopes of satisfaction and is concerned only with the maintenance of security. He shows, often with painful chagrin in retrospect, the autistic type of speech which is probably our second nature, and which we certainly show among our intimates when we are very tired and safe.[20]

Sometimes, when we are very tired, or when we feel secure with friends or family, our inner speech becomes our outer speech. We omit context and framing devices, we use images instead of words, we bare our inchoate shifting autistic soul without the interlocking armour of speech. The only difference between normals and schizophrenics is that the latter's day to day mask of language has more cracks in it, more slits through which can be glimpsed the autistic world common to all of us.[21]

We Were Deluded

During the thousandth year the number of pilgrims increased. Most of them were smitten with terror as with a plague. Every phenomenon of nature filled them with alarm. A thunder-storm sent them all upon their knees in mid March. It was the opinion that thunder was the voice of God, announcing the day of judgement. Numbers expected the earth to open and give up its dead at the sound. Every meteor in the sky seen at Jerusalem brought the whole Christian population into the streets to weep and pray.

(Charles Mackay, *Extraordinary Popular Delusions and the Madness of Crowds*)[22]

Traditionally we are a species that *was* deluded. The primitive animistic world of spirits, religion and magic is an error that we have now grown out of: Moses was an embittered Egyptian; Christ was a megalomaniacal schizophrenic; Muhammad was epileptic. One of the most striking things about *Madness and Civilization* is the weirdness, the craziness, of the theories of madness that Foucault describes – a world of spirits, elements, humours, coolings, heatings and frenzies.[23]

Now we can assimilate these bizarre realms into our history as early tentative gropings towards Wisdom: we can see religion as an imperfect grip on Absolute Spirit and alchemy as a necessary precursor to modern experimental science.

The problems with this retrospective and euphemistic interpretation have been often enough stated. Even Popper admits that science rests upon a swamp and the results of an experiment are partly, if not entirely, dependent upon the filters that we apply to our observations.[24] The positivistic interpretation of history has competitors – Kuhn, Foucault, Adorno – and we are no longer sure which is the right one. We are no longer sure whether our earlier delusions were a partial grasp of the truth. We are no longer sure whether our earlier delusions were delusional. We are no longer sure that we are no longer deluded.

D: I see. So God was trying to straighten you out, you thought?
J: Ya.
D: Tell me more about how you knew it was His voice when you heard

the thunderstorm.

J: 'Cause nobody talks that loud.

D: The loudness.

J: Yea, the strength in His voice. Said, 'OD,' like a giant, like a giant was screaming out loud.

D: Tell me, was His voice in the thunder or did you hear the thunder and then hear his voice?

J: No, I heard it in the thunder.

D: Was His voice the same as the thunder?

J: Yes, exactly the same as the thunder. He was speaking through the thunder.

(David Bradford, *The Experience of God*)[25]

The Megalithic Bio-Cruncher

For me, madness was definitely not a condition of illness; I did not believe that I was ill. It was rather a country, opposed to Reality, where reigned an implacable light, blinding, leaving no place for shadow; an immense space without boundary, limitless, flat; a mineral lunar country, cold as the wastes of the North Pole. In this stretching emptiness, all is unchangeable, immobile, congealed, crystallized. Objects are stage trappings, placed here and there, geometric cubes without meaning.

People turn weirdly about, they make gestures, movements without sense; they are phantoms whirling on an infinite plain, crushed by the pitiless electric light. And I—I am lost in it, isolated, cold, stripped, purposeless under the light.

(Renee, *Autobiography of a Schizophrenic Girl*)[26]

Sometimes I stare into the eyes of a person that I intimately know and their personhood collapses. Two white and slimy orbs twitched by tiny muscles, automatic irises swelling and squeezing in response to light, conditioned clichéd responses, a programmed neuro-matrix, an animal driven by instinct, an assembly of particles and fields, a machine, a *thing* ...

A massive machine with billions of complex parts. Interlocking, ticking. A matrix of components resonating in response to one another. Delicate tremors sweeping through it and occasional shock waves ripping, tearing the tiny parts apart from one another. Then, slowly, the parts reassemble: linking up, interlocking until order is restored.

My body, an infinitesimal part of this machine; an assembly of microscopic parts. Each cellular part a tiny machine moving about, transmitting, receiving, manufacturing substances. Each machinic cell assembled from tiny components supplying energy, mobility, protection, duplication.

A gigantic sea of intensities, a twisted and folded field in a state of continuous agitation. Waves, vibrating strings of knotted dimensions. Clouds of fuzzy particles showering backwards and forwards in time; splitting, fusing, joining; located everywhere and nowhere.

My mind, an indeterminate particle cloud modulated by events in the rest of the universe; millions of vibrating rays and intersecting forces traversing me, constituting me every second. My unstable body condenses into itself and diffuses throughout the universe; everywhere and nowhere; mingling with its surroundings; a body that is not the same body from moment to moment.

A vast web of meaning, sea of information. Wetware brain, virtual body, self-enclosed artificial spaces, an encoded invisible real. Software thought modulates digital flows; speech swaps information between different processing algorithms.

Modern chimeras, mathematical dreams, invisible visions pouring into the dark eye of the intellect. Schizoid scientific fantasies validated by consensus.

A Bright and Preternatural Light

> Often enough schizophrenics feel not farther from but closer to truth and illumination. One individual ... for example describes her madness as a land suffused with a bright and preternatural light; another ... recounts how his head was 'illuminated by rays'; and a third, the poet Gérard de Nerval, describes a crystal-clear sight in his psychotic episodes: 'it struck me I knew everything; everything was revealed to me, all the secrets of the world were mine during those spacious hours.'
>
> (Louis Sass, *Madness and Modernism*)[27]

According to Sass, madness is an involution in which a person becomes increasingly preoccupied with reality and language and develops a solipsistic hyperreflexive stance towards the world. This generates paradoxes through its self-undermining, reifies experiences as substantial independent entities, cuts itself off from instincts and emotions, and attributes an unspecifiable *particular* meaning to things:

> Madness, on my reading, is neither the psyche's return to its primordial condition, nor the malfunctioning of reason, nor even some inspired alternative to human reason. It is, to be sure, a self-deceiving condition, but one that is generated from within rationality itself rather than by the loss of rationality. The parallels between Wittgenstein and Schreber reveal not a primitive or Dionysian condition but something akin to Wittgenstein's notion of a disease of the intellect, born at the highest pitches of self-consciousness and alienation. Madness, in this view, is the endpoint of the trajectory consciousness follows when it separates from the body and the passions, and from the social and practical world, and turns in upon itself; it is what might be called the mind's perverse self-apotheosis.[28]

For Sass, madness is a condition of excessive intellectualization, not a lapse into Dionysian delirium. In madness all contact with the body and the passions withers away to leave an icy-clear transparent reason that locks itself up in paradoxes and knots as it tries to rationalize about itself. Madness is what happens when reason is pushed to its limit, when the totalizing claims of reason are taken *seriously*. Our highest cerebral moments are slashed by the cold-burn sting of schizophrenia. The madman is more reasonable than the man of reason; his hypertrophy of consciousness and conceptual life pushes philosophy and science a little further; he is more detached, more objective and more reflexive than these disciplines – their distilled essence. Our striving after truth is completed in the madman whose reach for the pure concept has left the blooming buzzing confusion of the phenomenal world behind. Compared to the enlightenment of the mad, the average wisdom of philosophers and scientists is a meagre thing indeed.

Madmen intensify reason, they are more reasonable than reason: they are *hyperrational*.

The Homogenous Zone of Madness and Reason

Hyper-Humans

… psycho-analytic research finds no fundamental, but only quantitative, distinctions between normal and neurotic life;[29]

…we must recognise that the psychical mechanism employed by neuroses is not created by the impact of a pathological disturbance upon the mind, but is present already in the normal structure of the mental apparatus.

(Sigmund Freud, *The Interpretation of Dreams*)[30]

Suddenly … we are *here*; thrown into reality from the nothingness of the beyond. We look around. There are other people here too. Collected together on the surface of a single sphere we all share one thing at least, that we popped out of nowhere and appeared on the surface of this planet. Our common origin and physiology bind us together: we are a crowd of open-eyed children staring with wonder at the world. This vast assembly of thrown people is the homogenous zone.

Each of us is a small part of the homogenous zone, a patch within it. Each patch has a certain way of being, a certain style. The homogenous zone traces a different contour within each of us.

Although the homogenous zone is contorted in different ways in each of us, a trace of every one of its different qualities is present in all of us. These qualities and their level of intensity are features of this space; presupposing it they are not ruptures within it.

The homogenous zone can be thought of as a piece of cloth woven from many different colours. Each section of this cloth has at least one thread of each colour running through it, but some parts have many threads of the same colour. This variability gives each section of cloth its own individual character.

The pattern of intensity of our qualities gives us a particular emphasis, strengths in particular areas. Some people are more abstractly intelligent, some are more technically or practically minded, and others have musical or artistic gifts.[31]

There may be people whose qualities are all low in intensity: people who are 'deficient', without any amplification at all. Such people exist a patch of the homogenous zone that is grey; a patch with only one thread of each colour.[32]

We have labels for people who intensify different qualities. Strong jumpers and fast runners are labelled 'athletes'; people talented at manipulating sounds are labelled 'musicians'. 'Schizophrenia' is a label for people who have more intense solipsism, more intense non-consensual visual and auditory perceptions, more incoherent speech, more intense self-reflexive intellectuality, and a greater capacity for unorthodox thought.

The schizophrenic *intensifies* certain qualities that we all share. She *exaggerates* the style of being called 'schizophrenic'. She is one possible contortion of the homogenous zone; her style of being is a feature of the zone that does not detach her from it.

If the schizophrenic is solipsistic, it is because we are all individuals who are cut off and divided from one another. If the schizophrenic hallucinates, it is because we all hallucinate virtual worlds around us (some normals do not agree with what the madman sees, but the process of seeing is the same in everyone). We all speak incoherently at times and make unintentional slips, errors and omissions when our unconscious surfaces in conversation (the schizophrenic does this more, but he does not do this differently). We all abstract and objectify and are self-reflexive to varying degrees. If the schizophrenic is thrown into a world that she invents hypotheses to explain, it is because we are all thrown into worlds that we attempt to understand using conceptual resources that are thrown to us (thrown as us). The schizophrenic's world may be different, but she is thrown into it and tries to understand it in the same way.

Our society associates more intense solipsism, more intense non-consensual visual and auditory perceptions, more incoherent speech, more intense self-reflexive intellectuality, and a greater capacity for unorthodox thought with schizophrenia, but madmen judge normals to be mad on different grounds – because they intensify *different* qualities. According to the normal, the schizophrenic is mad because he hallucinates, is solipsistic and because he incoherently slips, neologizes and omits; according to the madman, the normal is mad because her excessive greed and aggression will provoke a karmic catastrophe that will end the world in 2012 (see Figure 2).[33]

On the scale of qualities that the normal associates with madness, the madman is an amplified man. On the scale of qualities that the madman associates with madness, the normal is an amplified man.

The amount of amplification of these qualities also depends on the observer: relative to the majority of normals the schizophrenic appears

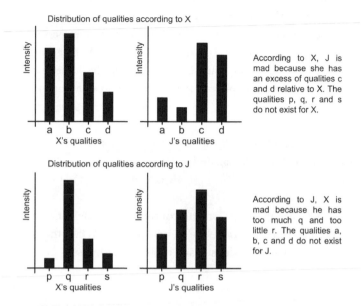

Distribution of qualities according to X

According to X, J is mad because she has an excess of qualities c and d relative to X. The qualities p, q, r and s do not exist for X.

Distribution of qualities according to J

According to J, X is mad because he has too much q and too little r. The qualities a, b, c and d do not exist for J.

Figure 2. The qualities associated with madness are relative

to have intense schizo qualities; relative to schizophrenics who have even more amplified schizo qualities the same madman appears normal. Who is classified as mad and who is classified as sane depends upon the level of intensity defined as normal.[34]

In some parts of the homogenous zone *all* of the qualities of a person are intensified or reduced relative to the average level. A person whose whole being is amplified relative to some normal person is labelled 'manic'; a person whose whole being is reduced relative to some normal person is labelled 'depressed'.

Disjunction and Delusion

... sanity or psychosis is tested by the degree of conjunction or disjunction between two persons where the one is sane by common consent.

The critical test of whether or not a patient is psychotic is a lack of congruity, an incongruity, a clash, between him and me.

The 'psychotic' is the name we have for the other person in a disjunctive relationship of a particular kind. It is only because of this interpersonal disjunction that we start to examine his urine, and look for anomalies in the graphs of the electrical activity of his brain.

(Ronald Laing, *The Divided Self*)[35]

Where two principles really do meet which cannot be reconciled with one another, then each man declares the other a fool and a heretic.

(Ludwig Wittgenstein, *On Certainty*)[36]

People who are far apart on the continuum of intensities find it difficult to understand or relate to one another. When they come into contact they may accuse each other of madness.

Disjunctions of intensity often become disjunctions of truth. The more insane a person is – the more she differs in intensity from some normal person – the more the content of what she says appears to be alien, false, wrong, crazy and untrue. From a stand-point of faith in her own world the self-appointed normal person experiences the madman's world as a delusion, a hallucination, as something that is *deficient* in the truth that she experiences within herself. Certain things that the madman says are *unacceptable* to her and madness becomes a reason given by the normal person for not believing what the madman says.

People with similar intensities of the same qualities see each other as mad if there is a significant difference between their systems of thought. Madmen are prolific in unorthodox beliefs and since these rarely coincide there are divisions between madness and sanity even within the walls of the asylum. A world in which everyone maniacally believed the same thing would have no madness in it.

People not only believe different things in the abstract: they also see and hear different sets of concrete phenomena. Some sleep with mermaids; others exist in a world that contains no living beings at all. Some hear angelic voices; others read minds, broadcast thoughts, and influence the weather and seasons. People who are far apart on this continuum of concrete phenomena declare each other deluded (Schreber thought that his psychiatrists were mentally blind, whilst they thought he was hallucinating).

Related to these differences are the kinds of theories that different people have. Madmen have a preference for theories about aliens, God, and the K.G.B., which are unattractive to sober well-educated psychiatrists. Scientists, psychiatrists and philosophers have strange theories about eternal underlying structures, bodies without organs and spaces of appropriation that make no sense at all to the intelligent madman. People with different theories accuse each other of madness.

These differences in intensity, beliefs, concrete phenomena and theories alienate people from each other. They no longer listen to one another and dismiss what the other has to say – the other is mad, he has nothing to say: he is *incapable* of saying anything meaningful.

Groups of people coalesce who share the same intensities, beliefs, concrete phenomena and theories. Although they may recognize a continuum between themselves and other people, they dismiss anyone who deviates too far from their consensual sanity. People outside of these groups are labelled deviants.

When these groups are large enough, or when they form a majority, the pressure of their numbers may convince the people labelled 'mad' that they are indeed mad and in need of treatment. In this case, the deviant minority accepts the judgement and standards of the majority, and at the same time acknowledges that they fall short of them. This temporarily stabilizes the deviant labels – if they are accepted by both the majority and minority, there is no one left to contest them.

However, even if the madman believes that he is deluded, he is still part of the homogenous zone, and if delusion is a matter of *consensus*, it is also *reversible*.

The Gorgon's Mirror

… there is a total space which is grouped around the Other, and this space is made *with my* space; there is a regrouping in which I take part but which escapes me, a regrouping of all the objects which people my universe. … The grass is something qualified; it is *this* green grass which exists for the Other; in this sense the very quality of the object, its deep, raw green is in direct relation to this man. This green turns toward the Other a face which escapes me. I apprehend the relation of the green to the Other as an objective relation, but I cannot apprehend the green as it appears to the Other. Thus suddenly an object has appeared which has stolen the world from me. Everything is in place; everything still exists for me; but everything is traversed by an invisible flight and fixed in the direction of a new object. …

But *the Other* is still an object *for me*. He belongs to *my distances*; the man is there, twenty paces from me, he is turning his back on me. As such he is again two yards, twenty inches from the lawn, six yards from the statue; hence the disintegration of my universe is contained within the limits of this same universe; we are not dealing here with a flight of the world toward nothingness or outside itself. Rather it appears that the world has a kind of drain hole in the middle of its being and that it is perpetually flowing off through this hole. The universe, the flow, and the drain hole are all once again recovered, reapprehended, and fixed as an object. All this is there *for me* as a partial structure of the world, even though the total disintegration of the universe is involved.

(Jean-Paul Sartre, *Being and Nothingness*)[37]

As my gaze sinks into the writhing pools of the madman's eyes I glimpse another world; within that world I observe another soul; within that soul I see the heart of a believer. Surrounded by incontrovertible realities the madman has *faith* in the world that he encounters. He *is* part of Al-Qaeda's plot to take over the world. He *is* being observed by aliens. He *is* the recipient of rays from God. Within this whirling world I see a tiny figure, a miniature effigy of myself. Within this world I *am* an American disguised as a doctor, a lifeless puppet controlled by aliens, a fleeting improvised man.

When my glance penetrates the cold eyes of the hospital psychiatrist I tentatively grasp another world; within that world I touch upon another soul; within that soul I palpitate the heart of a believer. Surrounded by incontrovertible realities the psychiatrist has *faith* in the world he encounters. He *is* assembled from an interplay of molecules and forces. He *is* no more than a twilit heap of interlocking instincts and drives crystallized around a complex formed during childhood. He *is* a palpitating mass of cosmic energy, a puppet in the hands of power. In this abstract world I encounter a tiny figure, a miniature representation of myself. Within this world I *am* a repressed homosexual, a man whose inhibitions inhibit the flow of energies at orgasm, an intricate machine formed from billions of complex parts.

When we study the madman we encounter a miniature world folded in upon itself; a world that interprets everything in its own terms; a world trapped behind its filters and limited to a single worldview. When we look a little closer at this world we see ourselves within it: distorted and caricatured, effaced or enlarged, we have become a devil or a demiurge, an operator or a spy, a machine or a fleeting improvised man.

But a reversal takes place. Once we have seen a miniature caricature of ourselves in the madman's world, we notice the miniature caricature of the madman that we have created in our own world. Once we have seen the way in which the madman encloses everything within his own way of thinking, we begin to question whether we are like that too, whether we squeeze the world through the fish-eye lens of our own certainties, whether our cursory rejection of the madman's ideas is a product, not of truth, but of the indubitability of our preconceptions.

The madman sees us as mad because we are too stupid to perceive what for him are self-evident realities. We look at the madman and wonder whether, perhaps, we are mad too. United with him in the homogenous zone, we see that he is exaggerated in a different way from ourselves, that he has different opinions, but we can no longer dismiss him with a label. Reflected in the madman's eyes we see ourselves as mad; exchanging places with him in the zone we attune ourselves to the sanity of madness, and awaken to the insanity lying at the heart of our reason.

This reversal is only possible within the homogenous zone – we can only exchange places with the madman because we have the same standing as him, because we have both been thrown in the same way, because we have both been *given* our thought, language, ontology and form of life. From our bedrock of truth we once saw the madman wallowing in the swamp of error. This arrogance drains away once we realize that the homogenous zone is suffused with the instability of being thrown. Without God, without external guarantees, now that the omnipotence of science is over, free flow and reversal becomes possible between ourselves and the madman.

This reversal reverses. We fall back into our own system of beliefs ... and fall away again. Although we see ourselves as mad through the madman's eyes, we still believe in our mad certainties. We cannot entirely reject them ... and yet they are absurd at the same time. Madness and reason swap places with each other in a confusing and despairing dance. Ceaseless fluctuation between madness and sanity over all parts of the zone.

We are left with the thrown zone of the human, its quirks and exaggerations and the concrete beliefs of the people constituting it.

Within one person some of these beliefs are a lived reality, a reassuring framework of certainties; within another, the same content is deluded nonsense, the fantastical production of a deranged mind. Given this instability, we can no longer take what we have been given to believe entirely seriously, and we are unable to dismiss the madman on grounds of madness. Perhaps we should be open to thinking about the world using the madman's language; open to the possibility that perhaps he might be right about the aliens, the C.I.A., about God having a special relationship with one human being, about psychokinetic control over the weather ...

> Human beings who are fortunate enough to enjoy healthy nerves cannot (as a rule anyway) have 'illusions', 'hallucinations', 'visions', or whatever expression one wants to use for these phenomena; it would therefore be desirable if all human beings remained free from such experiences; they would then subjectively feel very much better. But this does not imply that the events resulting from a diseased nervous system are altogether unfounded in objective reality or have to be regarded as nervous excitations lacking all external cause. I can therefore not share Kraepelin's astonishment which he expresses repeatedly (for instance Vol. 1, pp. 112, 116, 162, etc. 6th Edition) that the 'voices', etc., seem to have a far greater power of conviction for hallucinated patients than 'anything said by those around them'. A person with sound nerves is, so to speak, *mentally* blind compared with him who receives supernatural impressions by virtue of his diseased nerves; he is therefore as little likely to persuade the visionary of the unreality of his voices as a person who can see will be persuaded by a really blind person that there are no colours, that blue is not blue, red not red, etc.
>
> (Daniel Paul Schreber, *Memoirs of My Nervous Illness*)[38]

Planet of Fools

Once upon a time, in some out of the way corner of that universe which is dispersed into numberless twinkling solar systems, there was a star

upon which clever beasts invented knowing. That was the most arrogant
and mendacious minute of 'world history,' but nevertheless, it was only a
minute. After nature had drawn a few breaths, the star cooled and
congealed, and the clever beasts had to die. — One might invent such a
fable, and yet he still would not have adequately illustrated how miserable,
how shadowy and transient, how aimless and arbitrary the human intellect
looks within nature.

(Friedrich Nietzsche, 'On Truth and Lies in a Nonmoral Sense')[39]

Setting aside the possibility of alien lifeforms, God, and intelligences
from higher planes of consciousness, our culture has no outside. Six
billion people clinging to the surface of a rocky sphere *and that is it*.
We are aware that our beliefs are self-contained; we know that we
interpret what we see in terms of what we expect to see; we realize
that we *cannot* see what does not fit. However, because we are many
and not one, we seem to escape the privacy of language that
Wittgenstein criticizes:

Let us imagine a table (something like a dictionary) that exists only in our
imagination. A dictionary can be used to justify the translation of a word
X by a word Y. But are we also to call it a justification if such a table is to
be looked up only in the imagination? — 'Well, yes; then it is a subjective
justification.' — 'But surely I can appeal from one memory to another. For
example, I don't know if I have remembered the time of departure of a train
right and to check it I call to mind how a page of the time-table looked.
Isn't it the same here?' — No; for this process has got to produce a memory
which is actually *correct*. If the mental image of the time-table could not
itself be *tested* for correctness, how could it confirm the correctness of the
first memory? (As if someone were to buy several copies of the morning
paper to assure himself that what it said was true.)[40]

Our language-games are stable and our words retain their
meaning because we check up on each other. If one person makes
a mistake, a thousand will correct him. If someone makes a claim,
I can independently verify this claim. The problem with this

'independent' verification is that our culture as a whole lacks an outside. When we test our claims for correctness, we are not getting *independent* verification because any person that we ask will be at least partially within the same system of beliefs as ourselves. If I ask my neighbour to confirm that Schreber was deluded, I do not learn anything that I did not know before – I have done little more than purchase two copies of the same cultural newspaper. If my neighbour claims that Schreber was sane, I will think that she is insane. Dismissing her opinion as lunacy, I will work my way through my neighbours until I find one that agrees with me.

It might be thought that rigorously independent confirmation could be found within a wholly independent system of beliefs. One problem with this is that it might be impossible to formulate the claim that I want to verify within an alternative system of beliefs – a statement about computers cannot be confirmed by someone who has never encountered them before. Second, there are no wholly independent systems of belief within the homogenous zone because all people – simply through the fact that they are people – share a common form of life. A truly independent system of beliefs would have to have no connection with the human form of life, and any confirmation that this might offer is likely to be meaningless for us. Within our form of life, such a confirmation would hardly be a confirmation at all: it would be music, animal noises or random sounds – and no one hopes to get independent confirmation from random sounds.[41]

If there is no independent verification within the homogenous zone, the difference between an individual looking up a train timetable in his imagination and a number of individuals cross-checking each other vanishes. All language becomes private. When individuals are isolated, their old ideas silently mutate, and new ones are accepted less critically. Our culture also multiplies modifications: it blindly shifts, twists and drifts whilst all the time believing that it has never changed. New ideas are suggested and taken up; conservative elements attempt to preserve old ideas in response to innovation, but conservatism metamorphoses too – it is often a reaction to change, never a pure preservation.[42] Collectively, we do censure each other and check the cultural drift, but these censures and checks come from the culture that is drifting, and so they inevitably drift too. Nothing holds our culture fast to one position; there is no absolute outside that could tell us whether we are going crazy on our spherical island.[43]

In addition to the drifts in religious and scientific ideas, there are a couple of more subtle ways in which our culture changes over time. To begin with, our genetic material is constantly recombining and mutating, and so any language or thought structures with a neurological or genetic basis will be affected by these alterations, and we may be completely unaware of such changes if they occur. In *The Man Who Mistook His Wife for a Hat*, Oliver Sacks describes Dr. P. who gradually lost his ability to recognize faces and visualize narrative scenes. What is strange about this loss is that Dr. P. was not at all troubled by it because he no longer possessed any idea of what he had once had: 'Dr. P. was not fighting, did not know what was lost, did not indeed know that anything was lost.'[44] This man simply changed and a whole area of his experience disappeared without mourning or trace. When our brain and genetic makeup change our ways of thinking can alter without leaving any mark of this change upon us.

Against this it could be argued that evolution holds our neurology in check; that certain mutations will be thrown out because they leave a person too out of touch with reality to be able to survive or find food. This argument ignores the fact that people have survived for hundreds of thousands of years with structurally complex 'delusional' belief systems and animals also seem to do quite well despite their inability to grasp even the first principles of modern science. Some kind of stable and consistent view upon things may be necessary for eating and breeding, but the way in which this is put together can vary a great deal without affecting its bearer's chances of survival.[45] Most, if not all, of the *detail* of our complex human worldview is irrelevant to our longevity as a species.

The second subtle way in which our culture drifts is through the continual mutation and evolution of our languages. The division after Babel would have happened without divine intervention. One interpretation of linguistic change is given by Saussure, who describes how languages split up over time into local dialects, which grow more distinct from each other the further they are apart. This change comes about through accident, innovation, neologism, in response to writing, and through contact with other languages. Since a mutation in one word alters its relationships with other words, the possibilities of an entire language can be reconfigured by a single shift. According to Saussure, these language changes also affect the way we think because of an intimate link between the structure of our language and the structure of our thought. For Saussure, the objects of thought are constituted together with the differences in language, and so changes in the sounds of a language can also transform its conceptual possibilities:

> Psychologically, setting aside its expression in words, our thought is simply a vague, shapeless mass. Philosophers and linguists have always agreed that were it not for signs, we should be incapable of differentiating any two ideas in a clear and constant way. In itself, thought is like a swirling cloud, where no shape is intrinsically determinate. No ideas are established in advance, and nothing is distinct, before the introduction of linguistic structure. ... we can envisage the linguistic phenomenon in its entirety – the language, that is – as a series of adjoining subdivisions simultaneously imprinted both on the plane of vague, amorphous thought (A) and on the equally featureless plane of sound (B).[46]

> Once sound change has created a regular phonetic difference between two series of terms contrasting in value, the mind seizes upon this material difference and endows it with significance, making it a bearer of the conceptual difference.[47]

Within the structuralist picture, there is no overall direction or order governing change. The web of differences shifts over time in response to local idiosyncratic mutations. Furthermore, these changes are invisible to the people who speak the language: they cannot think about how they used to think within the framework of their new tongue.[48]

Microcosmically embodying this large-scale linguistic drift are the incoherent slips, neologisms and omissions of schizophrenics: an intensification of this process of linguistic and conceptual mutation. Our culture changes in this way all the time: contacting God, controlling the cosmos, drifting into madness in its festering flat in Peckham.

Planet Earth is a ship of fools floating through space, drifting through time on a voyage from nowhere to nowhere. We have gone insane on our island; the homogenous zone has lost it, flipped its lid after prolonged isolation. Or rather, the zone never had it; it has always been insane; we have always been foaming fools pouring out an endless stream of fantastical metaphysical, scientific, religious and cosmological imaginings.[49]

Problems and Objections

> ... the concept of 'mental disease' has proved of great value in the practice of medicine. It has advanced a set of testable hypotheses which have already borne fruit concerning the nature, causation and treatment of several of the very common and incapacitating forms of human suffering.
>
> (Martin Roth and Jerome Kroll, *The Reality of Mental Illness*)[50]

The most obvious objection to this interpretation of madness is that schizophrenia is a *disease* that was discovered by Kraepelin and relabelled by Bleuler. This disease of schizophrenia has a well-defined complex of symptoms (set out in the American Psychiatric

Association's document DSM IV), which progress in an orderly way and respond to drug treatment. In addition, there is some evidence that schizophrenia has a genetic component, and there are similarities between neurologically damaged patients and those suffering from schizophrenia. Furthermore, the argument that schizophrenia is a cultural product does not work because madness has been recognized in the West since the Greeks, and something akin to our notion of schizophrenia can be found in most other societies.[51] If schizophrenia is a genuine *disease*, then there is a real underlying difference between madness and normality that cannot be homogenized into a single space.

A first response to this argument is that beneath the veneer of medical confidence lies a 'disease' that is very poorly defined; a 'disease' that is perhaps no more than a cluster of 'symptoms'. In *Schizophrenia, A Scientific Delusion?*, Mary Boyle claims that scientifically respectable diseases are not just clusters of symptoms, but clusters of symptoms with definite *signs* that indicate the presence or absence of the disease. For example, you can *test* for diabetes by measuring the level of sugar in the urine, and a person who shows all of the symptoms of diabetes and tests negative does not have it and a different diagnosis must be found. In the case of schizophrenia, there are no tests that can be used to establish whether or not a person is suffering from it. Each of the 'symptoms', taken in itself, does not make a person schizophrenic,[52] and yet once they are brought together they become a disease with a hypothesized underlying abnormality: 'the variable cluster from which schizophrenia is inferred contains no sign, but only a number of presumably overdetermined behaviours called symptoms and which have never been shown to be systematically related'.[53] Boyle also describes how the group that Kraepelin isolated in his 'discovery' of schizophrenia included many people suffering from post encephalitic Parkinsonism and possibly syphilis. The modern schizophrenic is all that is left of this diverse group, after all the people with known diseases have been removed from it. It is possible that a single underlying cause will be discovered that explains the behaviour of this remainder, but it is also possible that a variety of diverse causes will be found that gradually remove people from the group of schizophrenics until there are no pure schizophrenics left. In the latter case, there would not be any people with the disease of schizophrenia – only people who manifest schizophrenic behaviour as part of the course of a different illness.[54] Boyle also offers a detailed criticism of the genetic evidence for schizophrenia.[55]

A second problem with *diseased* schizophrenics is that even if an underlying genetic, neurological or cognitive cause of schizophrenia could be found, it would not create an *essential* difference between the ideas and experiences of normals and those of schizophrenics. As Sass puts it:

> Implicit in a great deal of biological psychiatry is an asymmetry of explanatory principles. Normal (or healthy) forms of consciousness are assumed to be, to a great extent, under one's intentional control and, in addition, to operate according to rational principles and to be oriented toward the objective world. While these normal mental processes are certainly assumed to be *correlated* with physical events occurring in the brain, seldom are they viewed as being *mere* causal by-products of such events, since the meaningfulness and directedness they exhibit seem intrinsic to the psyche, to the realm of meaning rather than of physical event. But *ab*normal modes of consciousness, at least those characterizing the insane, have often been seen very differently: as involving a 'fall into determinism,' a lapse from dualism whereby the malfunctioning physical processes (in brain and nervous system) disrupt the mental or psychic stream, depriving it of its intrinsic rationality and meaningfulness.[56]

Schizophrenics may think in a particular way because of a gene or a neurological configuration, but normal people also think in the way that they do because of genes and a neurological configuration – both are equally dependent on the genes that patterned their brains and the present structure of their brains. If a majority of the population had the 'schizophrenic gene', normality would become abnormal and scientists would start to search for mutant genes in normal people. If a majority of the population had the same brain arrangement as the schizophrenic, this would become the normal way of dealing with reality, and a person judged normal today would become a mental patient. Which gene or neurological configuration is the *right* one is a matter of consensus, just as delusion is a matter of consensus. Shifting the problem down to a neurological or genetic level does not alter anything. Definitions of normal physiology are democratic.

Seen from a more general perspective, the medical model of schizophrenia and the homogenous zone are not that incompatible. Even the possibility of treatment is not excluded by the description of the zone that I am offering here. Some people may want to adjust the intensities of their qualities, and there is no reason why they should not attempt to do this with surgery or pills. However, the homogenous zone does not think that a real or fictitious disease can be used to create a qualitative difference between normal people and madmen, and it also rejects the way in which medicine uses 'disease' as a synonym for 'untruth' (and it may be impossible to interpret madness as a disease without bringing in the negative and normative connotations that this has in our society).

A second objection to the homogenous zone is that schizo-phrenics' 'delusions' can be *reduced* to their case histories. If we can reduce a madman's ideas to sexuality or an unfortunate childhood, there is no longer any need to take them seriously, and there will no longer be any reversal or exchange between normality and madness. The schizo will have simply *gone astray*. This dismissal by reduction can be clearly seen in the numerous studies of Schreber.[57] At first glance, Schreber's *Memoirs of My Nervous Illness* presents a radically different world, a unique interpretation of reality that would have been interpreted in an earlier age within the framework of religious visions. However, because Schreber is classified as mad, his beliefs and metaphysics are dismissed by contemporary critics by tracing them back to events in his childhood or other causes.

According to Freud,[58] Schreber's illness was caused by an outburst of homosexual libido. At first, this homosexuality was directed towards his doctor, Professor Flechsig, towards whom he felt a great deal of warmth and affection after his first attack of nervous illness had been cured. This erotic desire was not acceptable to Schreber – although it was fairly openly expressed throughout his illness – and so it was transformed into hatred. This hatred was projected outside of Schreber as the hatred of Flechsig for him, and this imaginary persecution enabled Schreber to openly acknowledge his love (transformed into hatred) for Flechsig, since he could now hate Flechsig in response to Flechsig's persecution of him. These four stages in the development of Schreber's paranoia are summarized below:

1) Schreber loves Flechsig.
2) Schreber hates Flechsig.
3) Flechsig hates Schreber.
4) Schreber hates Flechsig because Flechsig hates Schreber.

Later on, Schreber's erotic desire for Flechsig was transferred to God. This satisfied his ego and allowed his feminine fantasies fulfilment without conflict. Freud further reveals that Schreber's desire for Flechsig was actually an erotic desire for his older brother (who died before Schreber's illness). Schreber's transferral of affection from Flechsig to God during his illness probably repeated his earlier transferral of affection from his brother to his father after his brother's death. Freud found confirmation of this hypothesis in the fact that Schreber's relationship with God mirrored many of the features of his relationship with his father, with the similarities including a mixture of respect and insubordination in both relationships and the fact that both his physician-father and God were workers of miracles. This link between God and Schreber's father enabled Freud to interpret all the complexity, religiosity, and strangeness of Schreber's relationship with God as the working out of an infantile conflict with his father:

Thus in the case of Schreber we find ourselves once again on the familiar ground of the father-complex. The patient's struggle with Flechsig became revealed to him as a conflict with God, and we must therefore construe it as an infantile conflict with the father whom he loved; the details of that conflict (of which we know nothing) are what determined the content of his delusions. ... In infantile experiences such as this the father appears as an interferer with the satisfaction which the child is trying to obtain; this is usually of an auto-erotic character, though at a later date it is often replaced in phantasy by some other satisfaction of a less inglorious kind. In the final stages of Schreber's delusion a magnificent victory was scored by the infantile sexual urge; for voluptuousness became God-fearing, and God Himself (his father) never tired of demanding it from him. His father's most dreaded threat, castration, actually provided the material for his wishful phantasy (at first resisted but later accepted) of being transformed into a woman. His allusion to an offence covered by the surrogate idea 'soul-murder' could not be more transparent.[59]

A second reduction of Schreber is offered by Morton Schatzman, who compares many of Schreber's delusions and miracles with the treatments that Schreber received whilst he was growing up. Schreber's father was an authority on child rearing and his methods included cold baths, eye exercises and a strict emphasis on posture. He also invented a number of restraining devices that he probably tested on his children. These included a bar to maintain posture, a mechanism to prevent the child's head from falling forwards or sideways, and straps to hold the shoulders in position. Schatzman makes a number of connections between the exercises and restraining devices that Schreber may have been subjected to as a child and his later hallucinations, suggesting that Schreber's madness was in part a re-enactment of his early experiences. For example, Schreber's compression of the chest miracle may have been a memory of the bar that was used to maintain his posture, the little men on Schreber's eyes could be linked to the concentration and vigilance that he was forced to apply to his eye exercises, and the baths Schreber experienced as a child may have resurfaced as the miracles of heat and cold. Schreber's world is strange and alien to us because he had an unorthodox childhood: there is little reason to take his worldview seriously if it is little more than a re-enactment of his father's child-rearing experiments. As Schatzman explains:

> Schreber suffers from reminiscences. His body embodies his past. He retains memories of what his father did to him as a child; although part of his mind knows they are memories, 'he' does not. He is considered insane not only because of the quality of his experiences, but because he misconstrues their *mode*; he *remembers*, in some cases perfectly accurately, how his father treated him, but he thinks he *perceives* events occurring in the present of which he imagines God, rays, little men, and so on are the agents.[60]

Other reductions of Schreber include Canetti's explanation in terms of power and Sass's Wittgensteinian analysis, which compares Schreber's delusions with the end points of certain 'diseased' language-games.

The problem with these reductions of Schreber is that it is not just schizophrenic systems that can be dismissed on these grounds, but *any system whatsoever*. If we can dismiss a schizophrenic's theory because it is reducible to its antecedents, then we can also do the same with the theories of normal people like Freud, Schatzman and Sass. For example, Freud's psychoanalysis could be a product of his lust for power over his patients, perhaps Schatzman wants to explain Schreber in terms of his past because this explanation satisfies a yearning for security that he developed in childhood, and maybe Sass's conceptualization of Schreber in terms of solipsism is just a reminiscence of the time when Sass was locked inside a cupboard at the age of seven (Sass's problem is that he misconstrues the *mode* of his reminiscence; he imagines that he is analysing Schreber, when in fact he is just re-enacting an earlier closeted situation).

If theories can be dismissed because they are products of their creators' pasts, then we can dismiss all theories. This might be a reasonable position to take, except that this dismissal of all theories is itself a theory which, in turn, can be dismissed as a product of *its* past. If all theories are dismissed, including the theory that dismisses theories, then we are left upon strange oscillating ground that shifts between theories and no theories and dialectically emerges, falls and rises again as different aspects of the problem are brought to light. This is the territory of the collapsing hermeneutic circle, which it is the purpose of this book, but not this paragraph, to attempt to explain.

Reductions of schizophrenic worldviews also suffer from the problem that they are *reversible*. We can explain some features of *Memoirs of My Nervous Illness* on the basis of Schreber's homoerotic drives, but we can also claim that Freud wrote his essay on Schreber because ideas were planted into his head by Flechsig (or perhaps God). (This manipulation of Freud was probably an attempt to discredit Schreber further – unmanning him still more through a dismissal of his religious experiences.) Although the normal can explain the madman's deviation from the system of beliefs that he regards as true, the madman can also explain the normal's attempts to explain him as a deviation from the system of beliefs that he regards as true.

In conclusion, these criticisms of the homogenous zone can either be accommodated within its structure, or they rely on a double standard that dismisses the madman's beliefs because they are the product of his diseased brain and childhood and then fails to acknowledge that definitions of disease are democratic and normal beliefs are also products of brains and childhoods.

Collapse of the Homogenous Zone

The Limit

Some – farm houses – in a farm yard – time – with a horse and horseman – time where – going across the field as if they're ploughing the field –

time – with ladies – or collecting crops – time work is – coming with
another lady – time work is – and where – she's holding a book – time
– thinking of things – time work is – and time work is where – you see
her coming time work is on the field – and where work is – where her
time is where working is and thinking of people and where work is and
where you see the hills – going up – and time work is – where you see
the – grass – time work is – time work is where the fields are – where
growing and where work is.

(Anonymous schizophrenic patient)[61]

At the limit we no longer see another world opening up within the
chronic schizophrenic: just a wilderness of twisted words and
broken phrases – the empty blank stare of silence.

Neologisms, repeating words resurface; different personalities
scrap and bicker over the body's vocal apparatus.

At its limit, at the margins of madness, do we draw a line and
say that beyond this line the madman is no longer one of us; that
he has spiralled off into something no longer recognisable as
anything – a surface play of words and feelings; inertia immobility
and silence? Does an abyss now yawn between us and the
madman? Is there now an *essential* difference between us? Is he no
longer within the homogenous zone?

Or are our words the same as his: a mumbled mish-mash of
incoherent sounds and repetitions mixed with feelings, gestures,
thoughts; a raving delirious discourse; a rambling flood of sounds
vomiting from our mouths?

Sanity in the homogenous zone is always contaminated by
madness at its limit.

… just the mouth … lips … cheeks … jaws … never – … what? … tongue?
… yes … lips … cheeks … jaws … tongue … never still a second … mouth

on fire ... streams of words ... ... now can't stop ... imagine! ... can't stop
the stream ... and the whole brain begging ... something begging in the
brain ... begging the mouth to stop ... pause a moment ... if only for a
moment ... and no response ... as if it hadn't heard ... or couldn't ...
couldn't pause a second ... like maddened ... all that together ... straining
to hear ... piece it together ... and the brain ... raving away on its own ...
trying to make sense of it ... or make it stop ...

(Samuel Beckett, *Not I*)[62]

Circling Limits

Madness is the absolute break with the work; it forms the constitutive
moment of abolition, which dissolves in time the truth of the work; it draws
the exterior edge, the line of dissolution, the contour against the void.

(Michel Foucault, *Madness and Civilization*)[63]

A zone taunt and fluctuating between extremes. Ripping itself
into tiny shreds; spinning and dissolving into nothingness; bursting
apart with an aching clanging groan. Coalescing again into a
spinning sphere in a state of perfection from every direction.
Shudders and tremors trumpet the next explosion of this eternally
dissolving and returning dialectic.

Madness and sanity are variants of the same phenomenon:
everything that we see and fear in the madman can also be seen and
feared in ourselves. We are all mad children, we are all autistic, we
are all deluded, we are all abstract and solipsistic, and we all
madly cobble together systems of absurd beliefs on this lost planet
of fools.

The inhabitants of the homogenous zone are simultaneously
mad and sane. But if we are mad, we cannot describe our madness
because it becomes impossible to create a work, a theory or a
description. The hypothesis that we are mad is, like Descartes'

cogito, a moment of hyperbole that leaves reason and unreason behind; a moment of excess 'in the direction of the nondetermined, Nothingness or Infinity, an excess which overflows the totality of that which can be thought, the totality of beings and determined meanings, the totality of factual history'.[64] The hypothesis that we are mad is a leap into ... nowhere. Speech before this leap becomes (retrospectively) the discarded foam of fools. Speech after this leap bubbles up into the booming otherworldly laugh that echoes down the corridors of the asylums. Even the hypothesis that we are mad becomes meaningless and falls away from us. If we are mad we cannot know that we are mad. We remain in empty space for a while, and then fall back into reason; fall back into discourse, into the work. But once we are back inside the work we recommence our mad hypotheses, fly out to the hyperbolic point ... and return again. This *collapsing* hermeneutic circle is shown in Figure 3.

We cannot hypothesize that we are mad because this hypothesis states that we are no longer making hypotheses. It is not a possible conjecture. But where does this leave the statement that we are not

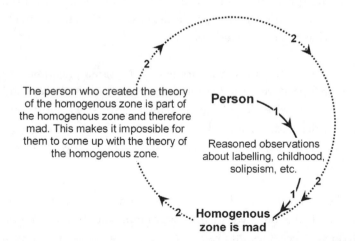

Figure 3. A mad homogenous zone is a collapsing hermeneutic circle

mad? Can this continue to speak when its opposite has fallen silent? If we cannot claim that we are mad, then 'We are sane' becomes a truism, a tautology, an affirmation that we are hermeneutically circling within reason. 'We are sane' no longer tells us anything about the world; it no longer describes a state of being or mind. At most it affirms the presence of meaning or reason themselves – but affirmations of meaning or reason have to be meaningful or reasonable, and we are caught again in the same vicious/virtuous circle.

'There is a cat' *says* something because there are other animals that the furry form in front of me could be – there is the possibility of *being wrong* about my attribution of catness to this animal. However 'The homogenous zone is sane' cannot be wrong because its opposite is not another statement, but the end of statements, the end of right and wrong, the impossibility of a speech that says anything. 'The homogenous zone is sane' is grammatically worthless – philosophical *nonsense*. This collapse of totalized sanity is shown in Figure 4.

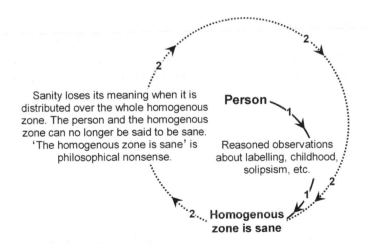

Figure 4. A sane homogenous zone is a collapsing hermeneutic circle

We have described a world in which no worldview is rejected because it is the *product of disease*. For our part, we think that there is a homogenous zone and this forces us to take the madman seriously (if the madman's beliefs are biologically determined, this must also be true of our own truths). But the madman disagrees, he does not see the homogenous zone the way we do; he has a *different* metaphysical picture of reality. We argue that it is a matter of opinion, that no one can *really* know whether or not there is a homogenous zone; but the madman is adamant, absolute, will not accept compromises: 'There is no homogenous zone and that is it!'. If we believe in the homogenous zone, we also have to listen to perspectives that reject it: we cannot use 'madness' to dismiss worldviews in which the theory of the homogenous zone has not the slightest shadow of existence.

The homogenous zone is forced to take the madman *seriously* when he claims that the homogenous zone is false. The homogenous zone starts out as a reasonable theory, believes in perspectives that reject it, vanishes and then reappears again once the rejecting perspective has been dismissed. It is the *unstable* hermeneutic circle shown in Figure 5.

The theory of the homogenous zone collapses because it is too crazy or too sane, or it destabilizes when it undermines the rejection of other beliefs on grounds of madness. If there were no homogenous zone, the theory of the homogenous zone could be sane, differentiated from other theories, and therefore true.

The collapse of an opposition is painful: schizophrenic philosophers, reasonable madmen; agitated struggling reason, calm clear hysteria. Faith in our own world; belief in mad alternative worlds. We gaze with wonder at the white-marble structures of reason; we dissolve into Dionysian delirium.

I have presented you with a mad world, an inverted world; a schizophrenic fantasy in which madness changes place with

normality – a world in which madness *is* normality. This is my
vision. There are other worlds, other visions, in which lines, barriers
and walls are erected between sanity and insanity, between
normality and schizophrenia. I am only a small patch in the fabric
of the homogenous zone and I can only offer you a personal
vision. You can dismiss me as deluded. You can ignore me, beat me,
burn me, tear out my eyes and lock me in a conceptual prison. But
I am already free and you are imprisoned – soon you will want to
join me in my homogenous zone and start ripping out the bars and

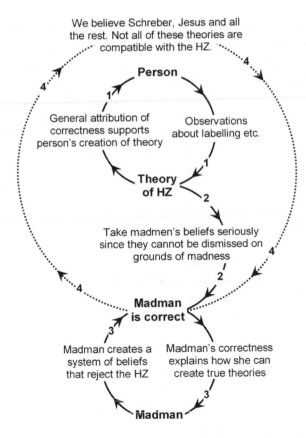

Figure 5. The homogenous zone is an unstable hermeneutic circle

tearing down the walls that you have created around me. Then, as you rest wearily upon your pick, you will suddenly realize that barbed enclosures and liberated spaces are just so many man-made ways of dividing space; valid for certain applications and purposes, but of no real importance or significance. Perhaps we can then relax together into our normality/madness, crack open a beer, light a pipe and chill out in the homogenous zone.

'Madness' in the Zone

Once we have understood the madman as a local amplification (or diminishment) of the homogenous zone relative to someone less (or more) amplified; once we have accepted everything that the madman has to say, what will become of 'madness' within the zone? Will we continue to think of the zone as simultaneously sane and insane, or will 'madness' and 'normality' dissolve into the detritus of history and join the vast crowd of surplus words that lie unused and abandoned from earlier times and places?

One possibility is that we could stop using 'mad' disease to dismiss someone different and continue to use it as a label for the collection of intensified schizoid qualities. This would leave us with an unstable culture of competing, incompatible and equally valid worldviews, and it would be impossible to dismiss any of them on grounds of madness.

But something would have been lost. The homogenous zone that I have described here is one that oscillates between madness and sanity; one that both reasons *and* spirals away into nothingness and infinity. If we eliminated the madness of madness, we would be left with a homogenous zone crosscut by multiple reasons that had forgotten that it ever glimpsed unreason. The worldviews of madmen would all be *understood* as contortions and exaggerations of the homogenous zone and there would be nothing left but a superfluity of reason; a rich dense weight of reason that is no longer contrasted with anything else. The homogenous zone would become hypersane.

Perhaps our vision of an alternative, of the other, of madness as something that opposes reason, is just a by-product of our inadequate understanding; a *misconception* generated by *insufficient* reason. Or perhaps a fundamental truth about our humanity can be found in the instability, thrownness and madness of the homogenous zone.

We cannot tell. We will have to wait and watch. Perhaps gods or aliens will come to reinject us with a notion of otherness. Baudrillard places his hopes in terrorism, viruses and catastrophe. Any of these could sustain the collapsing instability of the zone in a different form, even if the tag 'mad' is no longer used to label the flickering of the light of reason. But perhaps there is no otherness. We will have to wait and watch; wait and see what ends up re-creating history.

Why, thou sayest well. I do now remember a saying, 'The fool doth think he is wise, but the wise man knows himself to be a fool.' The heathen philosopher, when he had a desire to eat a grape, would open his lips when he put it into his mouth; meaning thereby that grapes were made to eat and lips to open.

(William Shakespeare, *As You Like It*)[65]

5 Labyrinths of Knowledge

These examples made it possible for a librarian of genius to discover the fundamental law of the Library. This thinker observed that all the books, no matter how diverse they might be, are made up of the same elements: the space, the period, the comma, the twenty-two letters of the alphabet. He also alleged a fact which travellers have confirmed: *In the vast Library there are no two identical books*. From these two incontrovertible premises he deduced that the Library is total and that its shelves register all the possible combinations of the twenty-odd orthographical symbols (a number which, though extremely vast, is not infinite): in other words, all that it is given to express, in all languages. Everything: the minutely detailed history of the future, the archangels' autobiographies, the faithful catalogue of the Library, thousands and thousands of false catalogues, the demonstration of the fallacy of those catalogues, the demonstration of the fallacy of the true catalogue, the Gnostic gospel of Basilides, the commentary on that gospel, the commentary on the commentary on that gospel, the true story of your death, the translation of every book in all languages, the interpolations of every book in all books.

(Jorge Luis Borges, *Labyrinths*)[1]

I have no idea who or what you are, but I can say that you and I have different points of view, different styles of being.

Your thoughts, obsessions, interests and idle talk are different from my own.

Our philosophical beliefs diverge: we argue differently for different things.

We may even have a different native language.

Perhaps you are an insect ...

In this chapter I will be discussing these differences between us.

If they are real, they provide evidence for what I have to say.

If there are no significant differences between us, this chapter will feel as if it has freshly sprung from your bright red cherry lips.

Aspects

> ... a study of continuous aspect perception can legitimately be viewed as philosophical investigation of human relationships with objects or phenomena *in general*.
>
> (Stephen Mulhall, *On Being in the World*)[2]

I look out of my window and see a naked woman running along the beach. The woman is separate from the beach, pressing into its sandy surface and springing on in a succession of graceful bounds. The meaning of the woman and the meaning of the beach are completely distinct for me. The woman is a sensuous vital erotic presence; the beach is a golden angled surface that I stroll on to see the sea.

Recognition dawns: she is my mother. In an instant the sexual possibility is replaced by the tender woman who cared for me as a child. Her breasts no longer arouse me: they were the source of the hot sweet milk that spurted between my infant lips.

As I look out of my window and watch the naked woman running along the beach, I am seeing an aspect, experiencing the situation in a particular way. On a postcard the same scene presents a different aspect to me: the woman and the beach fuse into a single 'holiday scene', and the meaning resonances of both are cut short.

A geologian sees the beach as a particular sand type; he hardly notices the woman at all. A fisherman assesses features of the beach, the phase of the tide and the condition of the sea in his attempt to ascertain where fish might be concentrating.

Aspects are present all the time in our lives: we see a tree, not a vertical columnar form with branching excrescences and green planar surfaces; we see a rose, not a convoluted red form with linear green attachment.[3] Some people are trapped forever within a world of geometrical forms; other people's daily lives are permanently furnished with cats, cars, TVs and trees.

An aspect is a whole way of seeing. Different ways of seeing discover themselves in different worlds.

I see a woman running naked on the beach and I can experience different aspects of her – see her in different ways. She is a finely tuned biological machine, a goddess, an assembly of soft curved surfaces of heady sensuality.

These aspects include myself. As she changes I change as well: I become a biological machine, a god, a man pinioned by the murmur of his erotic stirrings. These aspects may have complicated theories attached that penetrate my entire worldview.

> But how is it possible to *see* an object according to an *interpretation*?
> – The question represents it as a queer fact; as if something were being forced into a form it did not really fit. But no squeezing, no forcing took place here.
>
> (Ludwig Wittgenstein, *Philosophical Investigations*)[4]

Aspect change can be caused by theory. We look at the duck-rabbit in Figure 1 and see a duck. After someone has *told* us that they can also see a rabbit in the picture, the duck suddenly vanishes and a rabbit appears before us.

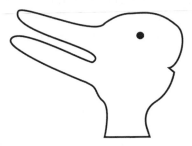

Figure 1. Duck-rabbit

Art, science and philosophy are mediums that open us up to aspects: they are aspect reflectors and generators. Turner's paintings of Venice lead us to see Venice in a different way; theories about genes and heredity generate a new experience of people; Heidegger's visions change our way of relating to existence. Art, science and philosophy are transformative because aspects are real, because we do see the world in a particular way, and because we can change this way of seeing.

Art, science and philosophy cause changes of aspect. However, this relationship is reciprocal: they emerge from aspects as well as create them. Art both reflects and transforms the culture that it comes from; normal science is determined by a paradigm, but scientific theories can create new paradigms.

We can *see* aspects, but for the most part we *inhabit* them. When we *see* an aspect we make a distinction between the aspect and the object. We look at an object and see an aspect of it. When we *inhabit* an aspect there is no distinction between what is seen or experienced and the object itself. When I am within an aspect the world is a certain way for me and this is not a representation of something else. The sadness of my friend is not an interpretation of his biological body: sadness seeps, burns and stirs within him; it pours out of his face and squeezes my heart in a sympathetic ache. My friend's sadness is an aspect *inhabited* by me: sadness stands before me in my friend, mingled with his blood, guts and bone.

> There are many occasions in which one is profoundly struck by the particular shade of consciousness manifest in someone's expression or behaviour; on such occasions, it is not just that we see *that* the person is fearful or joyful – we *see* the fear in his stare the joy in her face.
>
> (Stephen Mulhall, *On Being in the World*)[5]

Aspects are ways in which the world is: they are not solipsistic bubbles or subjective prisons. They can be shared by billions of people, or not inhabited by anyone. They are *cohabitable*.

The most global aspects do not appear to their inhabitants: they are taken for granted and other ways of 'seeing' are not even considered. A global aspect is taken to be self-evidently correct.

There is a spectrum of aspect differences. Some aspects agree upon almost everything, other aspects agree upon only one thing, and other aspects are radically incommensurable – they have no common ground, no common objects and no metaphysical worldview is shared by them.

Aspects can only contest one another if they have some common ground. Without this they are just speaking about different things altogether. Two aspects need to agree upon what x is and what truth is if they are to make opposing claims about the truth of x.

An evolutionist strikes a monkey with his staff and declares that this *Ateles belzebuth* is the result of natural selection. A creationist assays the monkey as the work of God's hand and a *debate* takes place that is based upon the fact that the aspects of the evolutionist and creationist overlap in many areas. They broadly agree about what a monkey is, what a monkey eats, the best way to cook a monkey, etc. Their *disagreement* about the origin of the monkey is founded upon their *agreement* about so much else.

The interpretations that different aspects offer do not always fight for supremacy. Victory can be independently achieved within each aspect by bending the facts round into systems with mutually reinforcing parts. Within each aspect the world is a certain way and theories within other aspects are either annulled or incorporated in a distorted form.

When two aspects disagree, it is possible that one is right and the other wrong, or both could be right or wrong. To decide the issue, some way has to be found to establish which side of the debate is correct (if any side of the debate is correct) and in many situations it will be *impossible* to resolve the debate in any way. Without resolution, the two aspects will simply stand before us, each as seductive as the other.

Within one aspect it is true that the monkey is the product of evolution; within a different aspect it is false that the monkey is the product of evolution. This disagreement could be resolved by a third aspect that integrated the two, but this would not necessarily be accepted by either party. Even if we consulted God on the matter, this would only add another opinion to the debate.

The clash between aspects brings them to our attention. If we all inhabited the same aspect, we would never become aware of aspects at all. We would all face the same world and make the same judgements about it – that world and those judgements would simply be true. However, different cultures, languages and forms of life have uncovered gaps between the worlds that people inhabit. The notion of an aspect developed from the experience of these fissures.[6]

Different aspects can affect one another. Parts of them can be exchanged through a kind of contact. But this exchange is not a conscious assimilation of the different. We just pick up parts of other aspects when we are exposed to them. If I hang around with a person long enough, I start to see things their way – and this has nothing to do with any conscious decision that I might make to do this.

Interpretation[7] takes place after assimilation: I absorb interpretations and then apply them. I interpret someone in one way for a while, and then, after assimilating part of their aspect, I start to interpret them in the way that they interpret themselves.

We only ever see one aspect at a time. The woman on the beach is *either* a sensuous erotic presence *or* she is my mother; the drawing is *either* a duck *or* it is a rabbit – it cannot be both a duck and a rabbit simultaneously.

When we look at an object we do not experience an *aspect* of the object: we experience the object. A little later we experience a different object. This second object is not experienced as an aspect of the first one: it is just there before us, appearing to us just as it is. It is only when we compare the two experiences that we begin to speak about *aspects* of a *single* object and start to detach the object from the aspects of it.

We see a drawing, we see a duck, we see a rabbit, we see some funny black marks on a piece of paper. We look at a drawing and see a duck. We look at a duck and see a rabbit. We look at a rabbit and see some funny black marks on a piece of white paper. We look at some funny black marks on a piece of paper and see a drawing. We can stay entirely within one aspect or we can make one aspect an aspect of another.

We often aspire to make one aspect fundamental: we wish to see all aspects as partial glimpses of one *true* aspect – an aspect so fundamental that it is no longer an aspect, but reality itself. In the duck-rabbit example we want to make the drawing fundamental: we want to see a single fixed *physical* drawing in a number of different ways. However, seeing a duck-rabbit as a drawing is just one way of experiencing a duck-rabbit.

This desire to make one aspect fundamental leads people to theories that distinguish between aspects and an objective world. Aspects are said to be *representations* of the world, and only one aspect is *the* correct representation. Science is a search for this single correct aspect.

However, aspects can be interpreted in other ways – there are other aspects on aspects. For example, Gadamer claims that aspects are indistinguishable from the world itself. Within Gadamer's aspect the world is the sum of an indefinite number of aspects.[8]

The aspects that we experience may be a categorically organized noumenal world, they may be the world itself, or they may be direct perceptions of an objective world. However, the question about which interpretation of aspects is correct could only be resolved by abandoning aspects and taking up a detached omniscient position. Without this, each interpretation of aspects is itself just another aspect.

> When we do relativize these matters to a background theory, moreover, the relativization itself has two components: relativity to the choice of background theory and relativity to the choice of how to translate the object theory into the background theory. As for the ontology in turn of the background theory, and even the referentiality of its quantification – these matters can call for a background theory in turn.
>
> (Willard Quine, *Ontological Relativity and Other Essays*)[9]

Positive scepticism sees reality as a labyrinth of aspects. As we pass from room to room we see things in a different way. In one room we see a duck, in another a rabbit, in another a drawing, in another a pattern of dark marks on a piece of paper. We can only escape from the labyrinth by finding a room in which the rooms do not exist.

This vision of the labyrinth is itself part of the labyrinth. The labyrinth of aspects contains a room within which it is a labyrinth of aspects. This room is positive scepticism. This chapter is a description of this room.

Positive scepticism began as an empirical theory. The positive sceptic looked around and saw people with diverse thoughts, languages, ontologies and forms of life. These people thought, spoke, acted and experienced very differently from each other and himself. When he reflected on this a little further he realized that there are also many *possible* thoughts, languages, ontologies and forms of life that, as it happens, are not currently inhabited by anyone. People who inhabited some of these alternatives might be radically different from the positive sceptic. After starting out with the vague naive belief that everyone around him was in agreement, investigations into the nature of knowledge shifted the positive sceptic into the uneasy spaces opened up by different aspects.

Positive scepticism is not a popular theory because aspect differences are not always apparent – we are systematically blind to the radical divergences between people. Wrapped up in our own aspect we tend to interpret things only within its framework and remain closed off from alternative worlds. We are also inclined to believe that everyone else could be persuaded to agree with our own view of things, and this helps to insulate us from the threat of other positions. Rarely do we believe that an encounter with the other will lead to the *loss* of our own opinions.

The first part of this chapter describes the way in which thought, language, ontology and form of life contribute to the formation of different aspects. The second part looks at positive scepticism in more detail, contrasts it with other forms of scepticism, and examines the self-reflexive limitations of this interpretation of knowledge.

Stepping Down into the Labyrinth

Introduction

The labyrinth of reality is an assembly of rooms opening out onto rooms opening out onto rooms. Connections between the rooms do not depend upon spatial proximity; from one room it is possible to access any other.

This labyrinth is irreducible to a single spatial plan. All that can be attempted is a taxonomy of the ways in which the rooms vary. Amongst the vast array of shifting aspects some features can be discerned that constitute aspects and enable them to differ. In this chapter I will examine how different thoughts, languages, ontologies and forms of life contribute to the formation of aspects.

Such a classification is useful, but it is by no means definitive – it does not attempt to articulate the differences between aspects *in detail*. Although I hope that this description will make the labyrinth plausible to other members of my culture, the real test of aspect theory lies in detailed studies that create new aspects or display differences between ones that already exist.[10]

The actual existence of some of the examples that I will be using is not important. This phenomenology includes rooms that have crumbled away, rooms that are waiting to be built, and rooms that may never be built.

A major limitation of this description is that it misses the inter-connection and interdependence of what it separates for the sake of clarity. I have separated thought, language, ontology and form of life, and yet a change in any one of these will delicately affect all the others. Adjusting the system of thought changes the language, language change alters ontology, an alteration in ontology transforms the form of life and a transformation in the form of life adjusts the system of thought. This section will describe many of the differences between aspects, but it will not attempt to capture the knitting together of all these elements into a whole. All that I can offer are some incomplete glimpses of the parts that are assembled within an aspect.

A final problem is that this description of aspects is an expression of *my own* aspect, and so I am doomed from the start to colour everything with my own thought, language, ontology and form of life. This description is offered in the impossible hope that the structuring principles of some of the labyrinth's other rooms will somehow shine through.

Thoughts

> … the questions that we raise and our doubts depend on the fact that some propositions are exempt from doubt, are as it were like hinges on which these turn.
>
> That is to say, it belongs to the logic of our scientific investigations that certain things are *in deed* not doubted.
>
> (Ludwig Wittgenstein, *On Certainty*)[11]

Things *are* a particular way for us. A reassuring framework of facts cossets us throughout our day to day existence. As children we were brought up to inhabit a particular way of seeing reality. In our culture this is a causal vision. I am here because mummy and daddy mated. We are here because of natural selection. IT is here because the big bang banged. Everything is processed by this vision. Furthermore, we are absolutely certain about it.

Certainties are a system of beliefs and judgements that stand fast for us. A collection of facts that we simply take for granted – the bedrock upon which our language-game rests. For Moore, these certainties included the duality of his hands, the pre-existence of the earth for millions of years, and the proximity of his body to the surface of the earth throughout his lifetime. My certainties include the belief that I am sitting in a cafe in Moscow, tapping words into my laptop and watching smooth streams of people flow past.

Many *ordinary* beliefs and facts can be refuted within a framework of certainties, but other beliefs constitute the framework and cannot be questioned without putting the whole belief system at stake. If I think that I have just seen my friend Rasputin in a black limousine, and it turns out not to have been him, then I will simply shrug and think no more about it. However, if I discovered that there is no such place as Moscow and I lost my hands in a farming accident at the age of five, then I would become completely disorientated: I would no longer know what to believe and any and every wild and fantastic belief would become equally plausible.

Certainties are not taught as additions to knowledge that we already have. Facts, evidence, and the arguments connecting facts and evidence are all learnt *together*: 'Light dawns gradually over the whole'.[12]

Ordinary beliefs may be acquired on the basis of evidence: we investigate something and reach conclusions that become ordinary beliefs. If the evidence is later thrown into question or refuted, the beliefs are thrown into question or refuted.

Certainties are not acquired on the basis of evidence: they are a network whose parts interlink and depend on each other – each certainty is evidence for the others in a kind of circle. Doubting and proving with evidence only take place *after* the network of certainties has been acquired – these procedures act against the backdrop of self-evident certainties.

However we can ask: May someone have telling grounds for believing that the earth has only existed for a short time, say since his own birth? Suppose he had always been told that, – would he have any good reason to doubt it? Men have believed that they could make rain; why should not a king be brought up in the belief that the world began with him? And if Moore and this king were to meet and discuss, could Moore really prove his belief to be the right one? I do not say that Moore could not convert the king to his view, but it would be a conversion of a special kind; the king would be brought to look at the world in a different way.

(Ludwig Wittgenstein, *On Certainty*)[13]

Moore and the king both speak the same language, but they have radically different beliefs about the duration of the Earth. Moore *knows* that the earth has been around for millions of years; the king *knows* that it has only been around since his birth. Moore claims that the fossil record *proves* that the Earth has existed for millions of years; the king dismisses the fact that rocks in the shape of skeletons were created at the time of his birth. Both sides of the debate see the matter in a different way and each has a different system of evidence to support his point of view.[14]

The foundational nature of certainties makes them indefinitely resistant to change. Although they may be overturned by new experiences, new experiences can always be discounted as illusory and the certainties sustained. An unusual experience may suggest to me that I am an angel inhabiting a human body, but if I am an atheist, I may dismiss this as anomalous brain chemistry.

Although we are never compelled to change certainties, it may still happen. Loss of love, a near-death experience, religious ecstasy or a journey into unreality can strip our certainties from us and hurl us into a cataclysm of doubt, despair and the sense that we are experiencing the world anew.

When someone *converts* to a new set of certainties, they are not convinced by arguments that they should change – their eyes are opened to a different way of seeing. After conversion new things exist, value judgements change and objects become beautiful and moving in ways that could not have been imagined before.

Certainties structure our world. If I see the world as the back of an enormous crocodile and you see the Earth as a spinning sphere in a vast expanding universe, then the aspects that we are inhabiting are very different. If I am the next incarnation of Christ and you are just an ordinary human being, it will be impossible for us to reach agreement, or even to effectively communicate, about certain matters.

Within each culture there is broad agreement about certainties.[15] However, there are many local divergences. Some people are certain that all men are bastards; others think them better than women. Some people are convinced that preservation of the environment should be the highest priority; others simply don't give a shit.

These differences are more accentuated between cultures. Some cultures believe in complicated pantheons of gods; others have faith in strange systems of intangible forces and particles. The justification and evidence for these beliefs also varies widely.

In *The Order of Things*, Foucault describes two major shifts in the Western framework of certainties that have taken place over the last few hundred years. Beginning with the sixteenth century's system of similitudes, he moves through the Classical age – characterized by its relation to order – to our modern epoch infused with notions of man, life, labour and history. Foucault deals with the thought systems of each of these periods in detail, bringing out with great subtlety both the mutual reinforcement of their parts and the tensions between them that lead to continuous compensatory movements.

Foucault's account starts with the organization of thought in the sixteenth century, which is based around resemblance:

> Up to the end of the sixteenth century, resemblance played a constructive
> role in the knowledge of Western culture. It was resemblance that
> largely guided exegesis and the interpretation of texts; it was resemblance
> that organised the play of symbols, made possible knowledge of things
> visible and invisible, and controlled the art of representing them. The
> universe was folded in upon itself: the earth echoing the sky, faces
> seeing themselves reflected in the stars, and plants holding within their
> stems the secrets that were of use to man.[16]

In this period each part of the world echoed all the others in a network of similitudes that extended throughout the entire universe. This network had four principle figures: *convenientia*, *aemulatio*, *analogy* and *sympathy*. *Convenientia* is a resemblance associated with the physical proximity of things that has two components: firstly, nature puts similar things in the same location, and so things that are naturally found together resemble one another, secondly, two things that are placed together influence each other and so further resemblance arises between them. Nature made the soul dense and heavy so that she could locate it in the heart of matter. However, once the soul is in place it starts to pick up the body's movements. *Aemulatio* is a form of resemblance that operates from greater distances. For example, the bright colours of flowers emulate the stars in the sky. The third part of this network, *analogy*, is a resemblance between relationships: 'the relation of the stars to the sky in which they shine may also be found: between plants and the earth, between living beings and the globe they inhabit, between minerals such as diamonds and the rocks in which they are buried'.[17] Finally, *sympathy* is an active principle that draws things together and mingles and assimilates them to one another. Fire is drawn up into the air, but as it moves up it cools down, mixes with the air, and loses its fiery quality. This mingling and assimilation is compensated for by *antipathy*, which maintains the isolation of things and keeps them in tension and opposition. This sympathy–antipathy pair is more fundamental than the other three forms of similitude because it is responsible for all movement and dispersion.

The next important part of this system is the recognition of similitudes: 'In order that we may know that aconite will cure our eye disease, or that ground walnut mixed with wine will ease a headache, there must of course be some mark that will make us aware of these things ... These buried similitudes must be indicated on the surface of things; there must be visible marks for the invisible analogies.'[18] The way in which similitudes can be recognized is through their *signatures*: each thing displays a sign that indicates what it resembles. The sympathy between aconite and our eyes is displayed in the similar appearance of the eye and aconite's seeds: aconite and the eye have *analogous* relationships between their parts and so there is sympathy between them. In this case, analogy is providing the signature for sympathy – one similitude is acting as the sign of another – and it turns out that the signatures for the other similitudes work in this way as well: each similitude is also a signature by which another similitude can be recognized. However, the same resemblance is never used twice and different resemblances are used for the signature and what it is a signature of. The sign of sympathy depends on analogy, the sign of analogy resides in emulation, the sign of emulation depends on convenience, and convenience in turn requires sympathy for its recognition. The sixteenth-century system of thought starts off with a system of resemblances, invokes signatures to explain how we come to recognize these resemblances, and then invokes resemblances again to explain the signatures:

> And so the circle is closed. Though it is apparent what a complicated system of duplications was necessary to achieve this. Resemblances require a signature, for none of them would ever become observable were it not legibly marked. But what are these signs? ... What form constitutes a sign and endows it with its particular value as a sign? –

Resemblance does. It signifies exactly in so far as it resembles what it is indicating (that is, a similitude). But what it indicates is not the homology; for its distinct existence as a signature would then be indistinguishable from the face of which it is the sign; it is *another* resemblance, an adjacent similitude, one of another type which enables us to recognize the first, and which is revealed in its turn by a third.[19]

In the Classical period this vast web of resemblances is replaced by *representation*, which divides things up into units or compares their level of complexity, and then displays the results in an ordered table. In this analysis signs play a key role. In the sixteenth century, signs were part of the world and their similitude with the world enabled them to represent it.[20] In the Classical period signs were detached from what they signified and became a transparent and neutral medium in which truth could be revealed:

> The simultaneously endless and closed, full and tautological world of resemblance now finds itself dissociated and, as it were, split down the middle: on the one side, we shall find the signs that have become tools of analysis, marks of identity and difference, principles whereby things can be reduced to order, keys for a taxonomy; and, on the other, the empirical and murmuring resemblance of things, that unreacting similitude that lies beneath thought and furnishes the infinite raw material for division and distributions.[21]

Although signs arose through the animal cries that give them birth, once they detached themselves from this origin they became entirely *arbitrary* conventions created and sustained by men.

This procedure of ordering things through signs was subdivided into *mathesis* and *taxinomia*. *Mathesis* is the ordering of simple natures using algebra, *taxinomia* is the ordering of complex natures, and each of these can be reduced to the other. Linked up with this is a *genesis* that explains the dependence of Order upon a resemblance situated at the margins of knowledge. Within this system it is only possible to compare things according to their identities and differences because an underlying similitude makes them comparable. This manifests itself in the imagination, which compares past impressions to present ones, analyzes impressions into simple elements, combines them with similar impressions, and lays them out in an ordered table:

> In any case, the Classical *episteme* can be defined in its most general arrangement in terms of the articulated system of a *mathesis*, a *taxinomia*, and a *genetic analysis*. The sciences always carry within themselves the project, however remote it may be, of an exhaustive ordering of the world; they are always directed, too, towards the discovery of simple elements and their progressive combination; and at their centre they form a table on which knowledge is displayed in a system contemporary with itself. The centre of knowledge, in the seventeenth and eighteenth centuries, is the *table*. As for the great controversies that occupied men's minds, these are accommodated quite naturally in the folds of this organization.[22]

What can be seen in both the sixteenth century and Classical period is the way in which the components of their thought depend on each other and work together. In resemblance the four similitudes act as signatures for one other; in representation *mathesis*, *taxinomia* and *genesis* are not separate domains but 'a solid grid of kinships that defines the general configuration of knowledge'.[23] This interdependence of the parts of each system of knowledge makes it difficult to directly compare concepts from the different systems – for example, both the sixteenth century and the Classical period made use of resemblance, but in the former, resemblance was the only form of knowledge – the resemblance between things was all there was to know – whereas in the latter resemblance was something marginal to knowledge that made it possible.[24]

What also emerges from Foucault's studies is the way in which knowledge completely regroups itself at different times. One set of difficulties and preoccupations guides people's thought for a while and then old problems are discarded along with their solutions and a new field opens up. In one period people were concerned with the similitudes between man and nature, God and nature, and man and God; in another period they were attempting to order natural history, general grammar and wealth into a table. Knowledge is guided by one configuration for a while, there is a rupture, it is guided by another configuration for a while, there is a rupture, and so on. As the thought system changes it is not always able to assimilate the past and learn from it: often it can barely think how the past was.[25]

I have used the work of Wittgenstein and Foucault to illustrate the way in which different aspects can be structured by different thoughts. However, I could have made the same point using Kuhn's theories about stable and revolutionary science, Winch's discussions of primitive societies, or Körner's theory of categorical frameworks. Any theory of thinking has to have ways in which thoughts can be different, and once we begin to think differently we start to inhabit a different aspect.

Languages

> At any rate it is important to imagine a language in which *our* concept 'knowledge' does not exist.
>
> (Ludwig Wittgenstein, *On Certainty*)[26]

We inhabit aspects suffused with language. Our sensual encounters with the world are inevitably interpenetrated by the streams of words that flow around our minds and through our mouths. We see someone and they become the evaluative judgements that pop into our heads about them; we walk down the street and flip out into unreal worlds constituted by imaginings and internal dialogues. Languages are a second world superimposed on and intertwined with the physical and emotional worlds. Words are traced in the sky, trapped beneath stones, and smeared across the faces of the people we love. A storybook world in which the word is flesh and dwells amongst us.

One way in which language structures aspects is through the effect that it has on our perception of the world. Whilst the more extreme claims of Sapir/Whorf are probably wrong, there remains a level at which language changes the way we see things. The words that we have to some extent determine the objects that we have and the way in which we think about these objects. One example of this is the Linnaean taxonomy, whose combination of genus name and specific epithet greatly enhances our perception of botanical reality. For example, an anonymous mushroom is very different from an *Amanita muscaria*, and our experience of a forest is substantially altered if we know all the plants' names – instead of just absorbing a general impression of forms and colours. Another example is the different loves that are possible in English and Spanish. Spanish has two verbs for love: 'amar' and 'querer'. The former is an intense eternal undying love; the latter a more familial neighbourly kind of love. For Spanish speakers there is a clear distinction between the two and they identify distinct emotional states. I querer my family, husband and friends all the time, but I amar someone only in exceptional circumstances (a Mexican woman will only say 'Te amo' when her soul trembles). Both of these words are translated into English as 'love'. The English speaker has no idea that two types of love are possible; for him there is just a single love continuum with varying degrees of intensity. The English 'I love you' serves both Christian and romantic purposes.[27]

Language also possesses a reality internal to itself; a reality composed of flows of sentences and phrases; an autonomous world that does not depend upon anything else. When we talk down the telephone or communicate through text there are no gestures of the eye or body, no touching of hands or lips. We are just answering one flow of words with another. These flows can be arranged in any way we choose, but if we want our moves to make sense, if we wish to be understood by the other, then we have to make them in accordance with the rules prescribed by our culture.

At the most basic level it is agreed within a language which words can be used and which cannot – the vocabulary of Swedish cannot be used to speak English. At the next level lies grammar, which defines the ordering of words and the different endings that can be used to give words different meanings. Beyond grammar, a looser organization of the language determines which patterns of word exchange are acceptable (and here language, thought and form of life start to become inseparable). Whilst grammar arranges the components, this looser organization defines the larger structures that can be brought into play at any point in the conversation.[28] 'I'm fine thank you' and 'Well, I'm a bit rough today!' are acceptable responses to the phrase: 'Good morning. How are you?', but 'The dinner drove redly backwards yesterday' and 'The fish wraps the sheet around the angel's cog' are not. A social context sets out a field of sense for each conversation.[29]

One way of understanding how these structuring principles of language operate is through Wittgenstein's notion of a language-game. In a game there are players, something that the game is played with, and rules that define how the game is to be played.[30] Chess is a game played by two people using wooden pieces and a board, with some of the pieces being allowed to move diagonally whilst others must advance one square at a time. Language is a game played with spoken and written pieces; some of these can be placed together, whilst other combinations are nonsensical. Once we have mastered a game's rules we cease to see them and focus instead on the possibilities that lie within their framework. When I play chess I consider moves that lie within the space of the game – castling, checkmating, etc. – and no longer worry about whether bishops should move horizontally or fret about the inability of pawns to jump over other pieces. The rules of chess structure a field of action that becomes a complete world whilst I am playing it. Without these rules my opponent and I are just messing around with a few pieces of wood; with these rules something clicks into place and a world opens up in which we can interact and participate. After we have struggled to master a game we start to speak: we begin to move naturally within it without being aware of it. Certain possibilities open up for us and others are automatically discarded. We learn to breathe in a different medium.

Chess is not the only game. Above the world opened up by the grammar of chess perch worlds structured by different rules, games played with different pieces. Beyond chess there are draughts, boxing, cockfighting, cricket, and all the other games that human beings invent. Each game has its own structure and when this becomes transparent we find ourselves immersed in a different world.

English is not the only language-game. Beyond English, language-games guided by different words and grammars encamp. We can drink vin rouge or vino rojo and past these milder variations there are surreal language-games, abstract language-games – language-games as different as chess and cricket.

Although the grammar of natural human languages can vary considerably, their structural variations are limited by the fact that they are all based around the human form of life. The form of life of people who hunt buffalo on wide open prairies is different from those who squat poky rooms in cities, but all people sleep, eat, make love and interact with objects and these activities help to structure the rules of the language-games that they play. However, whilst the human form of life may limit the language-games that we *naturally* play, there is no such limitation on the language-games that we *can* play. Sitting around in idleness we can invent and play as many different and varied language-games as we choose. We can inhabit languages that do not relate to or communicate anything; we can push the possibilities for organized flows of phonemes to their limits. These possibilities are hinted at in the languages that have developed in isolation from the human form of life – for example, mathematical languages, computer code, music and experimental literature.[31] The twentieth century's *leisure* has led to an efflorescence of these language-games.

Once the rules for a different language-game become transparent we start to freely move within them. An expert programmer no longer struggles with the code – he speaks it. We master the rules of a different language-game and dive into a different world.

The game of chess is not altered if it is played with ivory or scraps of rusty metal, but it does make a sensual difference if we caress jagged or slippery pieces whilst we play. A room lined with plush crimson velvet has a different consistency to one that is whitewashed and the textures and rhythms that line language give each its own particular feel. Even if the grammar of two languages is identical, a difference in their sounds creates a different atmosphere and textures our world in a different way whilst we talk. Although Western languages share a broadly similar grammar, our experience speaking them is different – each makes a different poetry possible. When we submerge ourselves in a new tongue everything becomes soft and squishy, hard and metallic, bouncy and rubbery. Vivid colours, pastel shadings, murky greenish hues. When we change the sounds that we sound we transform the texture of our world.

The texture of a language and its structure are to some extent interdependent since resemblance between the sound of two words can lead to a more natural flow between them. This effect is most noticeable in poetry, which depends both on the structures that are allowed by grammar and on the textures of the words. The textures of a poem have to harmoniously resonate together and at the same time the structure of its sentences needs to approximate consensual grammar if it is to communicate something intelligible. Poetry is a game in which the arrangement, colour and texture of the pieces is more important than winning with them.

Ontologies

> One kind of aspect might be called 'aspects of organization'. When the
> aspect changes parts of the picture go together which before did not.
> (Ludwig Wittgenstein, *Philosophical Investigations*)[32]

I emerge from the thicket, and a mushroom stands poised in the
clearing before me: velar remnants, cap, crowded gills, stem, ring,
stem and a basal bulb half buried in the moist autumn earth.

This mushroom is a distinct object that I separate out within the
general field of the clearing. Had I been bear watching, I would not
have seen it at all – it would have formed part of the general
background to the bears that I was observing.

The mushroom has parts. The velar remnants, cap, gills, stem,
ring or bulb can be made to stand out against the general
background of the mushroom. When I focus on the gills, they
become a distinct object for me and I cease to be consciously
aware of the basal bulb and cap.

The divisions between the parts of the mushroom can be nested
or they can overlap: one part can be broken down into smaller
parts or different overlapping divisions can be made. For example,
the mushroom can be divided into spore-bearing parts and
supporting tissues or it can be separated into top and bottom.

Through the microscope another field of partitions opens up:
divisions of the mushroom's flesh into hyphae, spores, and all the
structures within them. At higher magnifications further fields are
revealed.

When I emerged from the thicket *a* mushroom stood poised in
the clearing before me: a physically separate mushroom; similar to
other mushrooms and yet distinct from them.

The presence of *a* mushroom is also a form of partitioning. Not
because the mushroom is distinct from its forest backdrop, but because
we separate it from the millions of other mushrooms that bear its
likeness.

I could have said that there was *some* mushroom in the clearing – that a portion of the totality of mushroom stood before me. Instead, I separated the mushroom in the clearing from all other mushrooms; I partitioned the totality of mushroom into physically distinct objects. Mushroom became millions of mushroom*s* with parts that have many similarities between them.

This distinction between the totality of mushroom and physically distinct mushrooms is described by Quine as a distinction between mass and general terms:

> The contrast lies in the terms and not in the stuff they name. It is not a question of scatter. Water is scattered in discrete pools and glassfuls, and red in discrete objects; still it is just 'pool', 'glassful', and 'object', not 'water' or 'red', that divide their reference. Or, consider 'shoe', 'pair of shoes', and 'footwear': all three range over exactly the same scattered stuff, and differ from one another solely in that two of them divide their reference differently and the third not at all.
>
> So-called *mass* terms like 'water', 'footwear', and 'red' have the semantical property of referring cumulatively: any sum of parts which are water is water. Grammatically they are like singular terms in resisting pluralization and articles. Semantically they are like singular terms in not dividing their reference ... But semantically they do not go along with singular terms ... in purporting to name a unique object each.[33]

Mass terms do not divide what they refer to: there is just a mass of what they name. We do not describe a lake as *a* water, we say that there is water in the lake. The truck does not have a red on it; it is a red truck, a truck with a portion of red upon it.[34]

Masses indefinitely extend and have no internal parts.[35] However, they are still partitioned from one another – water can be distinguished from alcohol, even though there are not any individual waters or alcohols.

When I emerged from the thicket a *young* mushroom stood poised in the clearing before me. A mushroom at an early stage in its development – a mushroom that the days had not dilapidated.

Young mushrooms are plump, beautiful and firm. Older mushrooms are yellowing-soggy and scarred by the rasps of slugs.

Physical objects persist through time and change over this period, and we divide the span of an object's existence into stages. These divisions can be very crude (the seven ages of man) or articulated more finely (the stages of infant development).

The different states of a physical object are similar to its stages, with the difference that stages generally progress in a linear fashion. A mushroom can be healthy or diseased, soggy or dry; water can be frozen, liquid or gaseous. Different collections of an object's properties identify its distinct states.

Different stages of an object cannot be present together. An object cannot be both young and old at the same time, although some of its parts can be young and others old. The same is true of different states.[36]

States are distinct from the objects that are in the different states, but they can overlap with the properties that are used to identify the states.

When I emerged from the thicket, part of the clearing was white, firm, crimson, fragile, soft, slightly rubbery, loose, aromatic and tasty.

Part of the clearing has properties that are not present in other parts. There is fragile softness twelve centimetres from the ground and seven metres from me. Some sticky crimson below this, some rubbery white firmness and then some more fragile softness.

Some properties are overlaid (the ones from the different senses), whilst others cannot coexist at the same physical location. For example, aromatic and fragile can be co-present, whereas red and blue cannot. When I am focusing on one property, the others form a general diffuse background that is not perceived in any detail.

Properties can be indefinitely divided: we separate out different colours and make fine distinctions between shades of the same colour, temperatures can be measured to fractions of a degree, and we have a range of words and tests for different levels of hardness.

At higher resolutions we encounter different properties within the mushroom – the viscosity of fluids within the hyphae; the elastic rigidity of the spores. Further magnifications reveal the properties of molecules, atoms, electrons and quarks.

I have roughly outlined the ways in which reality is partitioned into objects, parts, stages, states and properties. Within each of these partitionings considerable variation can be brought about. To begin with, the objects that we are accustomed to can be joined together, split into smaller objects, or the divisions between them can be horizontally displaced. As we mature we learn to divide up reality by interacting with objects and making observations that help us to group them into coherent things – for example, apprentice ostlers derive their idea of single horses from the fact that horses' heads, bodies and legs move coherently together. The physical nature of our human bodies plays a large part in this (if our bodies were built from neutrinos, we would have a very different view of matter), but there is no reason why the divisions that we happen to have learnt within our human form of life should be rigidly adhered to in every ontology. For example, although we usually separate living biological creatures from inanimate objects and distinguish houses from furniture, nothing prevents us from overriding this division and seeing chair, floor and dog combinations as a single 'creature' and inventing a 'biology' that can handle this amalgam.[37] Each redivision of our customary ontology takes us into a different world, and these changes can extend all the way down to its atomic structure (the decision to group a number of electrons, protons and neutrons into a single atom is just one way of partitioning reality).[38]

A second way of altering our ontology is by dividing properties along lines that are finer, coarser, or superimposed over our own. For example, the Navahoe split our black into two colours and lump blue and green together[39] and it would be easy to go beyond this and create aspects with colours based entirely on the electromagnetic spectrum – colours individuated using a mathematical division of shades that is independent of the sensitivity of cells in the human retina.

Ontology can also be altered by shifting the boundary between objects and masses. In general, objects that can be individually recognized and physically handled are usually collected together under singular terms, whereas objects without these attributes are described using mass terms. For example, we can pick up and recognize individual apples and so we divide the totality of apple into individual specimens, but different waters lack stable boundaries and a fixed independent existence, and so we treat water as a mass term. Although these practical considerations have limited the partitioning of mass terms so far, there is nothing necessary about the balance between singular and mass terms that our society uses. This partitioning can be shifted by treating our current objects as masses or reinterpreting our current masses as aggregates of physically distinct objects. For example, if all objects became masses, then the world would change into a collection of masses that have different properties, but no physically distinct objects within them: there would be apple, tree and mama, but no individual apples, trees or mamas. According to Quine, our early experience of the world is likely to have been structured in this way:

> We in our maturity have come to look upon the child's mother as an integral body who, in an irregular closed orbit, revisits the child from time to time; and to look upon red in a radically different way, viz., as scattered about. Water, for us, is rather like red, but not quite; things are red, stuff alone is water. But the mother, red, and water are for the infant all of a type; each is just a history of sporadic encounter, a scattered portion of what goes on. His first learning the three words is uniformly a matter of learning how much of what goes on around him counts as the mother, or as red, or as water. It is not for the child to say in the first case 'Hello! mama again', in the second case 'Hello! another red thing', and in the third case 'Hello! more water'. They are all on a par: Hello! more mama, more red, more water.[40]

In the other direction, mass terms could be eliminated altogether by slicing masses up into multiplicities of individual objects. A beach would have a sand upon it, there would be a water on the ground and a grass in the park.

A fourth adjustment of our ontology can be brought about by moving the boundary between states or stages and objects. One possibility would be to treat all objects as different states of a single mass of matter (or energy) that extends throughout the entire universe. Another option would be to treat different stages as different objects. We speak about a single person being born, growing old and dying, but it would also be possible to take changes in the personality seriously and divide the different ages of man into different people. Many cultures have initiations into adulthood that go some way towards this, and it can also be found when there is high infant mortality and recognition of the personhood of children (by giving them a name) is withheld until they have attained a certain age.

This shift in the boundary between states or stages and objects also applies to properties. Although most properties are atemporal, they can include changes within themselves, as happens with Goodman's colour grue.[41] According to our atemporal division of colours, a grue object starts off green and becomes blue after the year 2000. Within Goodman's division, a grue object is grue before and after 2000. Before 2000 a tree by the lake is grue; after 2000 it changes into bleen. On the other hand, some grue jelly that I make before 2000 will continue to be grue after that date if I forget to keep it in the fridge. This way of partitioning colours could even be based around a form of life. For example, a culture that valued its bronze statues highly could use the single word 'broween' to describe their colour: whilst we would say that their statues change colour from golden brown to green, they would describe this as the maintenance of a single colour.

Finally, the distinction that we make between properties and physical objects can be altered. Although we speak about properties as if they were features of an objective world – 'honey is sweet', 'the brick is hard', etc. – they actually have more to do with the inter-action between our bodies and physical objects. Properties are situated at the interface between bodies and things: they are both objective features of things and the means by which we recognize and identify things, and this position can be pushed in either direction. On the one hand, the things that we recognize through properties can be eliminated in favour of a Berkeleyan world in which there are only properties (or ideas). On the other hand, a scientific language could be created in which all properties are described as physical states of things. Rorty imagines something akin to this in his fantasy of an Antipodean language that is stripped of all reference to subjective minds:

> In most respects, then, the language, life, technology, and philosophy of this race were much like ours. But there was one important difference. Neurology and biochemistry had been the first disciplines in which the technological breakthroughs had been achieved, and a large part of the conversation of these people concerned the state of their nerves. When their infants veered towards hot stoves, mothers cried out, 'He'll stimulate his c-fibers.' When people were given clever visual illusions to look at, they said, 'How odd! It makes neuronic bundle G-14 quiver, but when I look at it from the side I can see that it's not a red rectangle at all.' Their knowledge of physiology was such that each well formed sentence could easily be corre-lated with a readily identifiable neural state.[42]

All of these changes in partitions can have a profound impact upon our classification and theory since some of the objects that were previously grouped together fall into novel categories that may require new theories to understand them. For example, any attempt to describe a chair-floor-dog in the language of contemporary biology will fail to answer many of the questions that can usually be posed about a biological organism. A whole new way of seeing arises once reality is partitioned in a different way; fresh laws and languages may be needed to adequately express each ontology.

Forms of Life

If a lion could talk, we could not understand him.
(Ludwig Wittgenstein, *Philosophical Investigations*)[43]

We are bald creatures that walk upon our hind legs. We do lots of different things and make different noises when we are engaged in these various activities. Our central activities are working (some kind of complicated productive activity), eating, drinking, shagging and relaxing.

There are lots of other creatures that walk, work, eat, drink, shag and relax in different ways. Some are big and yellow with long sharp teeth and slitty pupils, others are small and light with pointy noses and thin twig-like legs. These other creatures accompany their various activities with a variety of sounds.

Other forms of life form aspects different from our own. Although there is a bridge between them and us (we empathize with them and see something of ourselves in them), there are also substantial differences: sensations from zero, six or a hundred legs; lust for feathered breasts or colourful shells; fear of open or enclosed spaces; different spreads of delectables and inedibles. Noises and smells that frighten other forms of life are familiar to us; noises and smells that terrify us are commonplace to them. Furthermore, our form of life *describes* the noises it makes as a transparent medium that represents the world. Other forms of life lack this unique attribute: they just make inarticulate bestial cries that do not represent anything at all.

At its margins the notion of a form of life vanishes into an indefinite haze. If we have enough in common with a creature we say that an aspect lies within it. Beyond this we have no idea what we can, could, or should attribute a world to.

These differences between forms of life are such that a human being who has been brought up in the human form of life can barely conceive what the aspects of an ant, eel, bat or cat might be like. However, these aspects can be *learnt* by a *Homo sapiens* that has not yet assimilated the human form of life.

Constructing the Labyrinth

As the source of authority, I have in mind principally textbooks of science together with both the popularizations and the philosophical works modelled on them. All three of these categories ... have one thing in common. They address themselves to an already articulated body of problems, data, and theory, most often to the particular set of paradigms to which the scientific community is committed at the time they are writing. Textbooks themselves aim to communicate the vocabulary and syntax of a contemporary scientific language. Popularizations attempt to describe these same applications in a language closer to that of everyday life. And philosophy of science, particularly that of the English speaking world, analyzes the logical structure of the same completed body of scientific knowledge ... All three record the stable *outcome* of past revolutions and thus display the bases of the current normal-scientific tradition.

(Thomas Kuhn, *The Structure of Scientific Revolutions*)[44]

The schoolboy *believes* his teachers and his schoolbooks.

(Ludwig Wittgenstein, *On Certainty*)[45]

Sitting on a park bench I look around and see a rose, a lawnmower and a man; each separate object has its own name and web of conceptual associations. The rose is an erotic flower, evidence for God's miraculous creation, an organ for attracting bees. The lawnmower is an aesthetic interplay of gleaming surfaces, a useful tool, a mutilator of grass. The man is a human being, my friend Jean, a weedy looking fellow.

This is my world, a world that emerged at the mobile site which is me; it is this that is constructed when an aspect is assembled in the child.

Within the infant a world is built – a system of thought, a language, an ontology and a form of life. A shifting blurred mass of emotions and colour condenses into a clear world, a global aspect inhabited by someone.

The child is the neutral stuff that is 'moulded' by thought, language, ontology and form of life. We bring up blank children to inhabit an aspect.[46] The development of aspects in the child can also be seen as the replication of aspects – as aspect breeding.

The thought, language, ontology and form of life of the child are partly determined by genetic factors and so biotechnology may be needed to splice in unusual aspects. However, even in its current form *Homo sapiens* is not limited to human thought, language, ontology and form of life. The aspects of wolves, bears and sheep can be placed in human bodies by allowing these animals to nurture them from an early age.

Their tongues hung out through thick red lips, they panted and frequently bared their teeth. They suffered from photophobia and day-blindness, and spent their days crouched in the shade or standing motionless with their faces to the wall. They livened up at night, howling and groaning and hoping to escape. Amala – aged one and a half – and Kamala – aged eight and a half – slept only about four hours in twenty-four. They had two means of getting about: on their knees and elbows for short distances and on their hands and feet for longer distances or for running. They lapped up liquids and took their food in a crouching position. Their exclusive taste for meat led them to indulge in the only activity of which they were capable: chasing chickens or rooting around for carcasses and entrails. Though they took a slight interest in dogs and cats, they were completely unsociable and used to snarl at humans, showing particular hostility to Singh's wife. When

anyone approached, they used to arch their backs menacingly and shake
their heads rapidly back and forwards to show their wariness.

(Lucien Malson, *Wolf Children*)[47]

Ancient, Modern and Positive Scepticism

Positive Scepticism

> For God, so to speak, turns on all sides and considers in all ways the general
> system of phenomena which he has found it good to produce in order to
> manifest his glory. And as he considers all the faces of the world in all
> possible ways – for there is no aspect which escapes his omniscience – the
> result of each view of the universe, as looked at from a certain position, is,
> if God finds it good to actualize his thoughts and to produce it, a substance
> which expresses the universe in conformity with that view.
>
> (Gottfried Leibniz, *Discourse on Metaphysics*)[48]

Positive scepticism sees reality as a bodiless beast with many faces:
a labyrinthine succession of different 'visions'.

The positive sceptic has encountered other aspects, collided with
visions radically opposed to his own. This made his aspect visible
as an aspect. Before this encounter his aspect was coextensive
with the world – there was no distinction between it and the
world. After this encounter his aspect continues to be the world,
but now there are other worlds as well.

Sometimes the labyrinth becomes visible when the dogmatic
foundations of an aspect are uncovered. Once a person's bedrock
certainties have been exposed, the possibility of aspects with
different dogmatic foundations opens up.

The collapse of a person's aspect can also throw them into the
labyrinth. The disintegration of everything that a person believes

in can open up a space in which everything is permissible; a space in which the world unfolds as a multiplicity of aspects. When a particle's velocity is collapsed into a precise measurement the particle becomes simultaneously present in all locations.

The positive sceptic does not rest with the visions that he encounters in his own and other cultures – although he takes much pleasure in exploring all of these. He creates and explores new vistas, populates new worlds with twisted morals and logics, constructs new rooms in his exploration of what aspects are possible for people.

The positive sceptic *falls into* the aspects that he creates. He imagines an aspect, develops it in detail, and suddenly a new world opens out in front of him.

A multiplicity of aspects is problematic for people who stick rigidly within one aspect and claim that their aspect is the only correct one. They experience positive scepticism as a threat, an attempt to invalidate their single correct worldview. However, the positive sceptic is not interested in invalidating aspects. For him each aspect is 100% objective and 100% correct. Theories are not undermined by the possibility of others – all possibilities are made real simultaneously. Positive scepticism is *hyper-objective*.

A plurality of aspects is also problematic if you believe that reality is some kind of in-itself that each of us has some kind of partial glimpse of. In this case the contradictions between aspects lock against one another and leave objective reality untouched. This picture is common in our culture and was important to the Pyrrhonic sceptics. However, this juxtaposition of aspects depends on a distinction between aspects and the world that they are an aspect of. Outside of this ontology these arguments have little relevance.

The positive sceptic deals with incompatible claims by describing them as an interplay between two aspects. One aspect rises to the surface, we inhabit it for a while, and then a different aspect rises to the surface. Claims are inhabited sequentially, not simultaneously.

The duck-rabbit is both a duck and a rabbit. Traditionally, this contradiction is held together and overcome by the fact that both the duck and the rabbit are ways of seeing a single drawing. Some people are convinced that the drawing is a duck and argue strenuously against the suggestion that it might be a rabbit. Other people admit superficial similarities between the drawing and a duck, but think it would be madness to take it for anything except a rabbit. A third group of people think that the issue of whether the drawing *really is* a duck or a rabbit is undecidable and abandon all hope for a theory that could illuminate the essence of the drawing. For his part, *the positive sceptic sees the drawing as an aspect as well.* Now there is no longer any thing to which two incompatible predicates can be attached. There are no neutral marks that can be interpreted in different ways because the 'neutral marks' have themselves become just one further way of seeing. We are left with a duck, a rabbit, a drawing, and the ability to move between these three ways of seeing.

Many people find positive scepticism unpalatable because the thought lurks at the back of their minds that everyone could somehow reach agreement – a fantasy of a world in which everybody is transparently in the truth. This thought generally takes the form: 'If only everyone could see things in the way that *I* see them – in the way that is, of course, self-evidently *true* – then we would all agree and understand things perfectly'. Rarely does it take the form: 'If only I could give up the beliefs that I hold – which may be mistaken – and take up beliefs that have been carefully checked by everyone else, then we could all agree'. Faith in the possibility of consensus creates resistance to the positive sceptic's vision of a labyrinth of aspects.

The positive sceptic does not reject the possibility that this utopia may come to pass. However, he also hypothesizes that peoples and cultures will continue to die before reaching 'the truth'; he conjectures that differences will remain between aspects that diverge as rapidly as they fuse. There *are* aspects in which there is a single communion of truth, but the distance between these aspects and positive scepticism only serves to confirm the positive sceptic's hypothesis that the Absolute has not yet been achieved on Earth.

The positive sceptic writes and speaks because he wishes to open other people up to his vision of the labyrinth. However, he recognizes that positive scepticism is itself just one aspect. His labyrinth of aspects is just one room in the labyrinth, not an absolute perspective on the whole. In his perambulations the positive sceptic has come across positive scepticism, and one day he may leave it behind. Given what he knows about thought, language, ontology and forms of life, he is forced into it, but he would also be happy to inhabit aspects in which there is no positive scepticism and only one truth – visions that flow along a single riverbed of certainties.

Excrescent Doubt

> Nobody ever *knows* that anything is so.
>
> (Peter Unger, *Ignorance*)[49]

The negative sceptic *doubts*. In her formative years she believed something with absolute conviction – she inhabited one aspect and excluded all others. One day she was caught unawares by a different aspect. She did not really believe in it, and yet its incompatibility with her original aspect robbed the latter of its former firmness. Now her old aspect is no longer certain, and yet she does not inhabit the new aspect either. The *possibility* of this other aspect has invalidated her own. How can she believe what she always believed when something completely different *might* be true? The negative sceptic could free herself from her agony by letting go of her old aspect and embracing the new one. Or she could dismiss the new aspect and continue to inhabit her original one. Or she could accept that reality is a multiplicity of aspects. Unfortunately none of these options appeal to the negative sceptic. She still desperately wants to believe that her original aspect is the *only* correct one and in a paroxysm of despair she reaches the conclusion that *no* aspect can be believed in in this way, no aspect is certain and a misty cloud of doubt will forever haunt her knowledge.[50]

The negative sceptic's exposure to another aspect has trapped her on the boundary between two aspects and deprived her of the certainty that either could give her. From this lack of certainty she concludes that certainty is impossible.[51] The positive sceptic is also between aspects, but his emphasis is completely different. For him, the possibility of other aspects leads to an explosion of knowledge, not to a holding back from claims to know. Different aspects do not conflict for the positive sceptic – they are *all* castles enchanted with the promise of a different world. Negative sceptics believe that the evil scientist controlling a brain in a vat and Descartes' demon are *possible*, but they fail to realize that it is possible to really believe in them; positive sceptics interpret anomalous events as bugs in the scientist's software and make propitiatory sacrifices to the demon in the hope that his deceit will be carried out more favourably in the future.

Pyrrhonism

The Skeptic Way is a disposition to oppose phenomena and noumena to one another in any way whatever, with the result that, owing to the equipollence among the things and statements thus opposed, we are brought first to *epoche* and then to *ataraxia*. ... By 'opposed' statements we simply mean inconsistent ones, not necessarily affirmative and

negative. By 'equipollence' we mean equality as regards credibility and
the lack of it, that is, that no one of the inconsistent statements takes
precedence over any other as being more credible. *Epoche* is a state of
the intellect on account of which we neither deny nor affirm anything.
Ataraxia is an untroubled and tranquil condition of the soul.

(Sextus Empiricus, *Outlines of Pyrrhonism*)[52]

In the course of his investigations into the world around him the
Pyrrhonic[53] sceptic has discovered that every theory he develops
about the world appears to be opposed by a different theory
claiming the opposite. Confronted by a person who dogmatically
believes *x*, he can see that a different theory proves *not-x*, leaving
two contradictory positions, *x* and *not-x*, and no way of choosing
one over the other. Without a way of deciding between the two
theories the Pyrrhonic sceptic has to suspend judgement about the
issue, either until he can show that one of the proofs is false, or until
he can discover a theory that can mediate between them. For
example, in response to the dogmatic assertion that honey is sweet
in its nature, the sceptic points out that honey tastes bitter to some
people, and so honey must be bitter in its nature as well. Since the
real nature of honey cannot be both sweet and bitter, it is impossible to decide what the real nature of honey is. Faced with this
dilemma, the Pyrrhonic sceptic suspends judgement and abandons
the debate. He is still willing to state that honey *appears* to him to
be sweet, but he is not interested in assertions that go beyond the
bare description of appearances.

This suspension of judgement (*epoche*) brings about a tranquil
state of mind (*ataraxia*). The Pyrrhonic sceptic had hoped to pacify
his mind by understanding the world and then, almost by chance,
he attains this by suspending judgement about the world. After
attaining peace of mind in this way the Pyrrhonic sceptic does not
close himself off from the possibility that truth might be found –
he does not claim that it is *impossible* to know anything. He is also
happy to describe the *appearance* of things. However, he is
personally no longer interested in discovering 'the truth' about the

world because he has reached tranquillity by a different path. He may give up philosophy altogether and take up a trade, or he may remain within philosophy so that he can help other people to achieve the same calm state of mind.[54]

Although the Pyrrhonic sceptic has a method and a clearly defined goal, he is not someone who believes dogmatically that dogmas are bad, *ataraxia* is good, and that *ataraxia* necessarily follows from *epoche*. In fact, all of these claims only *appear* to the Pyrrhonic sceptic to be the case: he does not believe that any of them are *really true*. The sceptic's phrases *express his condition*; they are not a new set of dogmas about reality. As Sextus Empiricus puts it: 'For concerning all the Skeptic slogans it is necessary for this to be understood first of all: we absolutely do not firmly maintain anything about their being true, especially since we say that they can be confuted by themselves, as they are included among the cases to which they apply – just as cathartic drugs not only flush out the bodily humours but expel themselves as well.'[55] The Pyrrhonic sceptic does not need his claims to be true because their main purpose is to alleviate the suffering caused by dogmatism, and this also makes the Pyrrhonic sceptics indifferent to the quality of their arguments (some are strong, whilst others are pitifully weak and unconvincing). What matters is the effect that the argument has upon the person being treated: if a weak argument induces *ataraxia* in the patient, then there is no need for a better one. More stubborn cases may require stronger solutions:

Because of his love of humanity the Skeptic wishes to cure by argument, so far as he can, the conceit and precipitancy of the Dogmatists. Accordingly, just as the doctors who treat physical symptoms have remedies that differ in strength, and prescribe the severe ones for people with severe symptoms and milder ones for those mildly affected, so too the Sceptic sets forth arguments differing in strength. And in the case of those who are severely afflicted with precipitancy he employs arguments that are weighty and capable of vigorously disposing of the Dogmatists' symptom of conceit, but in the case of those who have this symptom in a superficial and easily curable way, and are capable of being restored to health by milder persuasion, he uses the milder arguments. Hence the person motivated by Skepticism does not hesitate to advance at one time arguments that are weighty in persuasiveness and at another time such as even appear weak—he does this purposely, on the assumption that many times the latter suffice for accomplishing his task.[56]

Since the Pyrrhonic sceptic has suspended judgement about everything, he has no theories of his own that he could use to treat the dogmatist. Instead, he takes up the dogmatist's own arguments (or develops arguments within the dogmatist's framework) and demonstrates their opposition to one another. The Pyrrhonic sceptic *deconstructs* dogmatism; it is an *internal* critique without any dogmatisms of its own.

Although Pyrrhonic scepticism has a number of similarities with positive scepticism, there are important divergences as well. To begin with, the Pyrrhonic sceptic distinguishes between appearances and reality in a different way from the positive sceptic. The Pyrrhonic sceptic has given up the attempt to discover how honey *really* tastes, and so he contents himself with the way honey *appears* to taste. In contrast, the positive sceptic is not committed to this distinction (although she does not reject aspects that are). For her honey really is sweet, really is bitter, appears to be bitter and appears to be sweet: positive scepticism freely moves between these different levels and does not dogmatically stay within appearances at the expense of reality. A second difference is that the Pyrrhonic sceptic juxtaposes *philosophical arguments*, which he abandons in favour of the appearances of real life, whereas the positive sceptic deals with *aspects* that she encounters in life as well as philosophy. This situation of aspects within life gives them a positive value for the positive sceptic that is missing from the arguments offered by the Pyrrhonist. The positive sceptic cannot abandon theory for everyday life because she encounters and inhabits aspects in all areas of her life. There are no domains that she could move to if she suspended judgement about aspects; she is always irrevocably within an aspect, and even the attempt to escape from aspects is a further feature of the aspect that she is in.

The positive and Pyrrhonic sceptics also have different relationships to their identity. In the Pyrrhonist's case, there is something about them that makes the label 'Pyrrhonic sceptic' apply; something that sets them apart from other men.[57] They are people to whom honey *appears* sweet, who think that the attainment of *ataraxia* may be a good thing and who believe in the therapeutic power of scepticism. Sextus even admits that he has something like a 'system':

> If one defines a system as an attachment to a number of dogmas that agree with one another and with appearances, and defines a dogma as an assent to something non-evident, we shall say that the Skeptic does not have a system. But if one says that a system is a way of life that, in accordance with appearances, follows a certain rationale, where that rationale shows how it is possible to seem to live rightly ('rightly' being taken, not as referring only to virtue, but in a more ordinary sense) and tends to produce the disposition to suspend judgement, then we say that he does have a system. For we do follow a certain rationale that, in accord with appearances, points us toward a life in conformity with the customs of our country and its laws and institutions, and with our own particular *pathe*.[58]

The positive sceptic also has something like a system. She sees reality as a labyrinth of aspects and has a certain way of dealing with this way of seeing. However, whilst the Pyrrhonic sceptic is very comfortable with the move from *epoche* to *ataraxia* and the taking up of the common life that follows from this, the positive sceptic's preoccupation with aspects leaves her in a much less easy position: she is acutely aware of the limitations of an identity that is simultaneously problematic and inescapable. The Pyrrhonist thinks that he has left the labyrinth because he has discovered the multiplicity of rooms and suspended judgement about which is correct. In fact, all he has done is remain in the room called 'Pyrrhonism'. The positive sceptic accepts that it is impossible to escape – she knows that no cunning little leap will shake off an identity that clings to her like a shadow – but although she is nobly resigned to the labyrinth, she is secretly sadly tired of its stale air. Anything that she does will be a further exploration or creation of the labyrinth and she finds herself ceaselessly moving between aspects and exploring different visions. For her, nothing appears to be *the best* thing to do; no aspect shines forth as *the* correct aspect to be in. Unable to convince herself of the possibility of escape, the positive sceptic never leaves the flux of ambiguity and play: she is always right and always wrong and never comes to rest anywhere in the movement, preservation, overturning and resurfacing of aspects. The way of being of positive scepticism is to always be on the way; the system of positive scepticism is a ceaseless movement between systems.[59]

A Contrast Between Positive Scepticism and a Caricature of Relativism

Relativism is the claim that many (if not all) of the features of our experience are *relative* to the people who experience them. Reality appears as it does, not because it *really is* that way, but because it has been structured by our interpretations. I look out of the window and see a sheep: relativism tells me that the sheep that I thought I saw was almost entirely the product of my imagination. If my mind had not shaped it into an object and defined it as a domestic animal, the sheep would never have existed in this way. Relativism makes the self-evident sheep into a construct moulded from an unknowable objective reality.

This theory is often criticized because it makes a special exception for the relativist's own claims. Relativism describes a world in which people's interpretation of reality is guided by their culture and conceptual schemes, and yet it fails to interpret its own situation in the same way. The relativist is himself a person within a culture and conceptual scheme, and so the relativism that he creates must also be the product of a culture and conceptual scheme. Relativism relativizes *all* interpretations to their situation and so relativism itself must be relative to the relativist and of no general significance.[60]

The positive sceptic *does* believe the claims in the culture around him about thoughts, languages, ontologies and forms of life – it is these that led him into a vision of a multiplicity of aspects. However, he is not particularly interested in the claim that everything is *relative* to an aspect, or in debates about whether a theory is absolutely true, absolutely false or absolutely relative. Although he observes that some theories are present within some aspects and not others, he does not extend this observation into the claim that they are *merely* relative to aspects: situating a theory within an aspect just describes where it occurs; it does not make it any less or more absolute or true.[61] Each aspect remains absolute and yet there is a plurality of them. In a house one room might be painted yellow and another black, but the yellow does not undermine the black or fight against it: the yellow is absolutely yellow and the black is absolutely black. When we look at a duck/rabbit the duck is self-evidently and absolutely there for a while, and then it is there no longer and the rabbit is self-evidently and absolutely there in its place. Relativism is often felt to undermine different aspects and make them cancel each other out (with the exception, of course, of the relativist's own claims), whereas positive scepticism has moved beyond this negation into a plurality of absolute aspects.

A second important difference between positive scepticism and relativism is that although positive scepticism touches upon relativistic arguments to unveil the multiplicity of aspects, it is not committed to the metaphysics behind these arguments. The positive sceptic interprets the relationship between aspects and an alleged objective reality as something that itself varies between aspects. Within some aspects there is a distinction between aspects and an objective world; in other aspects the world is nothing more than the totality of aspects. The positive sceptic is interested in describing different aspects phenomenologically from the perspective of his own aspect; he is not interested in mediating between their different metaphysical claims.

Although positive scepticism may escape the relativist's performative contradiction, it is challenged by other self-reflexive problems. However, whilst the collapse of relativism is felt by its detractors to signal its unworkability, the collapse of positive scepticism is part of the way in which it works, and not something that invalidates it or should motivate a search for a better theory. Furthermore, relativism and positive scepticism are not the only theories to be challenged in this way. If they are pressed in the right places most other philosophical positions fall apart as well, and so it is likely that we will be struggling and living through some form of self-reflexive failure however we do philosophy.

Explosion into Transparency

Through language, theory, and text we close the openness that is the world. The closures we make provide our world – they are in a sense all that we have, and all that we could have. To want a final description of the world is to want more than this. We can provide many closures for our drawing – rabbit, duck, black lines on a white page, tiny particles impressed on a surface, analogy and of course drawing. Is it not ridiculous to want only one of these to be the 'true' version? Or perhaps that we might add all the interpretations together and thereby achieve a complete account? And so it is with the world. We do not have different accounts of the same 'thing', but different closures and different things. At any given point many closures are possible but this does not mean that any of them will do, or that they are all the same. Far from it, they are all different. *What matters* is not that there are a multiplicity of possible closures but that each closure textures the world and thereby enables us to do things in the 'world'. The choice of closures is not a merely theoretical affair, for it determines the possibilities of action available to us. Closures not only provide a world but are tools that enable one to deal with the world.

(Hilary Lawson, *Reflexivity*)[62]

Positive scepticism is a *position*; it makes definite claims about the way things are. It is a fixed way of being that does not attempt to theorize from nowhere, does not pretend that the theorizer does not exist.

Positive scepticism is extremely local. This Lower Clapton theory emerged at the end of the twentieth century, has a great deal in common with other sceptical positions and remains a product of its environing thoughts, languages, ontologies and forms of life.

Although positive scepticism is a finite philosophical position, it points beyond itself: it is a limited position that describes other possible ways to be. An aspect that situates itself amongst a multiplicity of aspects.

A map is a finite limited perspective; one opinion about the lie of the land. And yet a map points beyond itself – it indicates the possibility of places outside of the space occupied by the map. Even if the map is mistaken – for example, if the space occupied by the map is the only territory – it still remains part of its structure that it describes territories beyond itself.

Positive scepticism is a map that describes a territory populated by aspects. However, as you move over this territory, the map changes as well. Each part of the territory contains a different map of the whole.

How the different maps might be reconciled is not of interest to the positive sceptic. He has no idea whether one map correctly describes the whole territory, whether the combination of all the incompatible maps is the territory, whether the territory is created by the map, or whether there is no distinction between map and territory.

Positive scepticism interprets scientific realism as an aspect; scientific realism interprets positive scepticism as a mistake. Two

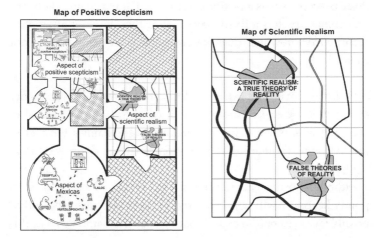

Figure 2. Relationship between the positive sceptic's map and the map of scientific realism

different maps are created in two different parts of the territory (see Figure 2).

At one point you are within positive scepticism; at another you are within scientific realism. The latter does not interpret itself as a map within the positive sceptic's territory.

Our theories about thought, language, ontology and form of life force us to take positive scepticism seriously – they all point towards the possibility of many different thoughts, languages, ontologies and forms of life. Furthermore, the multiplicity of theories about thought, language, ontology and form of life is an example of positive scepticism in practice.

One cannot depart from positive scepticism by arguing against it. Within the aspect of positive scepticism even the arguments against it tacitly endorse its validity.

One can escape from positive scepticism by moving to a point in the territory where the map no longer shows it: a point in the territory where positive scepticism is false or no longer exists. If you inhabit an aspect that negates or ignores positive scepticism, then you have escaped from it, even if positive scepticism continues to claim that you are in a labyrinth of aspects. There are rooms in which positive scepticism is relativistic nonsense, rooms in which cross-cultural differences can be explained more effectively, rooms without any of the problems posed and solved by positive scepticism.

I have presented the territory as if every point had a map, or at least the idea of a map or system. But at the limits of the positive sceptic's map, there is territory without maps or systems. Some aspects do not have anything resembling an interpretation or point of view.

Positive scepticism points towards mystical aspects, aspects incommensurable with everything, aspects that are not aspects. These are the flip side of the reality inhabited by philosophy: a flip side that haunts all other sides.

Radically different aspects are abysses in which positive scepticism ceases to exist: positive scepticism annihilates itself when it looks back from these aspects and gazes upon its own nonexistence. Positive scepticism is absent from these other aspects, and yet it is commanded by its own aspect to accept these different worldviews.

Positive scepticism starts off as a positive theory about thoughts, languages, ontologies and forms of life. Then its acceptance of hostile aspects negates it, this negation negates the acceptance of hostile aspects, and positive scepticism emerges again as a positive theory. This is the *unstable* hermeneutic circle shown in Figure 3.

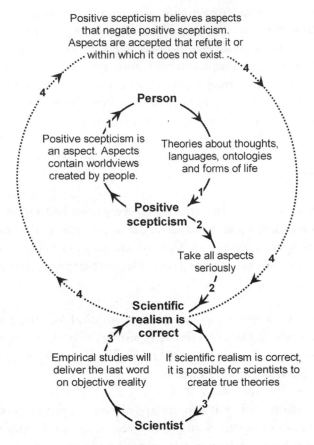

Figure 3. Positive scepticism is an unstable hermeneutic circle

Positive scepticism is a fixed point of view; it is an aspect that describes aspects. But aspects can only be inhabited sequentially, not simultaneously – they cannot be superimposed. The duck can only become a rabbit by ceasing to be a duck. The positive sceptic's description of aspects never leaves the aspect that is positive scepticism – it is always a duck talking about the possibility of becoming a rabbit. However, the human body that is the site for aspects *can* cease to speak within the framework of positive scepticism: she or he can abandon positive scepticism by taking on the thought, language, ontology and form of life of another aspect. When this site moves into a different aspect all of his or her saying becomes done by the aspect that he or she has moved to. When she or he is within Catholicism she or he speaks about a world built by God; when she or he is within positive scepticism, she or he describes reality as a labyrinth of aspects.[63]

The limit point of positive scepticism is a transparency in which the positive sceptic moves into and simultaneously occupies all other aspects. The positive sceptic ceases to judge aspects according to his system and evaluates them using their own systems. Different aspects cease to be different aspects and become whatever they say they are. The positive sceptic does not carry his identity with him into the other aspects – he is no longer a positive sceptic on the move. He dislocates himself from positive scepticism and abandons this amongst all the other identities. In a strange explosion into everything he becomes present in all aspects – even in the ones that he is not aware of. The positive sceptic becomes the labyrinth of aspects talking about themselves.

This limit point may not be possible or even conceivable. If we reached it, we would not realize that we had done so.

A simultaneous preservation, annulment and moving beyond. Positive scepticism is preserved in the expansion into other aspects, annulled by aspects in which it is denied or does not exist, and moved beyond as something that interprets and controls other aspects.

Positive scepticism *explodes* into transparency. The positive sceptic moves *outwards* to embrace all parts of the labyrinth.

Other aspects (and perhaps positive scepticism as well) are *imploded* by their internal contradictions. The arguments that normally support an aspect are turned against it or against each other. A self-justifying system becomes a collapsing system.

Implosion of the only aspect that a person believes in hurls them into a free space in which all aspects are equally valid. Once they had one fixed way of thinking; now every way of thinking becomes conceivable. Implosion breaks a person's mooring point and moves them suddenly into every room. A collapsed aspect is a black hole that passes to all points in the labyrinth – an implosion *into* transparency.

In this book I have flagrantly twisted arguments in my favour, blatantly cobbled together only the facts supporting *my* enclosed and self-justifying theoretical position. Fortunately I am not alone in my madness. We all offer hermetic fantasies to one another from our cosily enclosed worlds.

The aspect that placed itself on these pages is just one particular 'distortion' of a postmodern aspect that is common within our culture. I am only one among many inhabitants of an aspect in which reality is a labyrinth of aspects. In fact, none of the material in this chapter is mine at all: a collage of ideas assembled in me from a variety of 'famous' sources.

Perhaps it is the form and not the content of positive scepticism that is important. A form that functions as a mirror. As you study positive scepticism, as you accept and reject its arguments and dismiss the whole thing as nonsense, the form of your own theoretical position is reflected back to you. I could have picked any aspect to serve as your mirror, but this one seemed to have a particularly high reflectivity. A monad containing the entire universe within itself.

Positive scepticism cannot be argued for, but it can be evoked and embodied in a discourse that lives it out in practice. It can only hope to inspire people, for it will never convince them. In fact, positive scepticism predicts that people will reject it, that there will always be a gulf between positive sceptics and other people – a gulf that neither party will have any particular desire to erase.

But it is a good thing for the reputation of scepticism that there are so many people about who are not sceptics, to show that man is quite capable of the most extravagant opinions, since he is capable of believing that he is not naturally and inevitably weak, but is, on the contrary, naturally wise.

Nothing strengthens the case for scepticism more than the fact that there are people who are not sceptics. If they all were, they would be wrong.

(Blaise Pascal, *Pensées*)[64]

Endings ...

I would like to try and delineate a *fifth* response to nihilism, that borrows heavily from the work of Heidegger and Adorno. With this fifth response, it is not a question of overcoming nihilism in an act of the will or joyful destruction, because such an act would only imprison us all the more firmly in the very nihilistic logic we are trying to leave behind. Rather than overcoming nihilism, it is a question of *delineating* it. What will be at stake is a liminal experience, a deconstructive experience of the limit – deconstruction *as* an experience of the limit – that separates the inside from the outside of nihilism and which forbids us both the gesture of transgression and restoration.

(Simon Critchley, *Very Little ... Almost Nothing*)[1]

The Beginning of the Beginning

Tight choking black muffled noise; shifting writhing squashed; crushed; choking slide; heave slip-grasp ease; crush; cold-steel-pain; ease; sudden whack scream blurred light.

I was born – a fact that I can scarcely comprehend – and have memories of growing up that I can barely relate to. Blurred unreal glimpses of my past – doing things, seeing and hearing things, asking things, interpreting things. Memories as grainy as the 8 mm images that silently link them to existence.

I was *given* a system of thought, a language, an ontology and a form of life. I was *given* a way in which I could understand the commencement of myself.

Now I sit and contemplate the bloody thrust that threw me into the world. Retrospectively I dissect and interpret. My beginnings began when I started to look back on my history.

The Beginning of the End

Philosophy is the attempt to comprehend the world around us, the reality that we inhabit in our day to day lives. Over time this quest has separated into many sects. Some bear the escutcheon 'science'; others use 'economics', 'politics', 'philosophy' or 'religion' to describe themselves. We are people thrown into a world and talking about it.

As we struggle to comprehend reality we come across *limitations*: we encounter blind spots, self-cancellations of our descriptions, an excess of equally plausible descriptions. Cataracts cast dark spots over philosophy's clear vision.

We want to *describe* reality, but our most promising theories about perception and time cannot be proved or spoken about. We reach out towards the world and our theories slowly sadly surely melt away.

We want to *fix* reality, but it explodes into a labyrinth of mad aspects. This labyrinth appears differently within each room and is obliterated by many of them. All rooms shift uneasily between sanity and insanity.

Reality destabilizes. The world that we grew into as a child starts to crumble and fragment. Sliding systems, partial systems, vague drifting clouds of thought. We slip into madness; we watch madness tumble from our grasp forever.

This book was built within the territory that I have just described; it has attempted to circle some of the self-reflexive limits of philosophy and science. By creating more far reaching and coherent interpretations of some of our contemporary theories, I have tried to put the pieces of our worldview together more consistently and highlight the problems that emerge when this is done.

One of the aims of this work has been to show how we need to bear self-reflexivity in mind when constructing, criticizing or believing in philosophical and scientific theories. We need to know if theories are stable, unstable or collapse, and whether a criticism on these grounds matters; we need to know if theories are visible or invisible if we are planning to take them seriously as total systems. We may also have to revise our criteria for acceptable theories if few theories remain visible and if the notion of invisibility can be sustained as a theoretical concept. There are also questions about the status of stable hermeneutic circles. If these are the only theories that we can argue for, what is the point of such arguments? If we are *forced* to put them forward because we cannot speak about alternatives, are we not in some sense merely moving within their presuppositions?

I have also tried to show how self-reflexive limits cancel the cancellation of themselves; how philosophy has a strange habit of returning to its starting point. After a collapse that eliminates the evidence for the brain hypothesis or our ability to speak about objective time, we fall silent for a while, and then these theories miraculously return. After losing ourselves in madmen and other aspects, we lose this losing of ourselves and return to the homogenous zone and positive scepticism.

This book has forged a path from normal theories about the world to the strange ground that has formed its main subject matter. It is not just a few obscure metaphysical theses that are challenged by these problems, but our ordinary interpretations as well. Our *everyday* understanding of the world falls apart in the way that I have described – collapsing aspects do not just lie within the dusty tomes of past thinkers.

A variety of theoretical freaks have been trapped within the glass chapters of this volume. If we take these theories *seriously* and really *inhabit and believe in them*, we will come terrifyingly close to insanity. And yet these teratoid models *are* our everyday theories in a starker darker form with all their metaphysics and self-reflexive problems intact. This book has birthed monsters that were already part of our diseased imaginations.

My description of these problems has been inextricably trapped within the problems that it has described. This has been a book *about* philosophy and the world that was written *within* philosophy and the world and it has also *been* philosophy and the world. Although I have attempted to set limits to philosophy and science, and to enact these limits, I have not thereby hoped to overcome them. My main aim has been to open up ways in which we can limn these limits without seeking solutions. We can accept these limits, or move into a different room in which they no longer appear – a room that, perhaps, has nothing to do with philosophy.

The end begins when philosophy finds itself unable to escape from the limits that it discovers within itself. This end never ends because the attempt to wrap it up in a conclusion only succeeds in deferring it. So long as the end is a philosophical *theme*, it is an end that is just beginning.

The Ending of the End

I am a nihilist

I observe, I accept, I assume the immense process of the destruction of appearances (and of the seduction of appearances) in the service of meaning (representation, history, criticism, etc.) that is the fundamental fact of the nineteenth century, of modernity, is the radical destruction of appearances, the disenchantment of the world and its abandonment to the violence of interpretation and of history.

> I observe, I accept, I assume, I analyze the second revolution, that
> of the twentieth century, that of postmodernity, which is the immense
> process of the destruction of meaning, equal to the earlier destruction
> of appearances. He who strikes with meaning is killed by meaning.
>
> The dialectic stage, the critical stage is empty. There is no more stage.
> There is no therapy of meaning or therapy through meaning: therapy itself
> is part of the generalized process of indifferentiation.
>
> The stage of analysis itself has become uncertain, aleatory: theories float
> (in fact, nihilism is impossible, because it is still a desperate but determined
> theory, an imaginary of the end, a weltanschauung of catastrophe).
>
> (Jean Baudrillard, *Simulacra and Simulation*)[2]

Prescriptive limits are part of philosophy; they do not substantially
limit it at all. They extend philosophy by partitioning it into legitimate and illegitimate areas. The limits to philosophy that I am
interested in do not prescribe what we *should* say or do in
philosophy. They create a kind of play within which prescriptive
limits become less important.

We can only go so far within philosophy, within language, and
yet this limitation can extend indefinitely. A folded space in which
we can advance continuously without resistance, and which insen-
sibly returns us to the beginning.

The end extends endlessly or vanishes. As we keep attempting to
speak our speech slips and disintegrates into nonsense, sense or
silence.

This book can be interpreted as a modern mystical text. No
blood-dripping wounds of Christ to save us, but perhaps the first
stirrings of a cloud of unknowing that we can penetrate with a
loving longing dart.

When some theories are pushed to their limits they abolish
speech, but the practice of speech is not affected. We do not fall

silent – we keep our aimless chatter going – but our hopes for language die. We give up even though this giving up is completely unjustified. This giving up is a further move *within* the language-game, not an escape from it.

The end steps off a bus, quietly checks into a cheap motel, throws its hat and coat over a chair, unpacks its typewriter, pours itself a glass of whiskey and starts to type ...

Notes

Introduction

1. Martin Heidegger, *The Fundamental Concepts of Metaphysics*, translated by William McNeill and Nicholas Walker (Bloomington and Indianapolis: Indiana University Press, 1995), p. 21.

2. This notion of a picture or model that is embedded in a number of different theories can be found in Wittgenstein's analysis of the Augustinian theory of language, which is described by him as a pervasive worldview that underlies a number of accounts of meaning that are superficially quite different. According to Baker and Hacker's commentary on Wittgenstein, 'Augustine's picture of language might be represented not as an explicit theory, but rather as a proto-theory that shapes the development of many philosophical theories of meaning. It is like an invisible force, evident only in its visible effects; like a prevailing wind that affects the growth of a tree, it might show itself only in the asymmetric shape that it gives to explicit theorising.' (G. P. Baker and P. M. S. Hacker, *An Analytic Commentary on Wittgenstein's Philosophical Investigations*, Volume 1 [Oxford: Basil Blackwell, 1988], p. 46.)

3. See Hilary Lawson, *Closure* (London and New York: Routledge, 2001).

4. Ludwig Wittgenstein, *Tractatus Logico-Philosophicus*, translated by D.F. Pears and B. F. McGuinness (London: Routledge & Kegan Paul, 1961), § 4.113–§ 4.115.

1 Stable and Collapsing Theories

1. G.W. F. Hegel, *Logic* (first part of *Encyclopaedia*), translated by William Wallace (Oxford: Clarendon Press, 1982), Section 17, p. 23.

2. Hilary Lawson, *Closure* (London and New York: Routledge, 2001), pp. xxix–xxx.

3. Josef Bleicher distinguishes between the hermeneutic*al* circle, which is primarily methodological, and the hermeneutic circle which is the ontological condition of understanding binding us to tradition: 'I have chosen the terms "hermeneutical" and "hermeneutic" in order to signify

contrasting conceptions of hermeneutics itself; this choice is not an arbitrary one in that I hope that the former conveys a methodological orientation whereas the latter should indicate a more fundamental, philosophical concern. A similar distinction applies to their respective relationships to history: "historical" approaches strive for objective knowledge of past events in contrast to their "historic" significances for an interpreting subject *hic et nunc*.' (Josef Bleicher, *Contemporary Hermeneutics* [London, Boston and Henley: Routledge & Kegan Paul, 1980], p. 3.) In these discussions I will use 'hermeneutic' to label the type of circle that I am interested in, which will be distinguished from Bleicher's two meanings.

4   Bleicher's second meaning in footnote 3, above.

5   I am using the terms 'stable', 'collapsing' and 'unstable' to describe theories, not to evaluate them. Stable theories are not necessarily better than collapsing ones and the paradoxical structure of collapsing theories does not necessarily make them incorrect.

6   Alexandre Kojève, *Introduction to the Reading of Hegel*, assembled by Raymond Queneau, edited by Alan Bloom, translated by James H. Nichols, Jr. (Ithaca: Cornell University Press, 1996), p. 35.

7   Jacques Derrida, *Writing and Difference*, translated by Alan Bass (Exeter: Harvester Wheatsheaf, 1982), p. 281. See Charles Levin, *Jean Baudrillard, A Study in Cultural Metaphysics* (Hemel Hempstead: Prentice Hall, Harvester Wheatsheaf, 1996), p. 75, for more on the problematic status of Lévi-Strauss' structuralism.

8   Some of the other attempts that have been made to escape collapse are discussed by Lawson in *Reflexivity* (La Salle, Illinois: Open Court, 1985), pp. 16–22.

9   In *Reflexivity* Lawson makes this point about Nietzsche, Heidegger and Derrida. All three of these authors struggle to speak within a paradoxical self-reflexive position because they are convinced (and attempt to demonstrate) that all theories are beset by similar problems.

10   This is related to Hegel's theory of time, which I do not have space to go into here.

11   This structure is similar to a person who says: 'I am lying'. We start off believing a person who claims to be lying and accept 'I am lying' as a true statement. However, if 'I am lying' is a true statement, then its claim to be a lie must be true and so 'I am lying' must be a lie. But if 'I am lying' is a lie, then the person must be telling the truth and 'I am lying' becomes a

true statement again. 'I am lying' is a statement that compels us to reject it and this rejection leads us to accept it once again.

2 Evidence for the Brain?

1   Jean Baudrillard, *Simulations*, translated by Paul Foss, Paul Patton and Philip Beitchman (New York: Semiotext(e), Inc., 1983), p. 2.

2   This example ignores all the complications due to multiple reflections and assumes a single returning pulse.

3   To fit into the robot, the virtual model would have to be stored in a space smaller than the robot and it is assumed that this is the case here. However, the robot could store its virtual model in a remote computer that is larger than the robot that it is controlling.

4   Richard Dawkins, *Unweaving the Rainbow* (London: The Penguin Press, 1998), p. 277.

5   Bertrand Russell, *An Outline of Philosophy* (London: George Allen & Unwin Ltd, 1927), p. 148.

6   Although the liver also processes information from the environment – in this case chemical information gathered by the blood – this kind of information is not thought to be relevant to an explanation of our perceptual experiences.

7   Colin McGinn, *The Problem of Consciousness* (Oxford: Basil Blackwell, 1991), p. 40.

8   See J. R. Smythies' article on projection theory for some background and a convincing refutation ('Analysis of Projection', *British Journal for the Philosophy of Science*, 5, 1954). Thomas Baldwin has a more philosophical version of projection theory ('The projective theory of sensory content', in Tim Crane (ed.), *The Contents of Experience* (Cambridge: Cambridge University Press, 1992) and Max Velmans has an excellent discussion of many of the arguments covered in this chapter ('Consciousness, brain and the physical world', *Philosophical Psychology* 3(1), 1990, pp. 77–99).

9   We are unlikely to be able to detect McGinn's property P because we are perceptually and cognitively closed towards it and a more plausible property to account for projection has not been put forward.

10   Smythies, 'Analysis of Projection', p. 122.

11 Russell, *An Outline of Philosophy*; Thomas Metzinger, *Being No One*
    (Cambridge, Massachusetts: The MIT Press, 2003); Gregory Mulhauser,
    Mind Out of Matter (Dordrecht: Kluwer Academic Publishers, 1998);
    Steven Lehar, *The World in Your Head* (Mahwah, New Jersey: Lawrence
    Erlbaum Associates, Publishers, 2003); Dawkins, *Unweaving the
    Rainbow*. This chapter draws on all of these accounts to develop a
    coherent and convincing interpretation of the brain hypothesis.

12 Lehar, *The World in Your Head*, p. 8.

13 Ibid., p. 2.

14 These observations do not apply at the quantum level. Although it is
    assumed in this chapter that consciousness does not depend on
    quantum effects in the brain, some physicists, most famously Roger
    Penrose, have suggested that quantum effects could explain some
    features of the mind. See R. Gush and P. S. Churchland for an exami-
    nation of Penrose's claims ('Gaps in Penrose's toilings', *Journal of
    Consciousness Studies* 2(1), 1995, pp. 10–29). Even if consciousness
    is linked to quantum effects in microtubules, this has nothing to do with
    the way in which the brain senses its environment. At present we
    assume that the brain obtains its data through the eyes and nerves, not
    through non-local instantaneous quantum sensing.

15 Hilary Putnam, *Reason, Truth and History* (Cambridge: Cambridge
    University Press, 1982), p. 6.

16 Daniel Dennett claims that this kind of modelling would be impossible in
    practice (*Consciousness Explained* [London: Penguin, 1992], pp. 3–7).
    However, even if his arguments are accepted, this thought experiment
    could still be carried out in a restricted environment at the lower data rates
    required for video games instead of the real world.

17 Martin Amis, *Time's Arrow* (London: Jonathan Cape, 1991), pp. 13–14.

18 Stereograms can also have images that come forward as well as backwards
    from the surface of the cardboard. See *Stereogram* (London: Boxtree,
    1994) for examples.

19 Once objects are represented in the virtual environment it is easy to see
    how they can directly affect other brain processes and cause movements
    without the need for a second act of perception. The firing patterns of
    neurons that are creating the virtual piece of fruit on my left could
    activate other neurons in the superior colliculus to reorient my eyes. If
    the firing patterns of neurons that are creating my virtual stomach signal

that it is empty, then the neurons that release saliva could become activated by association.

[20] The section on evidence in the second part of this chapter will take a careful look at the relationship between phenomenal representations and the real world.

[21] Hans Reichenbach, *The Philosophy of Space & Time*, translated by Maria Reichenbach and John Freund (New York: Dover Publications Inc., 1957), p.16.

[22] Robert J. Stone, 'Virtual Reality: A Tool For Teleprescence and Human Factors Research', in *Virtual Reality Systems*, edited by R. A. Earnshaw, M. A. Gigante and H. Jones (London and New York: Academic Press, 1993), p. 200.

[23] Philip K. Dick, *Valis* (London: Gollancz, 2001), p. 191.

[24] Metzinger, *Being No One*, p. 140.

[25] Jacques Lacan, *The Seminar of Jacques Lacan. Book 1: Freud's Papers on Technique*, edited by Jacques-Alain Miller, translated by John Forrester (New York: W.W. Norton, 1988), p. 245.

[26] Antti Revonsuo, 'Consciousness, Dreams, and Virtual Realities', *Philosophical Psychology* 8 (1), 1995, p. 55.

[27] This relationship between virtual and real kilometres was suggested by Lehar's metaphorical link between the dome of the sky and the dome of the skull. This is a useful way of thinking about it, but it should not be taken literally since the brain's representation of its environment is highly distributed and although many maps of the senses have been found in the brain, it is still not understood how they are used to create an integrated spatial model.

[28] Robert Crookall, *Case-Book of Astral Projection, 545–746* (New Jersey: Citadel Press, 1980), p. 63. I have taken out Crookall's additions in square brackets.

[29] Ronald Melzack, 'Phantom Limbs', *Scientific American*, April 1992, p. 90.

[30] Approximately twenty per cent of people born with missing limbs also experience phantoms. See R. Melzack, R. Israel, R. Lacroix and G. Schultz, 'Phantom Limbs in people with congenital limb deficiency or amputation in early childhood', *Brain* 120 (9), 1997, pp. 1603–20.

[31]   Melzack, 'Phantom Limbs', p. 90.

[32]   Crookall, *Case-Book of Astral Projection, 545–746*, p. 34. I have taken out Crookall's additions in square brackets.

[33]   Lehar, *The World in Your Head*, p. 39.

[34]   Friedrich Nietzsche, *Beyond Good and Evil*, translated by R.J. Hollingdale (Harmondsworth: Penguin, 1977), § 15, p. 27.

[35]   It could be objected that this is true of science generally and so it cannot be used as a specific objection to the brain hypothesis. For example, Popper makes this claim about science in *The Logic of Scientific Discovery* (London: Hutchinson, 1968), p. 106.

[36]   It might be objected that some brain hypothesis theories allow for the possibility that the brain might be systematically blind to some aspects of its functioning. For example, within Thomas Metzinger's framework certain types of offline simulation or introspection are impossible (Metzinger, *Being No One*). However, whilst it could be a feature of the brain hypothesis that the brain cannot imagine or introspect all aspects of itself phenomenologically, this has little bearing on the brain's ability to cognitively discover and justify the brain hypothesis. If it turns out that one consequence of the brain hypothesis is that the brain cannot understand or justify the brain hypothesis, then the brain should give up on the brain hypothesis and look for a better theory. It is one thing to claim that we cannot imagine or access some lower level of our neurons' data processing; quite another to claim evidence for the belief that our phenomenal world is a virtual construct of the brain.

[37]   John Locke, *An Essay Concerning Human Understanding*, edited by Roger Woolhouse (London: Penguin Books, 1997), pp. 136–7.

[38]   Dennett, *Consciousness Explained*, p. 131.

[39]   I have excluded situation from this list, which Locke does not emphasize, and it is hard to see how an object's situation could be defined in non-relative objective terms.

[40]   I am using Locke as an example of someone who supports a distinction between primary and secondary qualities. This distinction had already been made before him by a number of people, including the Greek atomists, Galileo, Descartes and Boyle.

[41]   Mackie suggests that this distinction, which goes back to Aristotle, could be used to support Locke's analysis. See J. L. Mackie, *Problems from*

Locke (Oxford: Clarendon Press, 1987), pp. 28–32.

[42] This is not an argument Locke put forward, but originates in more ancient sources. For example, Sextus Empiricus discusses many cases of this type, such as the claim that things which appear white to us appear yellow to people with jaundice and reddish to those with bloodshot eyes. However, it could have easily been used by Locke to make his case and so I have included it here. Locke does discuss a similar example in which a person experiences both heat and cold when his warm and cold hands are placed in a bowl of warm water.

[43] This interpretation of Locke is taken from Mackie: 'It is clear that Locke adopted the distinction as part of the "corpuscular philosophy" of Boyle and other scientists of the time whose work Locke knew and admired.' (Mackie, *Problems from Locke*, p. 17).

[44] For these reasons I will be dropping number from the list of primary qualities for the rest of this discussion.

[45] k is a constant that can be calculated from measurements of P and V, but it cannot itself be directly measured.

[46] The modern metre is defined as 1,650,763.73 wavelengths of the orange-red emission line in the spectrum of the krypton-86 atom in a vacuum, but the general method of measurement is the same as the comparison of an object with the platinum bar in Paris, which I am using here to make my description as clear as possible.

[47] This is true for a realist interpretation of scientific entities, which most scientists and philosophers who are not philosophers of science tend to believe in. It is not clear whether the brain hypothesis or the hard problem of consciousness (discussed later in this section) would make any sense within an anti-realist interpretation of science, in which there is only one level of reality and scientific theories about the metaphysical nature of reality are reduced to predictive instruments.

[48] Russell, *An Outline of Philosophy*, p. 163.

[49] Ibid.

[50] It might be argued that there are *evolutionary* arguments for a resemblance between our ideas about primary qualities and the primary qualities themselves, but this has the problem that it applies equally well to colour, taste and smell. If it is evolutionarily advantageous for my idea of extension to resemble real extension, then it is equally evolutionarily advantageous

for my idea of colour to resemble real colour. Any attempt to show that primary qualities are more evolutionarily important will have to deal with the fact that taste, colour and smell are very important from an evolutionary point of view. It is also unclear why evolutionary control strategies could not be based on *consistent mis*representations.

51 G. W. F Hegel, *The Logic*, from *The Encyclopaedia of the Philosophical Sciences*, translated by William Wallace (Oxford: Clarendon Press, 1874), § 44, p. 77.

52 McGinn, *The Problem of Consciousness*, pp. 1–2.

53 Michael Heim, *The Metaphysics of Virtual Reality* (New York: Oxford University Press, 1993), p. 91.

54 Maurice Merleau-Ponty, *The Visible and the Invisible*, edited by Claude Lefort, translated by Alphonso Lingis (Evanston: Northwestern University Press, 1995), p. 3.

3 Impossible Speech about Time

1 Saint Augustine, *Confessions*, translated by R. S. Pine-Coffin (London: Penguin, 1975), p. 263.

2 Quoted from Antonin Artaud, *Collected Works*, Volume 3, translated by Alastair Hamilton (London: Calder & Boyars, 1972), p. 63.

3 Compare the responses of people in ordinary cinemas and people in IMAX 3D cinemas, who often cry out, try to touch the image, or even feel physically sick when they are first exposed to IMAX 3D films.

4 Marshall McLuhan, *Understanding Media* (London: Routledge & Kegan Paul Ltd, 1964), p. 22. Note that television, when McLuhan wrote *Understanding Media*, was black and white, small, and low definition, which made it very different from the television that we have now, which is almost as hot as film.

5 This assumes a projection rate of twenty-four frames per second and a semi-circular shutter that blocks off the light for half the time. A faster projection mechanism could use a shutter that blocked the light for less time.

6 This would impose practical (but not theoretical) limitations on the kind of film that could be shown. It would also be difficult to build machinery

that was fast, powerful, and silent enough to accurately exchange the frames with a smooth transition between them.

[7] In this thought experiment sounds, odours, sensations, emotions and thoughts are all encoded digitally. In traditional cinema technology, the sound runs in a continuous analogue optical strip alongside the film, whereas digitizing creates the illusion of continuous sound by breaking the sound up into a number of fixed amplitudes, each of which is held for a short period (the full technical details are more complicated, but this does not substantially affect my argument). The frequency at which sound fragments are exchanged in digital sound is much higher than the rate of exchange of cinematic frames (44,100 Hz opposed to 24 Hz), but in this thought experiment each fragment of image, sound, odour, sensation, emotion and thought is held stationary for 1/48th of a second and then exchanged. In practice this would result in extremely bad sound and thought quality, but the whole thought experiment could be repeated using 44,100 frames per second and a stationary period of 0.0000227 seconds without making any difference to my argument.

[8] I am examining here what the audience *might* think if their thoughts were not being projected into them. In fact, the thoughts of the audience are not applicable to their real situation because they are all being controlled by the film. This will become important in the fourth point, and in the later discussion of the relationship between time and language.

[9] Connected with this is the further problem that Roger would not experience any time at all if he was held *immobile* for 1/48th of a second and then wiped out for 1/48th of a second. This will be dealt with in the section on fixed and mobile moments.

[10] Although the lights become brighter, they continue to be switched off whilst the frames are exchanged.

[11] Henri Bergson, *Creative Evolution*, translated by Arthur Mitchell (London: Macmillan and Co. Limited, 1911), p. 321.

[12] For simplicity I have concentrated upon our experience of light in the realtime reality projector, but the same analysis could be applied to our experience of sound and other sensations.

[13] Deleuze uses the terms 'time-image' and 'movement-image' in his books on cinema, but I will be using them in a different sense here.

[14] Augustine, *Confessions*, p. 269.

[15] Ibid., p. 278.

[16] A much more sophisticated phenomenology of time perception can be found in Edmund Husserl, *The Phenomenology of Internal Time-Consciousness*, edited by Martin Heidegger, translated by James S. Churchill (Bloomington and London: Indiana University Press, 1966). The temporal phenomena described by Husserl can also be re-interpreted as changes in a sequence of static reality-frames.

[17] 'Activation' should not be taken in any temporal sense. A neuron is active or 'firing' when it has a certain chemical composition and inactive when its chemical composition is different.

[18] A. R. Damasio, D. Tranel and H. Damasio, 'Amnesia caused by herpes simplex encephalitis, infarctions in basal forebrain, Alzheimer's disease and anoxia/ischemia', in F. Boller and J. Grafman (eds), *Handbook of Neuropsychology* (New York: Elsevier, 1989), Volume 3, pp. 149–66.

[19] J. Zihl, D. Von Cramon, and N. Mai, 'Selective Disturbance of Movement Vision after Bilateral Brain Damage', *Brain*, 106, 1983, p. 315.

[20] Part of the eighth fragment of Parmenides, quoted from *The Fragments of Parmenides*, A. H. Coxon (Assen, Netherlands: Van Gorcum, 1986), p. 66.

[21] P. D. Ouspensky, *Tertium Organum*, translated by Nicholas Bessaraboff and Claude Bragdon (London: Kegan Paul, 1937), p. 119.

[22] If the continuity of the two-dimensional person was broken up, she would not notice, but then time could not be described as the third dimension of a two-dimensional world. To avoid digressions that do not affect my basic point I will assume continuity for this interpretation of the projection mechanism.

[23] Of course, this is just one way of expressing it. If time is the fourth dimension, then the individual reality-frames that I have described are from the beginning an abstraction from a continuum, not something that have to be made infinitely thin and stacked on top of one other in order to reconstitute it.

[24] A further consequence of time being a dimension of space is that time should be measurable in metres. Relativity theory claims that this is the case, with one second being equivalent to 299792458 metres (the speed of light is used as the factor of conversion). However, relativity does treat time and space differently when it calculates four-dimensional distance using $x^2 + y^2 + z^2 - t^2$.

[25] Ouspensky, *Tertium Organum*, p. 45.

[26] Ibid., p. 205.

[27] Within relativity theory there are at least two perspectives from which all the events in my life and the universe are experienced simultaneously. A person moving at the speed of light has their time infinitely dilated, and all of the events that they observe appear to be taking place at the same time (a photon that was created in the big bang and obliterated in the big crunch would experience the entire history of the universe as a single event). On the edge of a black hole, time is dilated in a similar way and the entire life of a person on earth appears to take place within a single moment for an observer in this position.

[28] Ouspensky, *Tertium Organum*, pp. 46–7.

[29] There is a further problem about the *shape* of this four-dimensional hyperblock. How can the universe have a shape unless it is situated within a greater environing space, a larger universe?

[30] Ouspensky, *Tertium Organum*, p. 122.

[31] G. W. F. Hegel, *Philosophy of Nature*, translated by A. V. Miller (Oxford: Oxford University Press, 1970), p. 35.

[32] If time is the nihilating nothingness outside of the plenitude of being, then it can creatively change the world as a whole. However, this reduces the world and all of the creatures in it to *object*s that are changed *by* time (instead of free subjects who make decisions *in* time). In a world with an open future, time is the only for-itself; and this for-itself nihilates an in-itself that includes human beings.

[33] Husserl, *The Phenomenology of Internal Time-Consciousness*, p. 99.

[34] Ibid., p. 152.

[35] Ibid., p. 100.

[36] Martin Heidegger, *Being and Time*, translated by John Macquarrie and Edward Robinson (Oxford: Blackwell, 1995), p. 329.

[37] Bertrand Russell, *An Outline of Philosophy* (London: George Allen & Unwin Ltd., 1970), p. 7.

[38] See George Edward Moore, 'A Defence of Common Sense', reprinted in *Philosophical Papers* (London: George Allen & Unwin Ltd, 1959).

[39] Damascius, *Commentary on Parmenides*, quoted from Richard Sorabji,

Time, Creation and the Continuum (London: Duckworth, 1983), p. 55.

40 It might be thought that the projector should project at an infinitely fast rate as well as continuously. However, as I pointed out in the discussion of the projection mechanism, the notion of time projecting at any particular rate is nonsensical.

41 Martin Nilsson, *Primitive Time Reckoning* (London: Humphrey Milford, 1920), p. 356.

42 Figure adapted from Roger Penrose, *The Emperor's New Mind* (Reading: Vintage, 1990), p. 259.

43 Ibid.

44 The *interval* is a combination of space and time which is analogous to distance in three-dimensional space. Just as distance is independent of the axes used to measure it, the interval is the same in all reference frames. In three-dimensional space the square of the distance is given by $x^2 + y^2 + z^2$; in four-dimensional spacetime the square of the interval is given by $x^2 + y^2 + z^2 - t^2$. This interval is spacelike when it is greater than zero and timelike when it is less than zero.

45 Penrose, *The Emperor's New Mind*, p. 259.

46 Saint Gregory the Great, *Morals on the Book of Job*, Vol. II, Book XVI, 45 (Oxford: John Henry Parker F. & J. Rivington, 1845), p. 253.

47 Alexandre Kojève, *Introduction to the Reading of Hegel*, assembled by Raymond Queneau, edited by Allan Bloom, translated by James H. Nichols, Jr. (Ithaca: Cornell University Press, 1996), p. 118.

48 For more on picturing see Moreland Perkins, 'The Picturing in Seeing', *The Journal of Philosophy*, 67, pp. 321–39; and Robert Sokolowski, 'Picturing', *Review of Metaphysics*, 31, September 1977, pp. 3–28.

49 Kojève, *Introduction to the Reading of Hegel*, p. 148.

50 Franz Brentano, *Philosophical Investigations on Space, Time and the Continuum*, translated by Barry Smith (Worcester: Croom Helm Ltd., 1988), p. 83.

51 Meister Eckhart, *The Essential Sermons, Commentaries, Treatises and Defense*, translated by Edmund Colledge and Bernard McGinn (New York: Paulist Press, 1981), p. 205.

52 Jacques Derrida, *Margins of Philosophy*, translated by Alan Bass (Exeter: Harvester Wheatsheaf, 1982), p. 63.

4 Merging Madness and Reason

[1]   Quoted in Maria Lorenz, 'Problems Posed by Schizophrenic Language', *Archives of General Psychiatry*, 4, 1961, p. 604.

[2]   Jacques Derrida, 'Cogito and the History of Madness', in *Writing and Difference*, translated by Alan Bass (London: Routledge, 1995), p. 62.

[3]   In a chapter that destabilizes the difference between normality and madness there should really be quotation marks around every use of normality, madness, schizophrenia and their variants. I have decided not to clutter up the text in this way, but these words should be taken with progressively larger pinches of salt and spice as the chapter progresses.

[4]   Schizophrenia is used in this chapter as the main example of madness. However, the central argument also applies to other thought 'disturbances' as well.

[5]   It should be noted that this chapter is not an attempt to give an account of madness *itself*, described from within the standpoint of reason (it hopes to avoid the mistake that Derrida criticized in Foucault). Since it is *already* madness itself, it does not pretend to describe madness from the outside, and one of the purposes of this chapter is to *embody* and *enact* the madness that it is describing.

At a different level, this chapter does offer a description of madness, a theory of insanity that could be said to misrepresent and oppress madness. To the extent that this chapter works in this way, it does not pretend to give an account of madness *in itself*. It is a theory of madness within the language of reason that pushes reason until it topples over into its opposite – a deconstructive theory of insanity.

A final cautionary note should be added: the homogenous zone is not intended to be some kind of archaic return to a distant point when madness and reason were united. The Greeks and the Renaissance both had medical treatments for madness and so do most (if not all) 'primitive' cultures. In some of these periods (perhaps especially in the Renaissance) there may have been more of an emphasis on the homogenous zone, but there has never been a time when there was no madness; when the mad and the sane played happily together. The homogenous zone is a schizophrenic delusion/structure of reality that our culture is creating/discovering today. It should be taken on its own merits and not in relation to a possible instantiation in history.

[6]   Michel Foucault, *Mental Illness and Psychology*, translated by Alan Sheridan (Berkeley: University of California Press, 1987), p. 77.

7   Howard S. Becker, *Outsiders* (London: The Free Press of Glencoe, Collier-Macmillan Ltd., 1963), p. 9.

8   Thomas J. Scheff, *Being Mentally Ill* (Chicago: Aldine Publishing Company, 1976), p. 33.

9   Ibid., p. 92.

10 Ibid., p. 47.

11 Raymond Cochrane, *The Social Creation of Mental Illness* (New York: Longman, 1988), p. 158. A great deal of caution should be exercised when interpreting the type of study that Cochrane cites which presents a very simplified questionnaire to those people in the community who are prepared to answer it (or are capable of answering it). *The Social Creation of Mental Illness* has more discussion of the type of information gained by these surveys and an example of a typical questionnaire.

12 The notion of a symptom of schizophrenia should be interpreted with a great deal of caution since this presupposes that it is a genuine disease. See the section 'Problems and Objections' for a discussion of this.

13 See note 52.

14 Frances L. Ilg and Louise Bates Ames, *Child Behavior* (New York: Dell Publishing Company, 1955), p. 173.

15 Jean Baudrillard, *Simulacra and Simulation*, translated by Sheila Faria Glaser (Michigan: The University of Michigan Press, 1996), p. 13.

16 E. Bleuler, 'Autistic thinking', in D. Rapaport (ed.), *Organization and Pathology of Thought: Selected Sources* (New York: Columbia University Press, 1951), pp. 401–2.

17 Although there are many parallels between the schizophrenic state and childhood, such as the presence of 'fantasy' friends, a lack of differentiation between subjective and objective, a low level of abstraction and self-reference (this last is claimed by some authors but disputed by Sass), there are differences as well and schizophrenia is not simply a regression to childhood or the 'primitive'. Although many schizophrenic behaviours are apparently childish, many of their beliefs are derived from the adult world (such as religious ideas, persecution by the state, telepathic communication, etc.). This is supported by the work of Norman Cameron, who tested schizophrenics on a number of tasks that he also presented to normal adults, senile adults, and normal children. In these experiments Cameron found that the schizophrenics' results were substantially different from

those of the other groups. (Norman Cameron, 'Experimental Analysis of Schizophrenic Thinking', in J. S. Kasanin (ed.), *Language and Thought in Schizophrenia* [Berkeley and Los Angeles: University of California Press, 1944], p. 59.) Critiques of the regression theory of schizophrenia can also be found in Michel Foucault, *Mental Illness and Psychology* and Louis A. Sass, *Madness and Modernism* (Cambridge, Massachusetts: Harvard University Press, 1994).

[18] Harry Stack Sullivan, 'The Language of Schizophrenia', in J. S. Kasanin (ed.), *Language and Thought in Schizophrenia* (Berkeley and Los Angeles: University of California Press, 1944), pp. 11–12.

[19] L. S. Vygotsky, *Thought and Language*, edited and translated by Eugenia Hanfmann and Gertrude Vakar (Cambridge, Massachusetts: The MIT Press, 1974), pp. 18–19.

[20] Harry Stack Sullivan, 'The Language of Schizophrenia', pp. 12–13.

[21] See Temple Grandin, *Thinking in Pictures* (New York: Vintage Books, 1995), for a good discussion of autistic experience and the continuum between autistics and normal people.

[22] Charles Mackay, *Extraordinary Popular Delusions and the Madness of Crowds* (New York: Farrar, Straus and Giroux, 1932), p. 257.

[23] Ronald Laing also makes this point: 'The madness of Europe is revealed not in the persons of the madmen of Europe, but in the actions of the self-validated sane ones, who wrote the books, sanctified and authorised by State, Church, and the repression of bourgeois morality. The history of madness documented here is the history of the projection into the few who were destroyed or forgotten, of the lunacy of the majority who won the day.' ('The Invention of Madness', in *Critical Essays on Michel Foucault*, edited by Peter Burke, Aldershot, Scholar Press, 1992, p. 26.)

[24] See Karl R. Popper, *The Logic of Scientific Discovery* (London: Hutchinson, 1968), p. 111.

[25] Conversation with John, a paranoid schizophrenic, cited in David Terry Bradford, *The Experience of God* (York: Peter Land Publishing Inc., 1984), p. 307.

[26] Renee, *Autobiography of a Schizophrenic Girl*, edited by Marguerite Sechehaye (New York: Signet, 1979), p. 44.

[27] Louis Sass, *Madness and Modernism*, p. 6.

28 Ibid., p. 12.

29 Quoted from Sigmund Freud, *The Standard Edition of the Complete Psychological Works of Sigmund Freud*, translated under the general editorship of James Strachey, in collaboration with Anna Freud, assisted by Alix Strachey and Alan Tyson (London: The Hogarth Press and the Institute of Psycho-Analysis, 1953), Volume V, p. 373.

30 Ibid., p. 607.

31 Intensity is always taken from zero – there are no negative values. If normal people were defined as zero, it would be necessary to speak about positive and negative amplification. However, the zero here is someone with a single thread of each colour.

32 This statement is a logical possibility, but should be taken with caution. It is possible that there are people who are flat, unresponsive and at degree zero of the human – for example, catatonic schizophrenics may be such people. However, many people who are labelled deficient have richness and intensity in areas that most of us neglect, as Oliver Sacks shows in *The Man Who Mistook His Wife For a Hat* (London: Duckworth, 1986).

33 This relativity may not be a cultural one since cross-cultural studies do indicate something akin to our medical notion of madness in most other cultures: 'All societies throughout the ages have recognised the existence of insanity or mental illness among some of their members, and have distinguished these from conditions such as feeble-mindedness, criminality, and incongruent gender roles or sexual behaviour. ... Furthermore, the indigenous descriptions of mental illness within very disparate cultures are extraordinarily similar and demonstrate the repetition of a few basic elements: incoherent speech, bizarre and idiosyncratic beliefs, purposeless or unpredictable or violent behaviour, and apparent absence of concern for one's own safety and comfort.' (Martin Roth and Jerome Kroll, *The Reality of Mental Illness* [Cambridge: Cambridge University Press, 1986], p. 5.) However, if the general diagnostic qualities that our normals associate with madness are confirmed by other cultures, different *explanatory* theories continue to disagree about the qualities that are said to be emphasized in the schizophrenic. Cognitive interpretations of schizophrenia postulate that certain processing modules are more or less amplified, chemical theories hypothesize that it is the neurotransmitters that are exaggerated, and Sass thinks that reflexivity and self-awareness are more intense in madmen. Even if these different explanations are felt

to complement rather than exclude one another, there remain divergences within our own culture between the qualities that normal people claim to be exaggerated in madmen and the qualities that madmen claim to be abnormally amplified in normals.

34 The qualities that are present throughout the homogenous zone are also relative. I have described the zone as a cloth woven from threads of many different colours. If the madman and normal disagree over which colours are associated with madness, they may also disagree over which colours of thread are used to weave the zone – the qualities that are common to all parts of it. Perception, communication and cognition are not absolutes, but part of the normal rational perspective – qualities of the zone *according to the normal*. The normal and the madman may also disagree over whether there is a homogenous zone at all. This is discussed in the third part of this chapter.

35 R. D. Laing, *The Divided Self* (Harmondsworth: Penguin, 1987), p. 36.

36 Ludwig Wittgenstein, *On Certainty*, translated by Denis Paul and G. E. M. Anscombe (Oxford: Blackwell, 1977), remark 611.

37 Jean-Paul Sartre, *Being and Nothingness*, translated by Hazel E. Barnes (London: Routledge, 1993), p. 255.

38 Daniel Paul Schreber, *Memoirs of My Nervous Illness* (Cambridge, Massachusetts: Harvard University Press, 1988), p. 224.

39 Friedrich Nietzsche, 'On Truth and Lies in a Nonmoral Sense', printed in *Philosophy and Truth: Selections from Nietzsche's Notebooks of the early 1870s*, translated and edited by Daniel Breazeale (New Jersey: Humanities Press, 1979), p. 79.

40 Ludwig Wittgenstein, *Philosophical Investigations*, translated by G. E. M. Anscombe (Oxford: Blackwell, 1994), remark 265.

41 The idea of the homogenous zone is not intended to dismiss or ignore the fact that there are a large number of different belief systems on our planet, and although these lack radical independence there remain substantial differences between them. When we move towards a concrete investigation of the content of what we are to believe, we are confronted by a wide variety of systems of thought, languages, ontologies and forms of life.

42 This is especially clear in the case of the Orthodox Jews. One might be tempted to believe that the austere clothes and hairstyles of the Orthodox Jews are the way in which Jews always used to dress prior to their

'corruption' by liberal ideas. However, their style of dress, and many of their customs, are recent innovations linked to the Jewish history in Eastern Europe. Prior to the Jewish Reform movement, Jews never dressed like this and there were no Orthodox Jews. Orthodox Judaism does not preserve an older style of Judaism: it started as a *reaction* to the reform movement that created something new. As Bruno Latour puts it: 'One is not born traditional; one chooses to become traditional by constant innovation.' (*We Have Never Been Modern*, translated by Catherine Porter [Cambridge, Massachusetts: Harvard University Press, 1995], p. 76.)

43 See also Georgina Warnke's discussion of Gadamer: 'We seem to be able to revise the prejudices we have inherited from the tradition only by assuming the validity of other prejudices the tradition contains.' (*Gadamer* [Cambridge: Polity Press, 1987], p. 91.)

44 Oliver Sacks, *The Man Who Mistook His Wife for a Hat*, p. 15. This particular change occurred because of brain damage, but the invisibility of change to the people undergoing it is also true of genetic alterations over time.

45 For example, despite considerable mob hostility, Joseph Smith Jr.'s non-consensual Mormon beliefs did not prevent him from fathering several children that survived into adulthood.

46 Ferdinand de Saussure, *Course in General Linguistics*, edited by Charles Bally and Albert Sechehaye, with the collaboration of Albert Riedlinger, translated and annotated by Roy Harris (London: Duckworth, 1990), p. 110.

47 Ibid., p. 157.

48 Structuralism is given here as an illustration of one mechanism by which concepts and language alter over time. If Noam Chomsky's picture is preferred, a similar account could be given that looked at the effect of genetic mutations on innate grammar. Any theory of language that explains how our current language and thought came about can also be used to explain how these will change over time.

49 A strange corollary to this drifting madness of the planet of fools is the way in which consensual sanity has fallen into what it defines to be insanity over the last hundred years. In *Madness and Modernism* Sass draws numerous comparisons between modernist and schizophrenic interpretations of reality and shows how the cultural products that we value most, and pay large amounts of money for, have a great deal in common with

the worldviews of the insane. During this century the middle ground of our culture has remained safely normal, but art, literature and philosophy have become increasingly hyperreflexive, alienated and schizophrenic. (It should be pointed out that this is not Sass's own claim, which is the attempt to understand madness using modernism, but a consequence that I have drawn from his book.)

50   Martin Roth and Jerome Kroll, *The Reality of Mental Illness*, p. 14.

51   This point is made by Cochrane: 'Schizophrenia is perhaps the only concept [of insanity] which seems to have an almost universal acceptance. In many cultures and indeed in many historical periods, extreme social and emotional withdrawal, auditory hallucinations, delusions and flatness of emotional response have been taken to be indicative of some serious psychological disturbance ... although it has not always carried the stigma associated with the concept of schizophrenia in the West. Equally it appears that there is a relatively uniform rate of schizophrenia across different cultures – sometimes estimated at between 0.5 per cent to 1 per cent of the adult population.' (*The Social Creation of Mental Illness*, p. 84.) Also see note 33.

52   This is true for all the symptoms listed in DSM IV except bizarre delusions or hallucinations involving 'voices *commenting*' or 'voices *conversing*'. These are said to be sufficiently symptomatic on their own as long as they match a number of other criteria (including continuous occurrence of symptoms for at least a month and social or occupational dysfunction). However, in practice even one symptom can be enough for a diagnosis of schizophrenia. For example, in the 1970s Rosenhan showed that claiming to hear a voice saying 'thud' was enough to be admitted into a psychiatric institution ('On Being Sane in Insane Places', in Thomas Scheff (ed.), *Labelling Madness*, New Jersey: Prentice-Hall Inc., 1975). The same experiment was repeated recently by Lauren Slater (*The Guardian*, January 31, 2004), who was not admitted onto a psychiatric ward, but was still diagnosed as having psychotic depression and prescribed antipsychotic medications.

53   Mary Boyle, *Schizophrenia, A Scientific Delusion?* (London: Routledge, 1990), p. 116.

54   Roth and Kroll would respond to Boyle's arguments by claiming that her absolutist conception of disease is mistaken and that medicine can be used to treat malfunctioning at both mental and physical levels. According to Roth and Kroll, the idea that schizophrenia must demonstrate specific

physical lesions or signs to be counted as a disease is a gross distortion of medical theory and practice.

55 Plomin et al. distinguish between genetic disorders that result from the mutation of a single gene (for example, phenylketonuria, a type of mental retardation caused by recessive mutations in the phenylalanine hydroxylase (PAH) gene on chromosome 12) from disorders that are linked to changes in several genes, none of which are individually necessary for the disorder to arise: 'Quantitative geneticists assume that genetic influences on complex, common behavioral disorders are the result of multiple genes of varying effect size. These multiple-gene effects can contribute additively and interchangeably, like risk factors, to vulnerability to a disorder ... Any single gene in a multigene system is neither necessary nor sufficient to cause a disorder. In other words, genetic effects involve probabilistic propensities rather than predetermined programming.' (Robert. Plomin, Michael J. Owen and Peter McGuffin, 'The Genetic Basis of Complex Human Behaviors', *Science* 264, 1994, p. 1736.) In the multigene case, which is probably the situation with schizophrenia, Plomin et al. claim that there is likely to be a continuum between normal and abnormal behaviour: 'If, as seems likely, multiple genes are responsible for genetic influences on behavioural dimensions and disorders, a continuum of genetic risk is likely to extend from normal to abnormal behavior.' (Ibid., p. 1735.)

56 Louis Sass, *Madness and Modernism*, p. 375. Bruno Latour makes a similar point about asymmetrical explanations in the sociology of knowledge, which takes 'modern' reason for granted and explains the deviance of other theories by invoking social factors: 'Error, beliefs, could be explained socially, but truth remained self-explanatory. It was certainly possible to analyze a belief in flying saucers, but not the knowledge of black holes, we could analyze the illusions of parapsychology, but not the knowledge of psychologists; we could analyze Spencer's errors, but not Darwin's certainties.' (*We Have Never Been Modern*, p. 92.) When the madman states that two plus two equals four, or that lithium has an atomic weight of three, his claims are *not* reduced to his biological state.

57 These include: Sigmund Freud, 'Psychological Notes on an Autobiographical Account of a Case of Paranoia' (in *Case Histories II*, translated by James Strachey, Harmondsworth: Penguin, 1979); Louis Sass, *Madness and Modernism* and *The Paradoxes of Delusion* (New York: Cornell University Press, 1994); Morton Schatzman, 'Paranoia or Persecution: The Case of Schreber' (in Thomas Scheff [ed.], *Labelling*

Madness); Elias Canetti, *Crowds and Power* (translated by Carol Stewart, London: Penguin, 1973). Sass gives a number of further references in the introduction and conclusion to *The Paradoxes of Delusion*. A dismissal by reduction can also be observed in Barbara O'Brien (*Operators and Things*, London: Elek Books, 1960), who carried this out on herself after her madness had passed, with the help of psychological and psychoanalytical literature.

58   This analysis is taken from Freud's 'Psychological Notes on an Autobiographical Account of a Case of Paranoia', in *Case Histories II*.

59   Ibid., pp. 191–2. Interestingly, at the end of his analysis and after a complete reduction of Schreber's cosmological vision, Freud opens up the possibility that Schreber's theories might have some truth in them after all: 'It remains for the future to decide whether there is more delusion in my theory than I should like to admit, or whether there is more truth in Schreber's delusion than other people are as yet prepared to believe.' (Ibid., p. 218.)

60   Morton Schatzman, 'Paranoia or Persecution: The Case of Schreber', in Thomas Scheff (ed.), *Labelling Madness*, p. 100.

61   Transcript of a description of a farming scene by a chronic schizophrenic patient (the dashes indicate pauses), in Christopher D. Frith, *The Cognitive Neuropsychology of Schizophrenia* (Hove: Lawrence Erlbaum Associates, 1993), p. 102.

62   Samuel Beckett, *Not I* (London: Faber and Faber Limited, 1973), pp. 11–12.

63   Michel Foucault, *Madness and Civilization*, translated by Richard Howard (London: Routledge, 1995), p. 287. I have translated '*oeuvre*' as 'work' to preserve the fuller meaning that is lost with 'work of art'.

64   Jacques Derrida, 'Cogito and the History of Madness', in *Writing and Difference*, p. 57.

65   William Shakespeare, *As You Like It*, in *The Complete Works* (Bath: Michael O'Mara Books Limited, 1992), Act V, Scene 1.

5 Labyrinths of Knowledge

1   Jorge Luis Borges, *Labyrinths*, translated by James E. Irby (London: Penguin, 1970), pp. 81–2.

2   Stephen Mulhall, *On Being in the World* (London and New York: Routledge, 1990), p. 137.

3   The second example is taken from Oliver Sacks, *The Man Who Mistook His Wife For a Hat* (London: Duckworth, 1986), p. 12.

4   Ludwig Wittgenstein, *Philosophical Investigations*, translated by G. E. M. Anscombe (Oxford: Blackwell, 1994), p. 200.

5   Mulhall, *On Being in the World*, p. 72.

6   Clashes between local aspects bring aspects to our attention. It may be impossible for us to become aware of clashes between global aspects.

7   Some aspects interpret things. In other aspects nothing like interpretation goes on at all.

8   See Hans-Georg Gadamer, *Truth and Method*, translated by William Glen-Doepel (London: Sheed and Ward, 1979), pp. 405–6. Bruno Latour's notion of the hybrid or quasi-object in *We Have Never Been Modern* provides a similar interpretation. Quasi-objects are not conceptual interpretations of natural phenomena, but networks in which subjective and objective components crisscross and interlink. Aspects can be interpreted as purely intellectual constructs superimposed on a neutral world, but they can also be seen as hybrids with their own reality; hybrids from which the purely natural and the purely social are derived.

9   W. V. O. Quine, *Ontological Relativity and Other Essays* (New York and London: Columbia University Press, 1969), p. 67.

10 The work of Michel Foucault is a good example of the latter approach.

11 Ludwig Wittgenstein, *On Certainty*, translated by Denis Paul and G. E. M. Anscombe (Oxford: Blackwell 1977), remarks 341–2.

12 Ibid., remark 141.

13 Ibid., remark 92.

14 Peter Winch makes a similar point about the Azande, who are as certain about the reality and efficaciousness of witchcraft as we are certain that it is superstitious mumbo-jumbo. The glaring inconsistencies that we see in the predictions of their oracle are explained by them in a way that reinforces their entire worldview: 'Of course it does happen often that the oracle first says "yes" and then "no" to the same question. This does not convince a Zande of the futility of the whole operation of consulting oracles: obviously, it cannot, since otherwise the practice could hardly have

developed and maintained itself at all. Various explanations may be offered, whose possibility, it is important to notice, is built into the whole network of Zande beliefs and may, therefore, be regarded as belonging to the concept of an oracle. It may be said, for instance, that bad *benge* is being used; that the operator of the oracle is ritually unclean; that the oracle is being itself influenced by witchcraft or sorcery; or it may be that the oracle is showing that the question cannot be answered straightforwardly in its present form.' (Peter Winch, 'Understanding a Primitive Society', in John V. Canfield (ed.), *The Philosophy of Wittgenstein*, Volume 13 [New York and London: Garland Publishing Inc., 1986], p. 256.)

[15] Madness is a category reserved for those who do not participate in this agreement.

[16] Michel Foucault, *The Order of Things*, translated by Tavistock Publications Limited (London: Routledge, 1997), p. 17.

[17] Ibid., p. 21.

[18] Ibid., p. 26.

[19] Ibid., pp. 28–9.

[20] This is not strictly true of the Renaissance interpretation of language. Originally language did resemble things when it was given by God to men. After Babel this transparency was lost and now only Hebrew retains a trace of this original similitude.

[21] Ibid., pp. 57–8.

[22] Ibid., pp. 74–5.

[23] Ibid., p. 74.

[24] This point is made by Dreyfus and Rabinow: 'The archaeologist finds that his elements (statements) are not only *individuated* by the whole system of statements, but that they can be *identified* as elements only in the specific system in which they make sense. Thus, although speech acts for Foucault as well as for Searle have some sort of fixed "information content" or "sentence meaning," whether or not two speech acts mean the same thing (that is, determine the same truth conditions) depends not merely upon the words that determine their information content but upon the context in which they appear.' (Hubert L. Dreyfus and Paul Rabinow, *Michel Foucault: Beyond Structuralism and Hermeneutics* [London: Harvester Wheatsheaf, 1982], p. 54.)

25 See also Kuhn's discussion of scientific paradigms: 'when paradigms change, the world itself changes with them. Led by a new paradigm, scientists adopt new instruments and look in new places. Even more important, during revolutions scientists see new and different things when looking with familiar instruments in places they have looked before. ... In so far as their only recourse to that world is through what they see and do we may want to say that after a revolution scientists are responding to a different world.' (Thomas Kuhn, *The Structure of Scientific Revolutions*, Second Edition [Chicago: The University of Chicago Press, 1970], p. 111.)

26 Wittgenstein, *On Certainty*, p. 74.

27 The ancient Greeks had three words for love: *eros* (erotic feeling), *philein* (friendship or fellow-feeling) and *agape* (total dedication) – see John Hospers, *Introduction to Philosophical Analysis*, Fourth Edition (London: Routledge, 1997), p. 260. There are also some interesting language-related problems with 'consciousness'. The problem of consciousness is the subject of a large and rapidly growing literature in the English language, but, as Kathleen Wilkes points out, it has only existed in English as a concept for the last three hundred years and there are still considerable problems in translating it into Chinese and Ancient Greek. (Kathleen Wilkes, '———, yìshì, duh, um, and consciousness', in A.J. Marcel and E. Bisiach (eds), *Consciousness in Contemporary Science* [Oxford: Clarendon Press, 1988].)

28 Searle's speech acts and Foucault's statements are at this level of language.

29 The move from association to association is also part of this area beyond grammar. In one language a word evokes a whole train of associations that may make no sense at all in a different language.

30 One difference between language-games and ordinary games is that language-games are played with absent as well as present pieces. A move in a language-game not only has to relate to the pieces that are in play at any point in time; it also has to be in harmony with the *background* field of statements that are legitimized by the language. When we speak we assume a whole field of other statements that make our statement intelligible. A move in the language-game is only legitimate if it relates to this background field in the correct way.

31 Gadamer distinguishes between artificial and natural languages and claims that only the latter are true languages: 'invented systems of artificial

communication are never languages. For artificial languages, such as secret languages or systems of mathematical symbols, have no basis in a community of language or life, but are introduced and applied only as means and tools of understanding. This is the reason that they always presuppose a living process of communication, which is that of language. The convention by means of which an artificial language is introduced necessarily belongs, as we know, to another language. In a real community of language, on the other hand, we do not first decide to agree, but are already in agreement.' (Hans-Georg Gadamer, *Truth and Method*, translated by William Glen-Doepel [London: Sheed and Ward, 1979], p. 404.) Even if we accept this distinction, there is no reason why the languages that we create should not be given to our children as the language that they already agree on. Infants could be brought up in Lisp instead of English.

[32] Wittgenstein, *Philosophical Investigations*, p. 208.

[33] Willard Van Orman Quine, *Word and Object* (Cambridge, Massachusetts: M.I.T. Press, 1960), p. 91.

[34] This distinction between general and mass terms is not strict and they can often be used interchangeably. For example, I might ask for two waters in a restaurant, or suggest that we go out on the water when we are windsurfing. On the other hand, I might ask for some lamb at the butchers, or offer to put some apple in the salad.

[35] This is not true at radically different scales. For example, water can be divided into parts at the molecular level.

[36] This is true within each aspect, but different aspects may attribute different stages to the same object. An ageing pop star might be a young painter.

[37] Something along these lines might be as follows: The chair-floor-dog is a 'creature' composed of a chair, a floor and a dog. In many ways its structure rests half way between amoebic and hydric. It attaches its fixed base to parallel vertical features in its environment and from this it extends its furry proboscis to find food. The chair-floor-dog reproduces using elaborate eggs, which it sends out from the main body. These eggs can either metamorphose into entirely new chair-floor-dogs or they can utilise the carcass of a dead chair-floor-dog for their development. The eggs can survive for up to eighty years without hatching, but an individual chair-floor-dog will generally only live for around fifteen years, after which its furry proboscis becomes exhausted and disintegrates.

[38] It could be objected that this idea of aspects partitioned differently from

our own is very close to the conceptual scheme–content distinction criticized by Davidson: 'Conceptual schemes, we are told, are ways of organizing experience; they are systems of categories that give form to the data of sensation.' (Donald Davidson, *Inquiries into Truth and Interpretation* [Oxford: Clarendon Press, 1984], p. 183.) This impression is not dispelled by the use of terms like 'partition', 'segmentation' and 'division', which all imply a distinction between a divisor and something else that is divided.

The main reason why I have settled on these terms is that an aspect with a different partitioning appears to us as the division or fusion of the partitions within our own aspect. The chair-floor-dog amalgamates *our* objects and so it makes sense to call it an alternative partitioning of them. Terms like 'partition', 'segmentation' and 'divide' are intended to express the fact that when we compare two aspects some of *our* objects, properties and states are divided, and others are joined – they are not meant to suggest that aspects are conceptual schemes which divide up a noumenal reality. The focus in this discussion is on the *contrast* between our aspect and another, which has little to do with the metaphysics of conceptual schemes. I could have spoken about an encounter with different object sets, but this would have missed the way in which we imagine these other object sets as different partitions of our own.

It must also be borne in mind that the origin of different partitioning 'schemes' is not discussed here. I am attempting to describe the partitions within our own aspect and the ways in which other aspects could be divided. If these other aspects could be experienced by us, it might be because a single amorphous mass of matter is carved up by our brains or language, or it might be for some other reason (and whether a different partitioning *could* come about is a matter for empirical investigation). The purpose of this section is to articulate the region of the labyrinth that is characterized by different object, state and property sets without projecting too much theory into it.

Finally, it is not clear whether Davidson would be entirely opposed to partitioning since his notion of an alternative conceptual scheme is for the most part tied up with the idea of a largely true but untranslatable *language*: 'the criterion of a conceptual scheme different from our own now becomes: largely true but not translatable.' (Ibid., p. 194). Since we can use a single language to describe a number of different ways in which reality can be partitioned (even if we have to invent new words or create complicated compounds), Davidson's criticism of conceptual schemes may not be applicable to the object, property and state partitioning that

I am discussing here. Theories about the objects, properties and states within one aspect may not be translatable into the theories about the objects, properties and states in another, but Davidson does not claim that all theories within a single language must be intertranslatable.

39 Mentioned by Max Black in his essay 'Linguistic Relativity: The Views of Benjamin Lee Whorf', *Philosophical Review*, 68, p. 231.

40 Quine, *Word and Object*, p. 92.

41 See Nelson Goodman, *Fact, Fiction, and Forecast* (Cambridge, MA: Harvard University Press, 1955).

42 Richard Rorty, *Philosophy and the Mirror of Nature* (Princeton, New Jersey: Princeton University Press, 1979), p. 71.

43 Wittgenstein, *Philosophical Investigations*, p. 223.

44 Kuhn, *The Structure of Scientific Revolutions*, p. 136.

45 Wittgenstein, *On Certainty*, p. 34.

46 This does not make aspects into merely subjective phenomena. It is just that if *we* are looking for aspects, we will not find them in rocks or furniture, but in people (and other forms of life as well). The fact that we happen to encounter and place aspects within people has no implications for what the world is like outside aspects, whether there is a world outside aspects, and so on. Furthermore, this 'biologistic' reading of aspects is just one interpretation of them – an interpretation that arises within my own aspect.

47 Lucien Malson, *Wolf Children*, translated by Edmund Fawcett, Peter Ayrton and Joan White (London: NLB, 1972), pp. 68–9.

48 G. W. Leibniz, *Discourse on Metaphysics*, in *Philosophical Texts*, translated by Richard Francks and R. S. Woolhouse (Oxford and New York: Oxford University Press, 1998), p. 66.

49 Peter Unger, *Ignorance* (Oxford: Clarendon Press, 1975), p. 95.

50 Most of Wittgenstein's *On Certainty* is a criticism of negative scepticism. According to Wittgenstein, the doubt of the negative sceptic can only be applied *within* her framework of certainties. It makes no sense at all to throw the *whole* framework into question and so the negative sceptic's attempt to doubt everything is senseless.

51 This boundary between aspects is itself an aspect, which creates the traditional paradox of negative scepticism: that the negative sceptic is certain about her universal doubt.

[52] Sextus Empiricus, *Outlines of Pyrrhonism*, translated by Benson Mates in *The Skeptic Way* (New York and Oxford: Oxford University Press, 1996), Book 1.4, pp. 89–90. I am using the work of Sextus Empiricus to illustrate the Pyrrhonic 'philosophy' because it is set out by him with great clarity and detail, and because the important sceptics before him (Pyrrho of Elis, Arcesilaus, Carneades and Aenesidemus) either wrote nothing or little of their work has been preserved. Furthermore, the work of Sextus is for the most part a compendium of the arguments of the earlier 'Pyrrhonists' and so it is a good example of this style of scepticism. *The Sceptics* by R. J. Hankinson (London and New York: Routledge, 1995) covers the other Pyrrhonists in depth.

[53] I will use the term 'Pyrrhonic' to describe all sceptics adopting the style of scepticism that began with Pyrrho of Elis, even if they do not explicitly assimilate themselves to this tradition.

[54] This psychological reconstruction can be found in much greater detail in *Scepticism* by Arne Naess (London: Routledge & Kegan Paul, 1968).

[55] Sextus Empiricus, *Outlines of Pyrrhonism*, Book 1.28, p. 117.

[56] Ibid., Book 3.32, p. 217.

[57] It could be argued that the Pyrrhonic sceptic only has a *past* identity. Once he reaches *ataraxia* he takes up a trade and becomes indistinguishable from everyone else. However, since everyone else is a dogmatist, the Pyrrhonic sceptic is presumably different from the common man in this respect. The Pyrrhonic sceptic could become an everyday dogmatist after achieving *ataraxia* (in which case this argument about identity would not apply), but if he continues to preserve his *ataraxia* through equipollence, then he remains a Pyrrhonic sceptic, even if he no longer practises philosophy.

[58] Ibid., Book 1.8, p. 91.

[59] This is true of positive scepticism as a theory, but a human being who happens to be 'hosting' positive scepticism may switch into a different aspect.

[60] A good statement of this argument can be found in Stephen D. Edwards, *Relativism, Conceptual Schemes and Categorial Frameworks* (Aldershot: Avebury, 1990), p. 5.

[61] This point is made by Nehamas in his discussion of Nietzsche's perspectivism, which has many features in common with positive scepticism: 'The general problem with both positive and negative approaches to perspec-

tivism so far is that they have been too quick to equate possible with actual falsehood, interpretation with mere interpretation. The claim, however, that a view is mere interpretation can be made only in light of a further interpretation, which is of course not a mere interpretation itself in that context.' (Alexander Nehamas, *Nietzsche, Life as Literature* [Cambridge, Massachusetts: Harvard University Press, 1985], p. 67.)

62 Hilary Lawson, *Reflexivity* (La Salle, Illinois: Open Court, 1985), pp. 128–9.

63 This notion of a mobile human site is also part of the way in which positive scepticism sees things. It is part of the positive sceptic's map of the territory beyond positive scepticism and not something that is common to all aspects.

64 Blaise Pascal, *Pensées*, translated by A. J. Krailsheimer (Middlesex: Penguin, 1981), p. 37, remark 33.

Endings ...

1 Simon Critchley, *Very Little ... Almost Nothing* (London and New York: Routledge, 1997), p. 12.

2 Jean Baudrillard, *Simulacra and Simulation*, translated by Sheila Faria Glaser (London: Semiotext(e)/ Pluto, 1990), pp. 160–1.

Index